INCOME
AND EMPLOYMENT

PRENTICE-HALL ECONOMICS SERIES

E. A. J. Johnson, Editor

INCOME

AND EMPLOYMENT

THEODORE MORGAN

Associate Professor of Economics,
University of Wisconsin; pro tem.,
Adviser to the Central Bank of
Ceylon.

Second Edition

PRENTICE-HALL, INC.　　New York　　1952

To *MARK*

Preface

THIS BOOK IS AN ESSAY IN MACROECONOMICS, WITH THEORY TIED close to data of the United States. The subject matter falls naturally into three divisions: the measurement of income, production, and average prices; the trend and determinants of production and productivity; and influences on, and policies toward, the levels of employment and of prices.

I am grateful for effective criticism and encouragement from Professors W. L. Crum, John T. Dunlop, Gottfried Haberler, George N. Halm, Alvin H. Hansen, Wassily Leontief, Yves Maroni, James N. Morgan, Andreas Papandreou, Joseph A. Schumpeter, and Sumner H. Slichter. Each of them gave his time and attention to special problems as they arose. Chapter 13 was improved by the criticisms of Professors David Easton and John Greene. Professors Albert G. Hart and Harlan Smith went over the whole manuscript with scrupulous care: many a page has benefited from their criticisms. Professor H. H. Burbank has my sincere thanks for useful suggestions and for an arrangement of my teaching schedule that gave me time to work on the book when I most needed it. Finally, I am indebted to my brother Donald for having first directed my interest toward the general field in which this book lies.

THEODORE MORGAN

Table of Contents

Charts

Tables

The Plan of the Book

THE NINETEENTH CENTURY VIEWED DEPRESSION AS MEDIEVAL
Europe viewed the plague—as an inevitable accompaniment of
this life, to be borne with resignation. It is unlikely that we
shall in the future retain the tolerance toward depression we
showed in the past. There are a number of reasons. It is contrary to common sense that some men should rust in idleness
while they and others lack goods. We in the United States have
been impressed by how completely we have employed our labor
force during wartime and by how well we have produced as
principal supply center of the United Nations. We have seen
fascist states and Soviet Russia obtaining full employment of
their resources, although their productivity has been much
lower than our own and their people have yielded up freedoms
we prize. Our own political parties have, of course, generously
accepted praise or dispensed blame for boom and collapse, and
so disposed us to look upon depression as controllable. Finally,
there are cooperating sentiments of personal apprehension,
humaneness, and prudence at work—apprehension lest we
should ourselves be impoverished and jobless, humane concern
lest others be so, and prudent fear lest social decay and hate
rot away the foundations of our society.

The question is not whether we are to seek effective action
against depression. The only question is whether we are going
to have policies set into effect *after* a crisis is upon us, so that
the action is hastily planned and hastily put into action—and
so relatively ineffective—or whether we are going to have a

1

program and facilities set up ahead of time to avert or meet the day of need. Recent advances in technical economics justify a tempered optimism: We can do the job if we set about it.

The chief purpose of this book is to present plainly, but with all important qualifications, the problems and policy alternatives faced by the United States' economy in maintaining productive and high employment. Chapters 7 to 18 deal primarily with the maintenance of employment. But policies directed toward high employment can readily have undesired effects through causing rising prices. And inflation, no matter what its cause, is a menace to the economy second only to depression. Chapters 19 and 20 are concerned with price level policy and with inflation.

High employment is an aim in itself because of the morale and educational values of work; but it is not the basic aim of the economic system. The basic aim is the highest production reasonably possible of those goods and services that best satisfy human wants; and high employment is best looked on as a means to, and a by-product of, this high production. Therefore, we are concerned throughout the book with production and productivity. As soon as we speak of production in the whole economy (or of income, its money equivalent) we face the problem of measurement, which is the subject of Chapters 1 to 3. The following chapters, 4, 5, and 6, discuss special aspects of total production—changes in total production and in productivity, production and price levels, and the behavior of certain main constituents of total production.

We start out, therefore, with the measurements of production and income; continue with a survey of changes in production and productivity; spend the main part of the book on the problem of maintaining effective high employment; and end by discussing the experience and problem of inflation.

CHAPTER ONE

The National Accounts

THE PURPOSE OF PRODUCTION IS THE FULFILLMENT OF HUMAN wants. Our wants for food, clothing, shelter, amusement, medical attention—for the long list of goods and services that minister to us—are met, more or less adequately, by the production of the economy.

It would be possible to measure national production by making a detailed list of the great variety of things produced: bathtubs, toy whistles, nitric acid, beauty "facials," spark plugs, research studies, beefsteaks, and so on. But this procedure would be most awkward. Our tabulation would require many volumes, and even so would give no plain and compact impression to anyone wanting a general notion of how well the economy is working. It might be possible, instead, to measure much of the national output by weight (pounds or tons), or by volume (cubic feet or cubic yards). But such measures would not represent well the significance for human consumption of such goods as diamonds and gravel, mercury and milk, electric motors and cotton textiles; and they would be unable to measure services, that is, labor time, devoted to fulfilling human wants.

The most useful common measure of the vast pile of goods and services that make up the national output in any period of time—say, a year—is the money value of those goods and services. We can define the national product of a given year as the money value of all economic goods and services produced in that year—that is, the money value of all products of business and government activity—of extraction (mining, forestry, fishing, and agriculture), manufacturing, transportation, trade, and direct services to consumers. We shall sometimes feel that money value is an inadequate measure of how well goods and services satisfy the wants of society, but it is much the best of the available measures.

The national product can be calculated for any time period we find convenient—for a month, a quarter, or, most commonly, for a year.

Three Ways of Measuring National Production

If a person has shoes shined for 10 cents, then production in the form of a shoeshine of the value of 10 cents takes place, 10 cents is spent for current production, and the shoeshine boy receives an income of 10 cents. If one receives a paycheck of $300 for a month of teaching, then the national product is increased by $300—the valuation of the teaching services, there is spending of $300 for a service, and also one receives a money income of $300. Or if a business contracts with a machine-tool firm to have a milling machine built for $100,000, then the value of national production increases by $100,000 as the machine is built, an obligation of $100,000 accrues, and $100,000 accrues as income to the employees, owners, and others who have claims on the machine-tool firm.

An easy generalization comes out of these examples: We can measure national production by adding up the value of all production, or by adding up expenditure for production, or by adding up incomes created in production. If our figures are accurate and complete, it does not matter which approach we use.

In most national income estimating, all three approaches are used somewhere, in different sectors of the economy and at different stages of calculation.

Justice, and the income accounts

One of the three equalities indicated above is that total income created equals value of product. This is not a sleight-of hand argument that peoples' incomes are precisely what they deserve. It is simply an accounting relationship: all income created in production is due to those who have claims on productive enterprises.

The best route to calculating the value of national production is through calculating the *national accounts*. These are tables showing receipts and expenditures of sectors of the economy.

The sectors of the economy

The sectors might be any parts of the economy that we are interested in and for which we can find data: farms and cities, for example; or the North-East, the South, the Middle West, the Rocky Mountains states and the Far West; or (for several countries of the Orient) the rural, plantation, and urban areas. In the United States, accounts have been estimated for five sectors: consumers, business, government, the rest-of-the-world, and "saving and investment."

The choice of these can be justified on the grounds that each is fairly united and homogeneous, with its own separate behavior and rationale; each is quantitatively important, and important toward explaining the economic life of the country.

Receipts and expenditures

The receipts and expenditures measured can be of several kinds. One can spend or receive expenditure (1) for goods or services produced currently[1]; (2) for nothing—these are gifts, or *"transfer payments"*; (3a) for goods produced in the past or not a product of economic activity (like old houses, arable land, or mineral deposits), or (3b) in exchange for an I.O.U.— a piece of paper promising future repayment.

Only (1) and (2) appear in the national accounts as presented below, and in the national income totals of the next chapter. (3a) is omitted on the grounds that these purchases cannot

---

[1] That is, in the time period with which we are concerned—say, the calendar year 1950. For foreign trade, it is the date of exporting or importing that counts.

serve as a measure of current production, which is our central concern. The exclusion of (3b) is a convenient simplification. A loan is not income, nor is it a measure of the value of production.

But (1), payment for current production of a good or service, plainly might be taken as a component of the value of national product, and it is obviously a part of the national income. And (2), a gift or transfer payment, though it does not serve as a means for valuing production, is just as plainly a component of "income" in some sense.

Hence if we select rightly among our sector receipts and expenditures, we can build up measures of national production, expenditure, and income.

Why Construct National Accounts?

The national accounts give information about the economic life of sectors of the economy, and about relationships among the sectors that is lost when only total national production, expenditure, and income figures are presented. This is one justification for their use.

But the main justification for their use and emphasis is a different one. It lies in the practical problem of measuring accurately the productive performance of an economy.

That problem is a tough one. No one who has actually set about the problem of calculation will underestimate its difficulty, nor the approximate character of the result. There are, on the one side, problems of classification and logic that repeatedly invite philosophic contemplation of what one is really about, and why he is about it. There is, on the other side, the perennial problem of the data available, which seldom approach in definition and accuracy what one ideally wants. The national income estimator must make the best use possible of partial data, of indirect data, of inaccurate data, of data that he knows is biased. He must guess judiciously in areas where the ice is thin.

It is here that the national accounts have a decisive advantage over direct estimating of total national product, spending, and income. They enable two kinds of checks to be made:

1. The receipts of each sector, rightly defined, must equal the expenditures of that sector.[2] Whatever goes in must be used somehow, somewhere. When in the course of our estimating, the two totals are not equal, we have a storm warning. We must re-estimate and re-check, until the logical equality is actually realized in the figures.

2. Since the rest-of-the-world is listed as one of the "sectors," our accounts are complete. We have listed all possible receivers of inter-sector receipts, and all possible sources of expenditures. Every payment comes from some sector listed, and goes to some sector listed (they may be identical). In other words every payment appears in the accounts twice.

The estimator, therefore, has the great advantage of being able to consider whether a given estimated figure is reasonable in two contexts, the paying account and the receiving account.

Can inaccurate accounts be useful?

If figures in the social and income accounts are so uncertain, if, as often happens for particular items, the national income specialist judges that his best estimate may be 10 per cent, 20 per cent, or even more off from the truth, is it worthwhile calculating them at all?

The more accurate the figures are the better. And in the United States some of the largest and most important items are

---

[2] How can this be when certain kinds of payments (3a and 3b above) are excluded? The answer is that any difference between income, as defined, and expenditures for current production and transfers, as defined, is considered "saving" of the sector concerned. For example, if consumers have $100 billions of disposable income, and spend $90 billions on consumer goods and services, then the difference of $10 billions is consumer saving. The equality holds: $90 billions *plus* $10 billions *equals* $100 billions. Nothing is asserted about what is done with the saving: some might go to buy land or real estate (not counted as consumer goods), some be lent or used to buy stocks, some held idle, and so on.

But the equality check is still useful, despite this seeming equality-by-definition. There is a direct and independent check of the accuracy of the sector saving figure in four of the five accounts, and in the fifth there is a check for the accuracy of total saving.

remarkably accurate. The U.S. wages and salaries' total is probably less than 1 per cent astray.

But even if only rough approximations, accounts are useful:

1. They refute those widely wrong statements that arise out of ignorance or political bias. For example, a few years ago a politician running for office in Massachusetts was able to claim that the special performance of U.S. manufacturing was miserably poor because only about one-fifth of its receipts went into wages. (The remainder, he alleged, went mainly into profits.) In 1900 or 1870 it would have been hard to prove him in flagrant error: the over-all accounts did not exist. Today anyone who has studied the U. S. national accounts knows and can show the contention to be false.

2. The social and income accounts of the economy direct attention to the variables of most importance to policy: the real volume of consumer expenditures, the quantity of investment, the balance of exports against imports, the trend of production per person, and the like. And so they raise the level of the never-ending public discussion over what are the right policies with respect to production, employment, and prices, and help toward the development of better policy. One major reason why we have in the past several years heard less traditionally confused interpretations of the burden of public debt is that the more important variables of national income analysis have attracted public attention.

3. The mere attempt to develop the social accounts focuses a spotlight on gaps in statistical information. To a person who has not worked with problems of national or international economic policy, it often seems that there is a surplus of statistics on all aspects of all problems. But when one has seriously gotten to work on these problems, the available statistics always reveal themselves lamentably few and filled with error. The formulating of the national accounts points up what additional data would be most useful and needed, encourages consistency in definitions and treatment, and so is the strongest possible

inducement toward strengthening the statistical arsenal of a country.

When a nation undertakes a program of economic development, one of the logical early steps is to improve its social and income accounts so as to measure accurately its progress and to help chart the future course. India's and Ceylon's effort to develop and improve their accounts were in 1951 a major stimulus to better organized statistical inquiry.

The Five National Accounts

In the remainder of this chapter are listed the five national accounts estimated by the Department of Commerce for the United States, for: (1) consumers ("persons," or households), (2) business, (3) government, (4) the rest-of-the-world, and (5) savings and investment. In each, the data are for the year 1950. A brief explanation of the sense of the accounts is given, and a survey of basic sources and methods of estimation.

Full information on sources and estimation methods is extremely detailed and complex, and in fact has not been published anywhere.[3] What is given here is elliptical and suggestive. It portrays the kinds of problems faced by national income statisticians, and the kinds of solutions.

In so doing it gives a sense of the range of error of the data (and hence of the degree of significance of changes in particular totals). And it describes the concepts into which the estimators try to fit their source materials (and hence indicates the uses, and misuses, of the final figures).

1. The account for consumers

The Department of Commerce estimates that in 1950 U.S. consumers had the receipts and payments shown in Table 1.

---

[3] The most complete report, from which the following information is mainly taken, is in the *Survey of Current Business, National Income Supplement,* 1951; Part III, "Sources and Methods of National Income Estimation," pp. 55-140; and Part V, "Statistical Section," pp. 147-216.

TABLE 1

PERSONAL INCOME AND EXPENDITURES, 1950 *

(in billions of dollars)

Expenditures		Receipts	
6. Consumer purchases 193.6		1. Income receipts from work... 146.4	
a. Goods and s e r v i c e s b o u g h t from businesses (10*a*) 184.5		Wages and salaries paid to employees (plus other labor income) :	
b. D i r e c t services (1*c*, 20*b*) 6.0		*a.* by business (13*a*) 123.2	
c. Interest paid (2*c*) 1.7		*b.* by government (22*a*) .20.1	
d. Net purchases f r o m abroad (29*c*) 1.3		*c.* by persons (including institutions) a n d abroad (6*b*, 28*a*) 6.0	
7. Personal income, taxes, fees, etc. (17) 20.5		*d. minus:* d e d u c t i o n s f r o m employees' pay for s o c i a l insurance (20*a*) .... —2.9	
8. Personal saving (31) 10.7		2. Income receipts from property. 27.3	
		a. Rents (13*c*) 8.0	
		b. D i v i d e n d s (13*c*[2], 28*c*) 9.2	
		c. Personal interest income (6*c*, 13*d*, 23*b*, 28*b*) 10.1	
		3. Mixed income receipts (from both work and property), to unincorporated enterprises, adjusted (13*f*) 36.0	
		4. Transfer payments 15.1	
		a. from g o v e r n m e n t (23*a*) 14.3	
		b. from business (14*b*) .. .8	
9. Personal outlay and saving... 224.7		5. Personal income 224.7	

* Adapted from the *Survey of Current Business, National Income Supplement,* 1951. p. 149. Final digits are rounded to the nearest number, and so subtotals may not add up exactly to totals.

On the receipts side, "personal income" of consumers was made up of receipts from work, from property, from mixed work and property, and from transfer payments. Since the concept of personal income is that of money income or its equivalent receivable in the time period concerned, a deduction is made (1*d*) for contributions taken out of the pay of employees to add to their social security credits. The income paid to employees for work performed made up 65 per cent of personal income; and if we add a pro-rata share of the mixed income arising from both work and property (going to unincorporated businesses), we have a total of 79 per cent of personal income received as a payment for work.[4]

On the expenditure side, the question faced is: What do consumers do with their incomes? They buy goods and services;[5] they pay income taxes and other fees and other charges directly to government; whatever they have is "personal savings."

In Table 1, as in the following accounts, there is a reference in parentheses after each item. Usually this indicates the identical item elsewhere, in the same table or in one of the other four tables. For example:

6a. Goods and services bought from businesses (10a) 184.5

We find (10a) in Table 2, the business account:

10a. [Consolidated net sales of business] to consumers (6a) 184.5

This expenditure of persons is a receipt of business.

Sometimes the reference is more complicated. In Table 1, interest is paid by persons (6c) to other persons (2c). Net interest is received by persons (2c) from other persons (6c), from business (13d), from government (23b), and from abroad (28b). We could, at the expense of making the tables more complex, always show separately the identical item elsewhere.

We have already seen why every item must be entered twice. Our accounts cover the whole world. Hence a receipt to any sector must be a payment from some sector.

(1) Over nine-tenths of the data for wages and salaries come to the Department of Commerce from the accounting records of businesses and government. Some eight-ninths of this portion are from industries covered by the Social Security and Railroad Retirement Acts, and are reported under nearly ideal conditions of regularity and accuracy: employers send

---

4 On the assumption that work and property incomes bear the same ratio within "mixed incomes" that they do separately.

5 Consumers pay interest in exchange for the service of being granted loans.

tabulations listing every employee to the Boards every three months. The employer has adequate incentive not to overpay, and the employee equal incentive to check against understatement (since social security benefits depend on the wage reported). But not all wages in these covered industries are reported: Some of the smallest firms (with not over 7 employees) are exempt, and also incomes above a fixed level (in 1951, $3600 a year). Such residual wages are small, and are estimated indirectly by several approximating methods.

Of the areas not covered by Social Security or Railroad Retirement: civilian payrolls of the Federal Government are reported monthly by the separate agencies. Military wages are estimated as the total of money wages and pay in kind. State and local government payrolls come from several sources: education payrolls from biennial surveys of the Office of Education, adjusted from Census data; most non-school payrolls from a quarterly survey of government units. Farm wages are estimated by the Bureau of Agricultural Economics, partly on the basis of a 1945 Census, partly from sample surveys. Pay to domestic servants comes from the 1940 Census of Population and Housing, projected to later years by an index of wage rates multiplied by employment.

Other, smaller items of wages and salaries come from various special reports, census returns, and surveys. Among them are wages and salaries received from non-profit hospitals and like organizations, religious organizations, educational services, Federal Reserve Banks, Forestry, from tips, and from services rendered to the "rest of the world."

The subtraction for social security contributions (1d) taken from the pay envelope or the paycheck can be totaled promptly directly from accounts of the administering agencies.

Included among the income receipts of employees from business, government, and persons is "other labor income." This is expenditure by employers that is part of the over-all payment for labor, but is not counted elsewhere or is not thought of as part of ordinary receipts from work. It includes employer contributions to private pension plans, health and welfare programs, and group insurance programs. Data are pieced together from a wide variety of sources: from unions, church organizations, and the Federal Reserve banks; from Bureau of Internal Revenue data for corporations (which come in three years late, and must be estimated in the meantime); from institutions of higher education, and the like. Compensation for injuries is also a part of "other labor income," whether the payments are actually received by employees, or by their dependents and survivors. The information is based mainly on data in the Insurance Yearbook and on reports from state funds and commissions and from the U.S. Employees' Compensation. The data are available with about a year's lag, and are estimated in the meantime. There are small additions to "other labor income" also for military reserve pay and pay to enemy prisoners of war (from Government sources), and a rough estimate for directors' fees.

(2a) Rental incomes are more difficult to estimate than wages and salaries and their supplements. The basic data are conspicuously inadequate, and estimates are built up laboriously from tax returns (individuals are required to list rental income on the Federal income tax forms), from census enumerations, and from sample surveys. Since it is not total rent, but rent after landlords' expenses that is wanted, complex estimates are derived for depreciation (taken on a 2 per cent per year basis for non-farm dwellings), taxes on the property, mortgage interest, and other expenses.

Owners who live in their own houses receive services from those dwellings for which they would have to pay rent if they did not own them. The Department of Commerce attempts to estimate this real income mainly from the 1940 Census of Population and Housing, carried forward on the basis of the surveys of the Bureau of Labor Statistics for its Consumers' Price Index. Rents from farm property are estimated separately from non-farm rents. The main source is data collected by the Bureau of Agricultural Economics. Net rents going to landlords living on farms are omitted, on the ground of being best regarded as income from farming, to be included under that heading, rather than income from ownership of property only.

Rental income added up to somewhat less than 4 per cent of 1950 total personal income.

(2b) Dividends are that part of corporate earnings (or corporate profits) that are distributed to stockholders. Corporate profits estimates come basically from the Bureau of Internal Revenue's annual *Statistics of Income,* or from the larger unpublished "Source Book," from which it is compiled. The totals reported from tax returns as Net Profit, Total Federal Corporate Income and Profits Taxes, and Dividends Paid are the starting point for calculation. The profit item, and taxes due, are defined by Federal tax law, court decisions, and administrative rules of the Bureau of Internal Revenue.

Depletion (for example, for lumber, minerals, or oil removed) is added to stated profits, since it is not considered a part of the using up of capital ("capital consumption") in the sense wanted in the national income accounts. Capital gains and losses are eliminated from profits: they are not a part of incomes created by current *production.*[6]

The tax return reports themselves are more than two years late, and estimation is needed in the meantime. And stated profits as given in the first reports are subject to a drastic increase, since the auditing of the Bureau, which goes on over about a fifteen-year period, regularly discovers much additional profits. (From the experience of one recent year, tax liability will eventually be raised through auditing by about 75 per cent!) The figures reported by the Department of Commerce attempt to forecast this eventual correction.

1950 dividends amounted to a little over 4 per cent of personal income.

(2c) Interest accruing to persons (about 4½ per cent of personal income in 1950) is estimated from a wide variety of

[6] See p. 46.

sources of varing reliability. The net interest paid by government is not counted as part of national income or product on the ground that it does not measure current production. It is counted instead as a special kind of tranfer payment. (If, to take a contrary point of view, one thought that such interest was the condition for added government production, then it *would* be counted as part of national income.[7])

Interest accruing to persons is estimated as a residual; (a) the total of interest paid minus (b) that paid to U.S. businesses and to foreigners. And so it is subject to the chance of cumulative error that afflicts all residuals. If, for example, (a) is slightly too large, and (b) slightly too small, then the remainder would be much too large.

Corporation income tax returns are the source for monetary interest paid by corporations. For interest paid by farmers, estimates of total farm debt, developed by the Bureau of Agricultural Economics from census and sample reports, are multiplied by relevant interest rates.

Imputed interest, that is, services received in lieu of money interest, is a large component. It is calculated in general for commercial banks and other financial intermediaries as the property income they receive, minus the money income they pay over to the owners of funds entrusted to them. In other words, a person who keeps money in a bank or like institution is considered to be getting in return two kinds of payments: a money interest payment (large or small or even zero), and a payment in the form of services in excess of any service charges paid. The main sources of data for banks are the published banking statistics of the Federal Reserve System, surveys carried on by the Federal Reserve, and statistics of the Federal Deposit Insurance Corporation. Government bodies, federal, state, and local, publish in their budget reports data on interest paid and received, summarized in part in the *Government Finances* publications of the Census Bureau.

(3) "Mixed income receipts from both work and property"

---

7 See p. 45.

accruing to unincorporated enterprises fall into three main divisions: (*a*) farm income, (*b*) that of proprietorships and partnerships (that is, unincorporated businesses), and (*c*) that of professional people (doctors, lawyers, engineers, accountants, and the like). Of these three, the first two are much the largest.

(*a*) Farm income estimates are prepared by the Bureau of Agricultural Economics. The five and a half million farm enterprises in the United States do not keep any uniform accounts of income and outgo. Often they keep no accounts at all. But over the course of many years, there has been built up a large body of *aggregative* statistics—both current data, and "bench mark" special studies, made from time to time. The procedure is to calculate the cash value of all farm crops and livestock products and deduct estimated production costs. The basic information comes from a Census of Agriculture carried out every five years, from the continuing Crop and Livestock Reporting System, which has a reporter in every significant farming township in the country, and from businesses that are concerned with the storing, processing, or marketing of farm products and farm supplies. For meat animals, most dairy products, cotton, tobacco, and sugar beets, only a few large firms are involved, and reliable information is collected without much delay.

Together with cash receipts from crops and meat and dairy products are counted the value of consumption on the farm of farm products (estimated from an annual mail survey), the rental value of farm homes, and of government payments to farmers. This total is adjusted for any change in the quantity of crops and livestock on farms (valued at year-end prices), in order to get a figure for gross farm income resulting from production of the given year.

Then there is a deduction for production expenses: depreciation of buildings and equipment, hired labor, taxes, farm mortgage interest, rents and government payments made to non-farm landlords, and current operating expense (feed, fer-

tilizer, livestock bought, etc.). These are estimated from a remarkably diverse group of sources.

Gross farm income minus production expenses gives net
farm income.

(b) The incomes of unincorporated businesses are the total
for about 65 industrial groups. Of these, three—retail and
wholesale trade and construction—have regularly made up
over half the total.

The basic data come from total receipts in industrial censuses.
These are multiplied by profit ratios in Bureau of Internal
Revenue summaries from the "business" schedules of individual
income tax returns and from compulsory reports filed by partnerships. These are adjustments for omissions and for depletion charges; and capital gains and losses are eliminated.

(c) Among the professions, most income goes to doctors,
lawyers and dentists. Incomes are estimated by multiplying
the number of people in independent practice (from tabulations of the professional associations), by net income as averaged from questionnaire surveys. Returns on these surveys
give cause for some doubt about their accuracy. Estimates for
engineer and accountant incomes are still more doubtful,
though their total is relatively small.

(4) Last among the components of *personal* income is transfer payments: old age and survivors' insurance benefits, unemployment insurance, railroad retirement payments, pensions, direct relief, veterans' allowances and benefits, disability pay, and the like. These are a part of personal income but
not of national income, since they are not payment for work
currently done.

Most transfer payments are from government agencies. In
recent years accurate and prompt information on nearly all
types of government transfers can be gotten from the agency
records, or (for the Federal Government) from Treasury summaries. The Social Security Administration summarizes much
of the available data from state and local government agencies.

The data for business tranfers come from weak sources.

Luckily the total is in any case small. Corporate reports on gifts to non-profit institutions are given in tax returns to the Bureau of Internal Revenue; other components are estimated from indirect and partial sources.[8]

This completes the items making up personal income.

On the expenditure side of the personal accounts, the largest item by far is consumer expenditures.

(6a) and (6b) 86 per cent of 1950 personal income went for the purchase of consumer goods and services. Also these same consumer expenditures made up 68 per cent of gross national expenditure.[9] Hence the accuracy of these estimates is a critical matter.

Unfortunately consumers seldom keep records of what they are doing with their money, and often do not know what they are doing. Even if they did have accurate records, the investigator would be faced with forty million households to survey.

The chief method of estimate used for consumer *commodities* (as distinct from services) is an indirect one, called the "commodity flow" method. Data are obtained for the volume of output of factories, farms and fisheries, valued at producer prices. Then the flow of these commodities is traced. Some are sold direct to consumers, the rest to foreigners, to wholesalers and to retailers. (Wholesalers obtain an additional supply from imports.) Wholesalers in turn sell mostly to retailers, but to some degree direct to consumers. The markup of wholesalers and retailers are estimated, and transportation charges and retail sales taxes are added in, to get the final total value of consumer commodities, at the prices actually paid by consumers.

The commodity flow method is indirect and requires complex adjustments. Its chief advantage is that it makes use of the detailed and complete Census of Manufactures, which covered in the year 1939 (still used in 1951 as a bench mark) about four thousand commodities. But the alternative is to

---

8 Cf. p. 29.
9 See Table 10 on p. 67.

use as a basis the Census of Retail Trade, which does not, in the main, classify by kinds of commodity but by a rather broad classification of kind of store.[10]

The Census of Manufactures was taken every odd year in the period 1929—39. There were none during the war years. Hence for 1940—1951 retail sales data have mainly been used to carry forward estimates based on the bench mark of the 1939 Census. This procedure involves growing possibilities of error as the years have gone on: both business and consumers might buy larger or smaller proportions from retail sellers, and goods handled by given kinds of stores might vary in type. There was a new Census of Manufactures in 1947, and of Retail and Wholesale Trade in 1948. These, though less complete than the pre-war censuses, were being used in 1951 to prepare new bench mark estimates for 1947—which will be checked against direct estimates for *total* retail sales.

For a small proportion of consumer expenditures—gasoline and oil, passenger cars, ice and most fuels—a "retail valuation" method is used. Estimated quantities bought by consumers are multiplied by average retail prices. For a still smaller proportion—food and fuel produced and consumed on farms—the basic information comes mainly from sample surveys.

Information on consumer *services* comes from a wide variety of sources. The Census of Population and Housing provides data on rents of non-farm dwellings and the Census of Agriculture on the rental value of farm houses. The final figures require complex adjustments, based in part on surveys, with considerable interpolating between Censuses, allowances for non-reporting, and estimating for depreciation and maintenance costs. The Census of Business has carried data on service industries like auto repair and care, motion picture admissions, cleaning and dyeing, barber and beauty parlour service, laundering, funerals and burials, photographic studios, hotels

---

10 The use of the Census of Retail Trade would not eliminate the need for estimating the part of sales to consumers not made through retail stores, and the part of retail stores sales not made to consumers.

and tourist cabins. In 1951 the 1939 Census was still being relied on, with projections forward based on various government and private reports. In some of these (like auto repair) there is a considerable problem of allocation between consumers and businesses.

There are regular annual reports by government and private sources for such consumer services as railroad, bus, and airline transportation, and telephone, bank, and financial institution services (both those charged for and those rendered without charge).

Sample studies are the main sources of estimates for such items as professional services by doctors, dentists, lawyers, and the like, for automobile insurance, and for payments to labor unions, for postage, and for telegrams.

(6c) Interest on personal debt comes from Federal Reserve data on consumer credit multiplied by interest rates as derived from samples for different kinds of debt.

(6d) "Net purchases from abroad" means the expenditure of U. S. residents on merchandise imports, travel expense, and the like, plus personal gift remittances abroad. It is entered minus the similar expenditures of foreigners in the United States. The estimates come from sources described below.

(7) Among "personal taxes, fees, etc.," by far the most important item is the Federal individual income tax, entered as recorded by the Bureau of Internal Revenue. Federal estate and gift taxes also fall under this heading, also reported by the Bureau. Fines, penalties, forfeitures, and various other charges to individuals are estimated from Trust Fund and Miscellaneous Treasury Receipts, as reported in the annual Budget of the United States Government.

(8) Personal saving is a residual. Take personal income (5), subtract consumer expenditures (6) and personal taxes, fees, etc. (7), and you have left what consumers did not spend or have taxed away from them, in other words, what they saved.

This series can be checked for accuracy against a Securities and Exchange Commission direct estimate of personal savings from changes in the assets and liabilities of persons. And it can also be checked against saving data from the Federal Reserve's annual sample survey of consumer finances, published in segments in the Federal Reserve Bulletin.

2. The account for business

Once again, we can look to the sources of all receipts to this sector of the economy—that is, to all businesses taken together; and, having totaled up all receipts, see what was done with them. As in the consumer account, sources of revenue are on the right, and expenditures, or allocations, from this revenue on the left. (See Table 2, p. 22.)

Businesses in the United States, corporate and non-corporate and including government enterprises, are here consolidated. That is, they are treated, with one qualification, as if they were all combined into one giant concern. We tabulate the value of production of this concern (which we list as receipts accruing to the concern, whether the product is actually sold or only exists as an increase in inventories available for sale). This giant concern allocates all revenue either as (13) incomes (wages and salaries, rents, interest to non-business lenders, and net earnings of corporations and partnerships and proprietorships accruing to their owners); or as (14) indirect taxes[11], charges and gifts; or sets it aside as (15) a depreciation allowance against the wearing out and obsolescence of buildings and equipment, since they must eventually be replaced if production is to continue.

The "one qualification" arises because of our special interest in how much capital goods are produced in the economy. And so the Department of Commerce, the United Kingdoms Central Statistical Office, and other measurers of national income feel it is useful to set up a separate account for "Savings and

---

11 Direct (that is, income) taxes on businesses are levied on the net earnings of corporations, proprietors, and partners. They are considered to be deducted out of those earnings. Indirect taxes are sales and excise taxes and like charges, which are not levied "directly" on corporations or on persons as such, but on their products or activities.

TABLE 2

BUSINESS RECEIPTS AND EXPENDITURES, 1950 *

(in billions of dollars)

Expenditures		Receipts	
13. Income originating from business 209.0		10. Consolidated net sales of business 248.3	
a. Wages and salaries to employees (plus other labor income) (1*a*) 123.2		*a.* to consumers (6*a*) . 184.5	
b. Employer contributions for social insurance (20*b*) 3.2		*b.* to government (22*b*) 18.1	
c. Rents to persons (2*a*) 8.0		*c.* to business on capital account (36) 44.5	
d. Net interest (2*c*) ... 3.5		*d.* to foreigners (29*a*) 1.1	
e. Gross corporate profits, adjusted 35.2		11. Change in business inventories (37) 4.3	
f. Income of unincorporated business, adjusted (3) 36.0			
14. Indirect business taxes, nontax charges, transfers, and adjustments 22.5			
a. Indirect business taxes and non-tax charges (19) 23.8			
b. Business transfer payments (4*b*) 8			
c. Statistical discrepancy (34) .... —1.8			
d. Current surplus minus subsidies of government enterprises (23*c*) .. —.3			
15. Allowances for capital consumption (32*a*) 21.2			
16. Uses of gross business revenue 252.7		12. Gross business receipts (and product) 252.7	

* Adapted from *Survey of Current Business, National Income Supplement*, 1951, p. 148. Final digits are rounded, and so subtotals may not add up exactly to totals.

Investment" (Table 5 below), showing the sources and uses of investment funds. (Any other kind of transaction could be similarly singled out, if we wished, even to accounts for toy balloons or tomato soup.) Since the capital accounts are set up separately, any transaction between another sector of the economy and this capital account appears once in the given sector account, and once again in the capital account.

As to the sources of the data given on the receipts side: (10a) "Consolidated net sales of business to consumers," comes from sources already indicated for purchases (pp. 18-20); (10b) "Business sales to government," is estimated on the basis of budget data of various government bodies in the United States. In general, statements of total expenditures are taken as the starting point, then various subtractions are made (for transfer payments, for purchase of land and existing capital assets,[12] for government loans and subsidies, and the like). Finally certain additions are made for government purchases of goods and services not entered in the original statements. The process is a roundabout one, but necessary because government basis data do not list goods and services bought separately. At this point we have government purchases of goods and services from all sources.

In order to get "government purchases from business," two series are deducted: compensation to government employees, and net government purchases from abroad (taken from U.S. balance-of-payments statistics). Because of its calculation by successive subtractions and additions, the resulting figure is peculiarly subject to error. It absorbs whatever errors not-offset-by-opposing-errors that exist in each of the constituent series.

(10c) and (11) "Sales to business on capital account" plus "change in business inventories" is the private capital forma-

---

[12] Since these are not a part of current production, and so should not be counted in government payments for *currently produced* goods and services.

tion (or private investment[13]) of the economy. It measures total production of business fixed works and structures, business equipment, and the change in stocks of raw materials and of partly finished and finished goods. There is no deduction for wearing-out or obsolescence of capital goods. (As a rule-of-thumb for borderline cases, capital goods are defined as durable production goods having an average life of over three years.)

The volume of private investment is critically important both for future productive capacity and productivity in the economy, and for determining the level of employment and trend toward deflation or inflation.

For 1950 the estimates run, in more detail:

```
Gross private domestic investment ...........................$48.9 billion
    10c. Net sales of business to business on capital account
        (36)  ...............................................  44.5
            1. New construction  ...........................  22.1
            2. Producers' durable equipment ...............  22.5
    11. Change in business inventories (37)  ...............   4.3
```

The data for (11) "Change in business inventories" will be discussed below (pp. 27-28).

(10c [1]). New construction is that of dwellings and other buildings, dams, bridges, roads, canals, and the like. Public construction is estimated separately, as a component of government purchases of goods and services.

The difficulties of getting information on private construction are considerable. Much construction is done by small firms that appear and disappear as the volume of business changes. Many firms have no fixed or recognizable place of business. Some construction is not done by "construction firms" at all. The final estimates are confessed by Commerce to be subject to considerable uncertainty as to coverage, valuation, and timing.

---

13 We use the word *investment* to mean *real,* or *physical,* investment—that is, the purchase of the kinds of currently produced output listed. It does not mean financial, or monetary, investment, which is the purchase of securities, or of goods whose production was completed during some past period.

The figures are built up by four general routes: (a) **Regular** formal reports are made by public utilities on their construction activity. These have excellent coverage and reliability. (b) Non-farm construction other than dwellings mainly comes from F. W. Dodge Corporation monthly summations of contract awards in the thirty-seven states east of the Rockies. An allowance is made for later contract cancellations. Values are fairly accurate for reported projects except during times of rapid price changes (when the final price paid will often be different from that first negotiated).[14] Estimates must be added in for omitted projects (such as construction carried on by property owners for themselves), and for the other eleven states. The allocation of a time period during which the building is supposed actually to take place can be no more than roughly correct. (c) Estimates for non-farm dwellings in areas where building permits are required come from those permits. The valuations are not accurate, being usually below the mark. An allowance is made for under-valuation. The time during which construction actually goes on can be estimated only roughly. Coverage is good for the given areas. (d) The remaining estimates have generally lower reliability than the above. For non-farm dwellings where no permits are required, sample surveys give data for units started and average construction costs. For farm construction, the Bureau of Agricultural Economics bases its figures also on sampling. There is considerable interpolation and extrapolation, and reliance on indirect information like sales of windmills, silos, and farm electric-lighting systems. Oil and gas well drilling rests on a 1939 Census of Mineral Industries, with projections onward from trade information on number of wells completed and costs per well.

(10c [2]). Data for most producers' durable equipment come from "commodity flow" estimates of the sort described under consumer purchases (pp. 18-19). But retail sales data could not be used to project onward the 1939 Census of Manufac-

---

14 Due to clauses allowing cost changes to be incorporated in the final price.

tures, since producers' durable equipment is bought in large volume direct from manufacturers and from wholesalers, and also since much of it goes to government use and export. For the 1946—50 estimates these are the main steps: manufacturers sales by major commodity groups (from 1946 surveys and later samples), *plus* transportation charges, *minus* exports, *minus* change in wholesalers' inventories, *plus* wholesalers and retailers' markups, *minus* government purchases. The Department of Commerce judges that its estimates for producers' equipment are somewhat more reliable than its estimates for consumer commodities.

Other methods are used for three special groups. "Business motor vehicles" consist of trucks, truck trailers, busses, and an allocation between business and consumers for passenger car sales. Statistics from *Automobile Facts and Figures,* published by the Automobile Manufacturers' Association, are the basic data. Expenditure of railroads on equipment is summarized by the Association of American Railroads up to and through the last World War, and by the Interstate Commerce Commission since. There is a small item for business purchases of ships and boats, in recent years from 1939 Census of Manufactures, extrapolated by data from the Bureau of Customs and the Maritime Administration.

(10d) "Net sales of business to foreigners," is discussed below (pp. 36-38).

Under business expenditures: wages and salaries to employees from business (13a), and rents to persons (13c), and net interest (13d) are in the main the same figures we have already looked at under receipts of consumers (1a, 2a, 2c). But personal interest receipts come not only from business, but also from government, from abroad, and from other consumers (or "households and institutions"). And business outlay for labor includes employer contributions for social insurance (13b), which are not considered part of personal income. The social insurance data come from regular contribution reports filed by employers with the U. S. Treasury or with the administering agencies. The reports come in late, usually by about three months, and are adjusted to time them with the wages and salaries on which they are levied. Some small corrections need to be made for reports that turn out to be in error, or that are delinquent.

(13) "Gross corporate profits, adjusted," breaks down as follows:

13e. Gross corporate profits, adjusted ....$35.2 billion
   1. Corporate profits tax liability (18) 18.6
   2. Dividends (2b) 8.8
   3. Undistributed corporate profits (32b[1]) 12.9
   4. Inventory valuation adjustment (32b [2]) ....—5.1

Total corporation profits are in part paid to governments in taxes (their obligations in 1950 added up to a bit over half of total earnings) ; in part distributed as dividends; and in part retained (or kept undistributed).[15] This latter part has been in recent years the main source of the funds that corporations have put into expansion of their plant and equipment.

(13e[2]) and (13e[3]) The sources of estimates of corporate earnings distributed and retained have been discussed above (p. 14).

(13e[4]) As for "Inventory valuation adjustment," any increase in inventories is of course a part of production; any decrease means that more has been sold than has been produced. Hence any measure of national production (or income) must include an allowance for the net *change* in inventories in the time period concerned.

But the final figure for inventory change is not too reliable. To calculate it, the difference must be taken between two relatively large and volatile totals (for the beginning and the end of the period); and so, here again, small errors in the totals can cumulate to large errors in the difference.

---

15 Dividends as reported in (13e[2]) differ from those reported in Table 1 (2b), and in national income totals, because dividends paid by business partly accrue to foreign residents, and because U. S. consumers receive part of their dividends from foreign businesses. This adjustment for international flow applies also to "Undistributed corporate earnings."

The original data on business inventories come from Bureau of Internal Revenue material from annual corporate tax returns. For non-farm, non-corporate inventories, data come from the Internal Revenue Bureau and from the Census Bureau. For agriculture there are the five-year censuses and periodic sample surveys in between. These are adjusted for omissions.

The main problem comes in valuing these inventories. What is wanted for national income purposes is the change in physical volume multiplied by average prices over the period concerned. But the inventory accounting methods of firms differ widely, and are usually inappropriate for national income purposes. Hence adjustment procedures are applied to underlying data, divided into groups in accord with the accounting procedure used. About one-tenth of the total non-farm inventories are thought to be originally estimated on a "last-in-first-out" basis. (Inventories are valued at the price of the last-bought stocks on hand, where those stocks have been bought at various prices.) Most of the rest of inventories are originally valued on a "first-in-first-out" basis. Adjustment procedures for these two main groups differ considerably.

The corporate inventory data of the Bureau of Internal Revenue are not available until at least two years after the event, and are based on preliminary data in the meantime.

(13f) "Income of unincorporated business, adjusted," is the same as item (3) under Personal Income (pp. 15-17).

(14a) "Indirect business taxes and non-tax charges," is, for the Federal Government, mainly excise taxes levied on the production or sale of commodities. Collections are reported monthly to the Bureau of Internal Revenue. As in other national income series relating to production, it is not the date of collection of these taxes and charges that determines when they enter the income accounts, but the date at which the liability arose in the course of productive activities. Some of these series need no time adjustment, others are shifted back one month, others six months. The adjustment to an accrual basis cannot be completely accurate, but is approximately right.

For the states, sales taxes are the main source of revenue. Data are from official reports. Other indirect state taxes often require uncertain allocations between "persons" and businesses. Local indirect business taxes are still less reliable. Except in recent years and census years, they are based on fragmentary data, and they also require estimating of incidence on business as distinct from persons.

(14b) "Business transfer payments," is estimated in part from corporate tax return summaries, which report separately corporation gifts to non-profit institutions. Other transfers are from indirect and incomplete sources. Among them are bad debts owed by consumers, net thefts from business, cash prizes, and injury payments (other than to employees).

(14c) The "statistical discrepancy" arises rather because U.S. data are abundant and accurate than because of their deficiency. It represents the difference between two independently calculated estimates of the value of "gross production or income"—one calculated by summing up the value of final products, the second, by summing up totals of and adjustments to income.

In countries where data are sparse, only one of these routes to the estimate of gross product or income is possible and the second is estimated from the first. Hence no "discrepancy" appears in the accounts. But its absence is no evidence of accuracy.

(14d) "Surplus minus subsidies of Government enterprises" represents the net receipts of government from its own "enterprises," and so is similar in its national accounts significance to indirect business taxes: both are payments accruing to government out of the receipts of enterprises. Federal Government enterprises range from the Alaska Railroad and Army Post Exchanges, to Federal Intermediate Credit Banks, the Panama Canal Zone and the War Shipping Administration. The profit and loss statements of Federal Corporations are modified to exclude capital gains and losses (since these do not arise from current "production," which national income accounts try to measure). There are other adjustments. State and local enterprise surplus is calculated—and adjusted—from the *Government Finances* compilation of the Census Bureau.

(15) "Allowances for capital consumption," represents a major issue. Part of the proceeds from business sales ought to be set aside as an allowance against the wearing out and obsolescence of buildings and equipment so that they can be replaced. Unless this is done, a business will estimate its profits too high —and if, for example, it distributes them as dividends, will eventually find its buildings falling down and its equipment worn out and obsolete, with no funds to replace them. It was distributing not profits alone, but its capital.

Or, from a somewhat different point of view: only part of the value of a firm's current production comes from labor and raw materials input. Part comes from the use of plant and equipment which, as it grows worn out and obsolete, transfers its value to the firm's current production. If production is to continue at the same level of efficiency, plant and equipment must eventually be replaced.

But the capital consumption allowances that appear in the national accounts are, mainly because of price changes in the economy, only a crude approach to a true measure of *economic* depreciation and obsolescence. Aside from any question of errors in the reporting, there are strong biases when prices are rising, and when they are falling. This becomes clear as we look at the calculation methods.

15. Allowances for capital consumption (32*a*) ....$21.2 billion
   a. Depreciation charges 17.7
     b. Capital outlays charged to current expenses........... 2.9
     c. Accidental damage to fixed capital 6

(15*a*) Most capital consumption is depreciation, and about half of depreciation charges are on (1) corporate property. The data come mainly from Federal corporate income tax returns and hence are two years or more late. (They are pieced together in the meantime from a number of less reliable sources.) Bureau of Internal Revenue regulations value capital assets at their cost, and permit the writing down (depreciation) of this value over their estimated average life.[16]

In recent years it has become possible to estimate depreciation in (2) partnerships and proprietorships (other than farms and real estate) from personal income tax data adjusted for omissions, and from reports to the Bureau of Internal Revenue required of partnerships in 1939, 1945, and 1947.

The remainder of capital consumption allowances originate in a wide variety of sources, via a wide variety of methods, and some are subject to much error.

Depreciation in (3) non-corporate real estate businesses comes from two sources. For rented non-farm dwellings, reported rents (from an intricate estimating procedure) are multiplied by (sample-derived) ratios of depreciation to rent. For owner occupied non-farm dwellings, data of the 1940 Census of Population and Housing are the basic source. They are projected forward through the 1940's by sample surveys.

All three estimates of depreciation so far assume that the value to be depreciated is *original cost*. Hence if prices are rising, the permitted allowances are too small to replace the goods when they are worn out or obsolete. If prices are falling, the allowances are too large. This is the bias, in an economic sense referred to above.

Depreciation on (4) farms, also an important item, is estimated by the Bureau of Agricultural Economics. It includes only depreciation of farm property of people living on farms. (Farm property owned by landlords living off farms falls under "real estate businesses.") Estimates are made separately for seven kinds of farm property, mainly on sample data for average useful life. The "value" that is depreciated is *replacement*

---

16 For national defense facilities acquired after 1939, taxpayers were allowed to depreciate over sixty months, later modified to a period ending not later than September 30, 1945. A new accelerated depreciation came into effect under the defense program initiated in 1950. National income depreciation allowances are adjusted to include those calculated under the wartime and defense program rules.

cost, not the original cost used in all the other estimates of depreciation.

(15*b*) Businesses often enter durable items of small individual cost as current expense rather than as capital outlay. But in the national accounts, producers' goods having a normal life of three years or more are considered investment or capital goods. Only if their life span is less than this would their cost logically fall in current expense. Hence a rough approximation for "capital outlays charged to current expense" is listed, in place of a depreciation allowance for this kind of capital equipment. The Census of Manufactures is the basic source of valuation for those kinds of capital goods that it seems likely are by current accounting practice charged to current expense.

Similarly oil and gas well drilling is usually charged to "current expense," although it is considered a capital outlay in the national accounts. And so the estimated outlays are entered under this heading.

(15*c*) The small item for "accidental damage to fixed capital" estimates loss to private business from fires, natural events, and other accidents. Data come from such sources as the National Board of Fire Under-writers, reports of state foresters, the National Safety Council (for motor vehicles accidents, and the Weather Bureau (for losses from storms).

3. The government account

The "Government" consists of all government bodies and their subdivisions—federal, state, and local. It does not include business enterprises owned by government, which are put into the business account.

The sources of government receipts are taxes and social security contributions. Government receipts are spent on currently produced goods and services, and on transfer payments, including interest and net subsidies to government enterprises. There may be a budget surplus on this income and product account (receipts are greater than expenditure), or a deficit.

TABLE 3

GOVERNMENT RECEIPTS AND EXPENDITURES, 1950 *

(*in billions of dollars*)

Expenditures		Receipts	
22. Purchase of goods and services	42.5	17. Personal income taxes, fees, etc. (7)	20.5
a. Wages and salaries, plus supplements to employees (1*b*, 20*b*)	20.9	18. Corporate profits tax liability (13*e*[1])	18.6
b. Net purchases from business (10*b*)	18.1	19. Indirect business taxes and non-tax charges (14*a*) .	23.8
c. Net purchases from abroad (29*b*)	3.4	20. S o c i a l insurance contributions	7.0
23. Total transfers and subsidies	19.3	*a.* From e m p l o y e e s (1*d*)	2.9
a. Transfer payments (4*a*)	14.3	*b.* F r o m employers (6*b*, 13*b*, 22*a*)	4.0
b. Net i n t e r e s t paid (2*c*)	4.7		
c. Subsidies minus current surplus of government enterprises (14*d*)	.3		
24. Deficit (—) or surplus (+) on income and product transactions (33)	+8.0		
25. Government expenditures and surplus	69.8	21. Government receipts	69.8

* Adapted from *Survey of Current Business, National Income Supplement,* 1951, p. 149.

Several kinds of government transactions are not counted among government receipts or expenditures in the national income accounts. As we have mentioned before, borrowing and debt repayment do not appear in the government accounts or in any other of the national accounts. They are not a part of income, nor do they measure production. And since in these income and product accounts, we are concerned with the purchase of currently produced goods and services, we also exclude purchases of land, of previously produced buildings and equipment, and of other already existing capital assets.

All government bodies are consolidated in the account so that one reckoning can be presented. Hence transfers of funds from one government body to another do not appear.

The budgetary statistics of the various government bodies, from which these figures are totaled are readily available and highly reliable. But in most years they do not cover all government units and the classifications in the budgets are seldom what are wanted for national income accounts. The data are available six months to a year or more after the event, and are subject to rough estimates in the meantime. There are also some problems of timing, to match budget flows with the related production and income flows. The data are good, but not ideal, for national income purposes.

4. The rest-of-the-world account

The "Rest-of-the-World" is viewed as a sector of the economy much like the other sectors. The Department of Commerce presents the account in this fashion:

TABLE 4

Receipts and Expenditures of the Rest-of-the-World, 1950 *
(in billions of dollars)

Expenditures	Receipts
28. Net payments of factor income to the United States. +1.3	26. Net foreign investment in the United States (38) .... —2.3
a. Wages and salaries (1c) .... .02	
b. Interest (2c) 2	
c. Dividends (2b) 4	
d. Branch profits (32c) . .7	
29. Net purchases by the United States .... —3.6	
a. From business (10d) 1.1	
b. From Government (22c) .... —3.4	
c. From persons (6d) .. —1.3	
30. Net current payments to the United States .... —2.3	27. Net foreign investment in the United States .... —2.3

* Adapted from *Survey of Current Business, National Income Supplement,* 1951, p. 149

"Net foreign investment in the United States," or simply "net foreign investment," is defined as net receipts from transactions involving goods, services, and gifts. That is, it is the value of exports of goods from the United States, *plus* U.S. services rendered to foreigners, *plus* money gifts from them[17], *minus* the value of imports of goods and services, *plus* money gifts to foreigners.

For 1950, the total is negative, which means that the United States—business, government, and persons counted all together—owed foreigners more for goods, services, and gifts than foreigners owed to the United States. The main cause was heavy purchases by the U.S. Government after the outbreak of war in Korea (a total of $3.6 billion for the whole year).

How was the 1950 net import of goods and services (including gifts) paid for? In some way, purchasing power had to be put into the hands of people abroad who sold to the United States. Partly this was accomplished through lending and direct investment (that is, through buying real estate or other property), partly through gold flows:

Net capital movement to the U. S. .... $2.3 billions
    Net long and short term lending, and direct investment. .4
    Export of gold from the U. S. 1.7
    Errors and omissions 2

The major item was the gold we transferred to foreign ownership. In addition, lending to the United States and purchasing of assets in the United States by foreigners was $ .4 billions more than the opposite flow; and these, like the gold, provided foreign funds with which to pay for the net imports.

There is still a discrepancy of $.2 billions between the total of the goods, services, and gifts items; and the net capital movement calculated separately. The cause lies in errors

---

17 If this way of treating gifts seems confusing, consider that a money gift to U. S. residents from foreigners implies a payment falling due to the U. S., in just the same way that an export of merchandise implies a payment falling due to the U. S. So likewise for gifts to foreigners, and imports.

and omissions in both accounts. It is the goods, services, and gifts account that enters national income totals. But in most years it is uncertain which account is the more accurate.

The data for net foreign investment come from the official balance of payments of the United States, as calculated by the Balance of Payments Division of the Department of Commerce. The figures are published quarterly in the Survey of Current Business and occasionally in special bulletins.

(28a) "Wages and salaries" are those received by U.S. residents from foreign governments (with basis fragmentary reports from some foreign missions) and from international organizations (with data from those organizations, *minus* the corresponding outpayments.

(28b) Interest is a larger item. Interest paid (1) to the U. S. Government is reported by the receiving agencies; (2) to holders of foreign bonds sold in the U.S. by regular questionnaire surveys of paying agents in the U.S., corrected for coverage by comparison with a 1942 Census by the Treasury of U.S.-owned assets abroad; (3) to U.S. corporations by their foreign branches and affiliates, from the same 1942 census carried forward by sample reports, income tax returns, and corporate reports to stockholders and to the Security and Exchange Commission; and (4) "other foreign interest" received, by applying average bond yields to bonds held, as estimated from the 1942 Census and from Foreign Exchange reports. Interest *paid to* foreigners is derived from tax returns to the Bureau of Internal Revenue, and from an extrapolation of a 1941 census of foreign-owned assets in the U.S. Plainly there is room for error to creep in among these approximations.

(28c) and (28d) Dividends and branch profits are estimated by the same general methods aplied to interest. The 1942 bench mark census, extrapolation on a sample basis, and tax reports to the bureau of Internal Revenue are the mainstays.

(29) More important quantitatively than these "factor incomes" is the balance of "purchases," which includes mainly merchandise, transportation, and travel. *Plus* items are ex-

ports of goods or services from the United States, or the equivalent; *minus* items are imports into the U.S., or the equivalent. Only the net balance is given, and the amounts are broken down into three groups: transactions with business, Government, and persons. Usually the net balance, or difference, is small compared to large and volatile totals for exports on the one hand, and imports on the other. Hence the net balance is subject to cumulating errors in the totals.

Merchandise trade is by far the largest item under "purchases." The estimates are primarily from declaration forms filed with the Collector of Customs, and from reports of Federal Government agencies that buy from and sell to foreigners. There is adjustment for trade not giving rise to financial claims—for example, shipments of grain to Canada for storage.

The Customs valuations are not always the true values. Customs has no financial interest in exports, nor in duty-free imports, nor in the valuation of imports on which "specific" duties are levied (so much per pound, or per cubic foot, or per unit). There are probably many cases of wrong valuation in these categories, despite some checks. And even imports dutiable on an *ad valorem* basis (as a per cent of the "value") may be under the law assessed at a different value than that paid in the foreign country.

U.S. ocean freight revenues from foreigners, 1948 and later, come from reports filed with the Maritime Administration or from direct inquiry. The revenues for earlier years are estimated from average tonnages carried of various commodities, multiplied by appropriate freight rates. Payments to foreign ship operators for all years are estimated by the latter procedure.

For travel expenditures of U.S. residents abroad, and of foreigners in the U.S., the basic procedure is to multiply numbers of travellers by average expenditures as estimated from sample questionnaires. All foreign visitors' travel expense in the U.S. is considered purchases from U.S. business; travel of U.S. residents abroad is divided between "business" and "personal" outlay.

Gifts of money from U.S. persons and institutions are included in "sales by the rest-of-the-world to persons" (since the money is due to the foreigner just as if the U.S. had imported goods). Gifts by the U.S. Government are similarly included with "sales from abroad to government." Foreign money orders handled by the Post Office are a main basis of estimate, though these must be adjusted upward to approximate a complete coverage. Institutions (like the Red Cross, and the Friends' Service Committee) report in a yearly questionnaire; and of course the agencies of the Federal Government keep official records of gifts abroad.

5. The savings and investment account

Savings and investment are singled out for special attention for two main reasons: because of the importance for productivity and maximum total output of the rate of purchase of new buildings, machines and inventories; and because of the importance of the flow of saving and of investment for analyzing tendencies toward inflation or depression.

On the right in Table 5 are the savings of persons, the gross savings of business, and the Government surplus (the excess of its tax receipts over its expenditure on income account). If Government expenditure exceeds taxes, this entry is the Government deficit, and is negative.

This "gross saving" is equal to "gross investment," the components of which are listed on the left.

This last national account is the first in which equality between receipts and expenditures, that is, between gross private savings plus government surplus and gross investment, is not immediately obvious. And as a matter of fact this equality is much the most interesting one found in the national accounts, since most of the discussion of the past decade and a half about the cause and cure of depression and unemployment on the one hand, and inflation on the other, have been phrased in terms of the saving-investment relation. But we postpone our

TABLE 5

GROSS SAVINGS AND INVESTMENT ACCOUNT, 1950 *
(*in billions of dollars*)

Expenditures		Receipts	
36. Business purchases of capital goods (10c) 44.5		31. Personal saving (8) 10.7	
37. Change in business inventories (11) 4.3		32. Gross business saving 29.7	
38. Net foreign investment in the United States (26) .... —2.3		*a.* Capital consumption allowances (15) 21.2	
		b. Undistributed (domestic) corporate profits, adjusted 7.8	
		1. Undistributed (domestic) corporate earnings (13e[3]) 12.9	
		2. Corporate inventory valuation adjustment (13e [4]) ... —5.1	
		c. Foreign branch profits (28d) 7	
		33. Government surplus (24) .. 8.0	
		34. Statistical discrepancy (14c) .... —1.8	
39. Gross investment 46.6		35. Gross private savings and government surplus 46.6	

* Adapted from *Survey of Current Business, National Income Supplement*, 1951, p. 149. Final digits are rounded, and so subtotals may not add up exactly to totals.

inquiry on this matter until toward the end of the next chapter, after we have looked at the construction and meaning of the measures of national income.

The individual items of the savings-and-investment account have all been discussed before.

Interrelationships of Industries—Leontief's Input-Output Table

The national accounts are not the only way of showing interrelationships among the sectors of the economy. It is possible to show in one table (a) the distribution of the outputs of various sectors of the economy, and correspondingly (b) from what sources the inputs used by each of these sectors were obtained.

Table 6 is a simplified presentation of such an input-output table for the United States in 1939.

One can read the table in this fashion: Each sector of the economy listed on the left, and reading down, supplied goods and services of the given values to the other sectors of the economy listed at the top, and reading across. For example, the agriculture and foods industry produced an output valued at $17,059 million. Of this total, an amount of goods valued at $555 million was bought by the minerals and manufacturing industries; $643 million was bought by the transport and trade industries; $14,522 million was bought by consumers (households).

Or one can look on the relationships in a reversed fashion: The inputs of the sectors listed at the top came, in the indicated quantities, from the sectors listed at the left. The government, for example, bought goods to the amount of $559 million from the minerals and manufacturing industry, paid its employees (households) $7,897 million; and so forth.

Of the total input of any sector the proportions which come from each supply sector (including households, which supply labor) change only slowly over time. The relations indicated among the units of the economy by such a table, therefore, furnish a useful guide to the relationships we should expect within the moderately close future.[18] Analysis of these actual interrelationships can lead to prediction of changed size of output and changed distribution of outputs and of inputs of specific industries, in response to changes in over-all employment, or to transition from war to peacetime production. A table showing total outputs of different industries, without any indication

---

[18] Cf. Wassily Leontief, "Economic Statistics and Postwar Policies," in *Postwar Economic Problems,* pp. 163-64. Seymour E. Harris. New York: McGraw-Hill and Co., 1943.

TABLE 6

INPUT-OUTPUT RELATIONSHIPS, 1939 *

(*in millions of dollars*)

	I	II	III	IV	V	VI	
	Agriculture and Foods	Minerals and Manufacturing	Transport and Trade	All Other Industries and Inventories	Government	Households	Total Outputs
I Agriculture and foods...	....	555	643	1,330	9	14,522	17,059
II Minerals and manufacturing	1,329	....	2,730	16,265	559	12,152	33,035
III Transport and trade...	2,261	5,977	....	1,653	100	689	10,680
IV All other industries	9,103	13,410	1,817	....	7,435	34,562	66,327
V Government .	1,073	384	32	9,712	....	2,594	13,795
VI Households ..	4,167	14,212	2,548	40,024	7,897	....	68,848
Total inputs	17,933	34,538	7,770	68,984	16,000	64,519	

* Calculated from data of the Bureau of Labor Statistics, Postwar Division of the Employment and Occupational Outlook Branch.

of the channels of use of those outputs, omits the detail of interconnections that an input-output table can present.

Such a table can be developed in as little or as much detail as we like. We might class separately households, and all other "industries," including government. Or we might have fifty or ninety or more divisions, depending on the data available and on our purpose. Hence input-output relationships, no less than the national accounts, offer a bridge between the whole economy and as many subdivisions as we wish and can calculate.

CHAPTER TWO

The National Income

No ECONOMIST HAS HAD THE COURAGE TO TRY TO ESTIMATE the accounts of the whole world, even if such figures could be useful. National accounts are what the name implies, figures for a given nation. This limitation causes vexing problems. Some people live and work in one country but are citizens of another. Some of the property in one country is owned by residents or citizens of other countries, and interest and dividends on the property are paid across national borders. As international trade proceeds, goods, and services are provided both for and by the foreigner.

The national income or product might be calculated to include all the goods and services produced in a given nation. It would exclude all production abroad even if the owners are residents of the given country, and it would include domestic production even if the output goes to benefit foreign owners.

The Department of Commerce uses a different principle. Its data apply to continental United States, excluding the territories and possessions. The production and income measured are those attributable to resources supplied by *residents* of continental United States. "Resources" include both work and property. The actual production may or may not go on within the continental borders.

Measuring versus appraising

On this matter the Department of Commerce makes a reasonable decision. But there are other reasonable decisions that might have been taken instead. Every statistician concerned with calculating national income must make up his mind on borderline matters. Should he, for example, include (a) theft from businesses, (b) income of servants, (c) the services of housewives, (d) the rental value of houses lived in by their owners, (e) unemployment relief, (f) the value of furniture produced in a home wood-working shop for home use, (g) the value of shaves self-administered at home instead of administered by a barber? [1]

The decisions of the national income estimator hinge partly on his own or the prevailing social philosophy as to what is *productive economic* activity, and partly on the kinds and reliability of data available. Hence his estimate is not an objective statement of fact, such as a surveyor's measure of the acreage of a plot of ground, where the thing to be measured is known and the only question is how accurately it can be measured. What constitutes "national income" is itself subject to a range of valid uncertainty; and accuracy of measurement is a separate, though related, problem. Nonetheless, there is usually fairly close agreement between different careful estimates; for example, between Kuznet's data for the United States and of the Department of Commerce estimates.

We have met many specific problems of inclusion and exclusion in Chapter 1, in surveying the national accounts. Below we discuss them more generally as background for building up national income totals.

The Payments Approach: The Problem of Transfer Payments and Other Non-Income Payments

If we try to measure national income or product by adding up incomes created in production, we have, as we have seen,

---

[1] In the U. S. accounts: (a) and (e) are transfer payments, part of personal income (available for allocation by "persons" either for consumer goods and services, income taxes, or saving) but not a part of national income or product; (c), (f), and (g) are excluded from both personal income and national income; (b) and (d) are included in both.

the pitfall of a double count to avoid. The national income is a measure of production. But people often receive money payments without producing goods and services in exchange. These are transfer and other non-income payments. If we are adding up payments to get a total for the national income, we must exclude all non-income payments.

Suppose a carpenter gets $4000 for his work during a given year, interest of $20 on a loan he has made, $30 rent from leasing out a plot of land, and $400 as his share of earnings in a partnership arrangement in which he makes furniture in his spare time. He also receives a G. I. benefit of $500, a repayment of a loan of $300 he has previously made, and proceeds of $1000 from sale of a car. These sums total $6250.

Of this total $4450 should be entered as part of the national income or product (the payment for work, plus interest and rent, plus his share of the mixed work-and-property income of the partnership). The G. I. benefit of $500 is a transfer payment, and is added in to make a total of $4950 of "personal income," which does not measure production but is available for spending by a person in one way or another. The repayment and the proceeds from selling the car are not a part of income in any sense. They are only changes in the form in which the carpenter holds his property—money replaces the automobile and the I.O.U.

For the whole economy, this implies that national income (or product) equals the total earnings of work and property created in current production of goods and services. It includes wages and salaries, interest, rents, and the earnings of businesses (since these are part of the value of production accruing as income to the owners of the businesses). There is no deduction for any taxes that are levied on these incomes and siphon off a part.

Transfer payments to persons (gifts, grants, prizes, bad debts, thefts, old age and survivors' insurance benefits, unemployment insurance, railroad retirement payments, pensions, direct relief, veterans' allowances and benefits, disability pay, and the like) [2] make up a part of "personal income," but not of national income.

Loans and loan repayments, purchases of land, purchases of property produced in earlier years, prepayments for goods and services to be produced in times to come, are not part of the current national income or product in any sense.

A difficult decision must be made with respect to the interest that the government pays on the national debt. Does the interest paid measure a part of national production, in the same way that interest on loans to persons or business is taken to measure a service rendered? Or is government interest simply a transfer payment?

The Department of Commerce, reversing a previous stand, now considers such interest a transfer, and bars it from being counted as part of the national income. Most of the government debt was created to finance wars and current running expenses. If it did not lead to the creation of more capital goods, serving in turn to swell current output (the argument runs), it should be excluded. Its inclusion would distort upward postwar "product" as compared with prewar product.

(But, one might answer, does not winning wars make national product larger than if the war had been lost? Commerce would throw out this connection between government borrowing and national production as too philosophical and uncertain.) [3]

Other exclusions from national income

Even among human activities often thought of as "productive" are a number that do not enter the national income accounts. We cannot in our estimate of national production include all satisfaction-giving activities of the residents of a country. The attempt to do so would mean trying to measure the worthwhileness of life as a whole, rather than of its eco-

---

[2] Some of these can be considered payment for past services. But they are not payment for services rendered during the current year (or half- or quarter-year) for which income is being reckoned.

[3] *Survey of Current Business, National Income Supplement*, 1951, p. 48.

nomic aspects only. And as we try to value activities and products that are never bought and sold, such an attempt also involves us in extremely doubtful estimates. How much is the satisfaction worth that we obtain from an afternoon of fishing or of tinkering with the car? How much are the services of the housewife worth to her family? How much is our work on the flower bed and in mowing the lawn worth?

With only a few exceptions, estimates of national production include only goods and services that appear for sale on the market.

The exceptions are for a few closely allied flows of income and product, omission of which would make for anomalies in the accounts. Wages and salaries paid in kind rather than in the form of money are included (especially important for farm labor), as are also: the rental value of owner-occupied houses; food and fuel produced and consumed on farms; and services rendered without charge or with partial charge to their clients by financial institutions (such as commercial banks, which clear checks and keep accounts for their customers, making no charge or only a small charge for the service).

The bootlegger and the burglar may labor zealously for economic gain. Should their incomes be taken to measure a contribution to national income? Or perhaps a half or a third of their incomes? Commerce excludes all illegal activities—theft, bootlegging, smuggling, racketeering, drug peddling, gambling, and the like—from its measures of national income. The transfer payment effect of thefts and bad debts is measured and included in personal income.

As already indicated (page 14), capital gains and losses are excluded from national income. One might buy a house for $8000 and sell it for $9000, or buy a share of stock for $90 and sell it for $105. The seller is of course better off (if the prices of things he buys have not risen equally). But production of goods and services has not taken place; the society has no more houses or capital equipment at its disposal than before the transactions took place. Our figure for the national income is intended to measure the productive activity in the economy. Hence capital gains and losses have no place in it.

The Total Product Approach: Avoiding Double-Counting

The previous several pages have dealt with measuring national income or product by the payments approach, and with the problem of including only the right items. If we try to measure national income by adding together the value of all production, we have a similar problem of inclusion and exclusion.

We want, of course, to include all the output of the economy. It is all too easy, in building up the estimates, to forget some of the items. It is probable that the national income estimates of most countries are to some degree too low for this reason.

A parallel problem is how to avoid double- or multiple-counting of the products. In the course of production most businesses use up some of the output of other businesses. For instance electricity produced in the course of the year is partly used up in the mining of coal; the coal mined goes partly into the production of electricity, automobiles, and railroad transportation. And so on. But if we add into our figure for national production, for example, both the value of electricity produced and the value of coal used up (which is the output of a coal mining business somewhere in the economy), we shall be counting the value of the coal twice. We will emerge from our figuring with a mistakenly high estimate for national output. At first glance it looks as if we were in a miserable tangle of complications.

The solution is to count in national output, explicitly or implicitly, only the *value added* by each business. From value of output of the business we subtract value of supplies bought from other businesses and used up in production. If we total the value added by all enterprises in the economy, we shall arrive at a figure free of double-counting. This total measures the *final output* of goods and services in the economy, excluding *intermediate products* used up in producing the final products.

Actually the summing up of net value added by each business and industry is not a convenient road to estimating national production. But any method used, to be logically accurate, must lead to a total equivalent to this sum. The logic of net-value-added is a useful check on other methods.

The general presumption actually followed by the Department of Commerce is that purchases that are resold are used up in further production, that is, they are intermediate products that should not be counted separately. Purchases that are not resold cannot make up part of the cost, and hence part of the value, of other goods and services; and so they do enter the count of final output.

The result of this general presumption is that purchases by consumers, government, and foreigners, purchases of capital goods by business, and inventory changes are counted. Purchases of raw materials used up by business in the course of production are excluded.

This presumption turns out in practice to be in some degree arbitrary and there are qualifications to its application. But it is necessary to have such a rule for borderline cases where the motivation for buying and using products is not clear-cut. Production needs often influence consumer purchases, and consumer purchases often are utilized for productive ends. Hence any measure of total production is to some extent conventional in its exclusions and inclusions.[4]

National Income and Economic Welfare

Are national income figures a useful guide to the economic welfare of a people? If the national income rises, are people better off in material things? If it falls, are they worse off?

In 1950 the average person in the United States had a share of about $1590 in the national income. (*a*) Before we can say anything about the command over goods and services this

---

[4] *Survey of Current Business, National Income Supplement,* 1951, p. 31.

figure signifies, we need to know how high prices were. How far would this income go in the buying of goods and services?

(*b*) The money value figures that enter national income totals may not reflect the social value of production. The money value of whiskey output probably overstates its social values: it takes no account of the social cost of drunkenness, despite the Men of Distinction. Conversely, a state can draft its men into the army or compel its citizens into forced labor, and the social product resulting from their work may greatly exceed the cost figures at which it enters the national income accounts.

(*c*) "Non-economic" kinds of production, especially the services of housewives, do not enter the national accounts. This procedure tends to give an upward bias to national income accounts during decades when the economy is becoming increasingly commercial. When the housewife takes an outside job and hires a neighborhood girl to take care of the house, two new incomes enter the national accounts. But production has not increased by so much.

(*d*) There is no indication in national income figures of the effort and unpleasantness required to produce the income. Nor is any account taken of the amount of leisure in the society, though this is a part of material welfare. During past decades these omissions have tended to make national income series understate the rate of economic progress.

(*e*) The data measure production and not consumption. A large, or small, part of total output may consist of consumption goods, which alone contribute immediately to material welfare. About eight-ninths of United States output in past decades has consisted of consumer goods, but in Soviet Russia before World War II consumer goods were only a little over two-thirds of total output.

(*f*) Figures for total national income take no account of how unequally the national output is distributed.

(*g*) The data we have on "consumption" are for *expenditures* on consumer goods and services, not for the satisfaction consumers obtain from their purchases. There is not necessarily a parallel between consumer spending and consumer satisfaction. During World War II production of automobiles, radios, and washing machines for civilians nearly stopped, but we kept on using these devices. We simply made the ones we had last longer.

This is a weighty list of qualifications. But it does not imply that national income has no significance for measuring welfare. It is only that the figures must be interpreted. Figures don't lie, but they can be misleading. National income totals are more useful in portraying changes than absolute levels. Breakdowns of the totals are indispensable in showing the shares going to one or another group, the proportions of different types of goods in total output, the effect of unemployment on production, and the like.

The Measures of National Income

So far we have spoken as if there were only two measures of income: personal income and national income. Unfortunately things are more complicated. There are several measures, each of them useful for special purposes, and all interrelated.

We start with the smallest measure of income, which turns out to be *not* a measure of production.

Disposable personal income

The income that people have available for spending on consumer goods and services, or for saving (that is, for *not* spending on consumption), is called *disposable personal income.*

In 1950 these three items [5] were:

Consumer purchases (6) ....$193.6 billions
plus Personal saving (8 or 31) .... 10.7   "

equals Disposable personal income .... 204.3   "

[5] The figures in parentheses refer to the location of these items in the national accounts of Chapter 1.

Personal income

But people are not free to "dispose" of their incomes until they have paid over to federal, state, and local governments their personal income taxes and other *direct* taxes and fees (including estate and gift taxes, fines, penalties, forfeitures, and various incidental charges) levied on persons.

Disposable personal income plus direct taxes equals *personal income*. In 1950:

Disposable personal income	$204.3 billions
plus Personal taxes, fees, etc. (7 or 17)	20.5 "
equals Personal income (5 or 9)	224.7 "

Net national income (expenditure, or product) at factor prices

This is the measure usually called simply the "national income." The name is well chosen. It is the measure of income and production used more often than any other, and it is for most uses the most important of all the income aggregates.[6] It is the total of employee earnings, interest, rent, and business incomes, arising out of current production. Hence it values current production at the prices (or costs) of the factors of production (labor, receiving wages and salaries; loans of money, earning interest; productive property, paying rent; and business, and perhaps entrepreneurship, receiving a residual income called profits).

National income is the value of resources whose product is divided, year after year, among consumer goods and services, government services, additions to plant, equipment, and inventories at home, and financial assets abroad.

To get from personal income to the total-income-created,

---

6 *Survey of Current Business, National Income Supplement,* 1951, p. 23; *Measurement of National Income and Construction of Social Accounts,* United Nations Studies and Reports on Statistical Methods No. 7, Geneva, 1947, Appendix by Richard Stone, pp. 23, 36-37.

which is national income, we make the following adjustments:

1. Transfer payments, for which no productive service is rendered in return, are as we have seen a part of personal income, but not a part of national income. They must consequently be subtracted from personal income. They include transfer payments from government, from business; and interest on government debt, also treated as a transfer (p. 45).

2. Three items must be added in, to get from personal income to income created. Contributions to social insurance funds are a part of income created, but are siphoned off before payments to persons are made. Similarly, a part of the income created in the economy is drawn off by federal and state governments as income and excess-profits taxes on corporations, and so does not become income payments to persons.[7] Finally, corporations retain any part of income created but not passed on to suppliers of factor services as "undistributed corporate earnings."[8]

Table 7 shows two ways of building up to the total national income, by adding the prices (or costs) of the factors of production, and by making the appropriate subtractions from the additions to personal income.

Or we can show how this same national income originates in four of the five "sectors" of the economy, or in different "industries." (See Table 8.)

The national income is a *net* concept. The sense in which we can speak of it as measuring net production will become clearer as we discuss below two larger measures of income and production. But the central notion behind *net* is an everyday sort

---

7 The concept of national income used by the Department of Commerce prior to 1947 excluded corporate income and profits taxes. They were instead put together with indirect business taxes (page 55). The 1947 revisions, following the procedure given above, applied to all national income estimates from 1929 on.

8 The savings of partnerships and proprietary businesses are considered to be made out of income payments to the individual owners. Likewise, the income taxes paid by partners and proprietors are personal income taxes like those on other persons.

TABLE 7

NATIONAL INCOME BY ADDING UP FACTOR COSTS AND BY ADJUSTING
PERSONAL INCOME, 1950

(*in billions of dollars*)

By Adding Up Factor Costs		By Adjustments to Personal Income	
Wages and salaries paid to employees, plus "other labor income" (1a + 1b + 1c or 13a, 22a, 6b, 28a)	149.3	Personal income (5 or 9)	224.7
		minus Transfer payments, including government interest	—19.8
plus Social insurance contributions from employers (20b, or 6b, 13b, 22a)	4.0	Government transfer payments (4a or 23a)	14.3
plus Net interest	5.4	Business transfer payments (4b or 14b)	.8
Personal interest income (2c, or 6c, 13d, 23b, 28b)	10.1	Net interest paid by government (2c, 23b)	4.7
minus Net interest paid by government (23b or 2c)	4.7	*plus* Contributions to social insurance funds	7.0
plus Rent income of persons (2a or 13c)	8.0	from employees (1d or 20a)	2.9
plus Business profits, before deduction of income taxes and adjusted for inventory valuation	72.2	from employers (6b, 13b, 22a, or 20b)	4.0
Gross corporate profits (13e, 28c, 28d, or 18, 2b, 32b [1], 32b [2], 32c)	36.2	*plus* Corporate profits tax liability (13e [1] or 18)	18.6
Income of unincorporated business (3 or 13f)	36.0	*plus* Undistributed domestic corporate profits (13e [3] or 32b [1]), plus foreign branch profits (28d or 32c), adjusted for inventory valuation (13e [4] or 32b [2])	8.5
equals the National Income	239.0	*equals* the National Income	239.0*

* As in previous tables, final digits are rounded, and subtotals may not add up exactly
to totals.

of concept. When we speak of a man's income being $3000
a year, we mean that he could spend that much during the
year, and still be as well off at the end as he had been at the
beginning. His income is the maximum he can spend on his
consumption needs without dipping into his capital (that is,
without drawing down his savings account or selling some of
his stocks or bonds, or selling other property or letting it run
down).

TABLE 8

NATIONAL INCOME BY SECTOR ORIGIN AND BY INDUSTRIAL ORIGIN, 1950 *
(in billions of dollars)

By Sector		By Industry	
Income originating among persons (= households, including institutions)	7.7	Agriculture, forestry, and fisheries	17.7
		Mining	5.0
Direct services (6b or 1c, 20b)	6.0	Contract construction	12.2
		Manufacturing	74.1
Interest paid (6c or 2c)	1.7	Wholesale and retail trade	43.3
Income originating from business (13)	209.0	Finance, insurance, and real estate	20.3
Income originating in government (= wages and salaries paid plus supplements), (22a, or 1b, 1d, 20b)	20.9	Transportation	13.2
		Communications and public utilities	7.2
		Services	22.0
Income originating in the rest-of-the-world (= net payments of factor incomes to the U. S.), (28)	1.3	Government and government enterprises	23.4
		Government	20.9
		Government enterprises	2.5
National Income	239.0	National Income	239.0

* Survey of Current Business, National Income Supplement, 1951, pp. 148-149, 159.
Because of rounding, subtotals may not add up exactly to totals.

Just so for the whole economy. The net production of the whole economy in a year is the flow of goods and services that can be drawn off and consumed without leaving the economy any less productive than it had been before (that is, without decreasing, on the whole, the quantity of factory buildings, machinery, goods in process, and so forth, that will be used to produce output during the next year).

All measures of national production, this one and the two others below, are, as already indicated, *value added* concepts. Suppose that from the value of output of each business in the economy (measured at factor prices, and after an allowance for depreciation is taken out), we subtract the value of supplies bought from other businesses and used up in production. The remainder is what is available for income payments to individuals who have supplied work, loans, or rented property to the firm, plus social-security taxes, plus the profits of the firm. If we sum up this net value-added for all businesses of the economy, and add in the cost of services rendered to government by its employees and to consumers by people who work for them (plus any further social security taxes these latter pay) and the net incomes paid U. S. residents by foreigners, then we have exactly what we have already called "national income," by the kind of summation shown on the left in Table 8.

Net national income (expenditure, or product) at market prices

The goods produced in the economy come on the market for sale.[9] But they are sold at prices that exceed the incomes paid to or accruing to the resources used in production. The difference is due to the indirect taxes imposed by government (sales, excise, customs, and others, imposed on products or business functions rather than on the incomes of persons or businesses). Add these taxes in, and we have a measure of net national income at market prices, often called "net national product."

Suppose that the employees, individual suppliers of raw materials, and owners of a business had paid or had accruing to them in return for their services, $100,000 at the end of the year. If the government levies a tax of $15,000 on the commodities produced, it is for $115,000 that the goods sell in the market. The output of the business valued at market prices is $115,000.

There are a few other items that also contribute to the discrepancy between national product valued at factor prices, and national product valued at market prices. If businesses pay out gifts or prizes or suffer thefts, these transfer payments are not part of national income, but they must be covered by business receipts from sales on the market. Government-owned enterprises do not pay indirect taxes on their products, but if

---

9 With a few exceptions. See p. 46.

they have a surplus accruing to government, this should enter the account just like an indirect tax; or if there is a loss, subsidized by government, this counts like a negative indirect tax. Finally, there is the "statistical discrepancy" between gross national production estimated from adding up values of products and that estimated from adding up income claims. It might enter the account elsewhere, but is put in here as being the least objectionable and awkward place.

The 1950 figures run:

National income	$239.0	billions
plus Indirect business taxes and nontax charges (14a or 19)	23.8	"
plus Business transfer payments (4b or 14b)	.8	"
plus Current surplus minus subsidies of government enterprises (14d or 23c)	—.3	"
plus Statistical discrepancy (14c or 34)	—1.8	"
equals Net National Product	261.5	"

Gross national income (expenditure, or product) at market prices

This measure is usually called simply "gross national product." It is the third and last of the measures of production, and the most general of them all. It attempts to measure total production, without any deduction for depreciation.

1. Suppose we add up (a) the total sales of all business enterprises plus any increase in inventories. We will avoid the double-counting involved, for example, in counting the coal consumed in an electric power plant in addition to electricity produced: this also will be a net-value-added concept. But we will make no deduction for depreciation of plant and equipment or for other reserves. (b) We include also direct services rendered to consumers by individuals, and interest paid on consumer loans. Finally, there are payments (c) by government for the services of its employees, which can be taken as valuing government production at cost, and (d) net payment of factor incomes by foreigners to U. S. residents. The total is gross national product.

2. Or suppose we add together total sales to consumers of goods and services, the total domestic sales to business of capital

goods plus any increase in inventories, government purchases of goods and services, and net foreign investment. These are all at market prices and there is no deduction for depreciation or other reserves. These added together also make up gross national product.

What relation has this gross national product to the net national product at market prices that we arrived at above? They are alike in that both include all the incomes created by the services of factors of production. They are alike also in that both include all the indirect taxes levied, which raise the price at which goods are sold above the value of the factor services.

They differ because gross national product alone includes the capital consumption allowances (pages 30-32), which, very roughly, measure the wearing out and obsolescence of plant and equipment.

The 1950 relationship is:

```
Net National Product  ...................................  $261.5 billions
plus Capital consumption allowances  (15 or 32a) ..........   21.2     "
    Depreciation charges (15a)  .....................   17.7
    Capital outlays charged to current expenses (15b) ..    2.9
    Accidental damage to fixed capital (15c)  ..........     .6
                                                          _____
equals Gross National Product 10  .......................   282.6     "
```

The Uses of National Income Concepts [11]

We have emerged from our national income inquiry with an embarrassment of riches. We have no less than five measures of national income: (1) *gross national product* (or income, or expenditure) at market prices, (2) *net national product* (or income, or expenditure) at market prices, (3) *national*

10 Rounding error explains the discrepancy.

11 Cf. S. Kuznets, *National Product in Wartime.* New York: National Bureau of Economic Research, 1945, pp. 27-31; and *National Income, A Summary of Findings.* New York: National Bureau of Economic Research, pp. 117-121. Also Richard Stone, *Measurement of National Income and the Construction of Social Accounts.* Geneva: United Nations, 1947, pp. 36-37; and Department of Commerce, *Survey of Current Business, National Income Supplement,* 1951, pp. 22-23.

income (or net national income, product, or expenditure) at factor prices; and then the two totals that are not measures of production: (4) *personal income,* and (5) *disposable personal income.*

If we are concerned only with percentage changes overtime in national production, it usually does not matter greatly which of the first three measures we use, since they are highly correlated with each other.[12] But if we are concerned with total amounts, or with amounts of change, then it is important to distinguish among them.

Gross national product

The *gross national product* has three special uses.

(a) For short-term studies of perhaps a decade or less, gross national product is a useful, perhaps the most useful, measure of a country's production. In such a short period, the total of *all* commodities and services produced may carry the most significance. The fact that some of gross output must eventually go to make up for depreciation can be partly or entirely neglected. Our buildings and equipment must be replaced eventually, but not necessarily now.

(b) The gross-national-product concept of the Department of Commerce, which we have followed, measures the revenues from sales of all private production (with adjustment for inventory change) plus the cost value of government production. It is also a measure of gross or total expenditure, at ordinary market prices, by all spending agencies for currently produced goods and services: by all consumers, businesses (which buy plant, equipment, and inventories), and government bodies (with adjustment for net foreign buying). (All of these can be figured on a smaller, or net, basis. The spending of businesses for plant, equipment, and inventories can be taken net, after an allowance for capital consumption is subtracted,

---

[12] The correlation coefficient of the Department of Commerce old series *national income* and *gross national product* was .996 between 1929 and 1941. The coefficient was lower after 1941

rather than gross; and the spending of consumers, business, and government can all be figured at the factor costs of goods and services purchased rather than at market prices.)

In studying prosperity, depression, and inflation, and their causes, we are concerned with the volume of spending of these three groups, and their components. There is decided convenience in using a measure of national income and product that consumer, business, and government spending add up to without adjustment. One avoids difficult problems of allocating capital consumption allowances, indirect taxes, and subsidies, that one would have to face if, say, National Income were used instead.

Hence the gross-national-product concept is ordinarily most useful for studying business cycles and inflation.

(c) We possess no acceptable measure of the total of all transactions in which money figures in the economy—the total of all payments, gifts, and loans—although we know this total is several times larger than the value of gross national product. Nevertheless, a series for all transactions with which to compare the flow of money in the economy would be very useful. The gross national product is the most significant stopping point between net national income and total transactions, and in reasoning about monetary matters can often be used as a substitute for the latter.

Net national product

Of the net measures of production, *net national product* at market prices can be more readily deflated to allow for price changes in the economy than can national income. But due to the usual high correlation between the two, the advantage is not a major one.

The decisive count against the U. S. measure of net national product is that depreciation allowances cannot be calculated on a basis that can be compared with the totals for gross investment. Hence net national product does not mean what it seems to imply, consumption plus government expenditures plus net investment, but, rather, something ambiguous, neither fish nor fowl. Only if an accurate measure for net investment could be calculated, could net national product be unambiguous.

The measure is not used very often. The Department of Commerce concludes with unusual flatness: "As a practical matter, a meaningful measure of net capital formation, and hence of net national product, cannot be calculated."[13]

National income

More than any other aggregate, this deserves the name the *national income*. It is the total of factor earnings; it is also an estimate of the value of national production at factor costs paid out.

For measuring normal income accruing to the people of the nation, for measuring normal production, and for analyzing problems concerned with the productivity of resources, it is the best tool. For example, if we want to study the trend of national production, to see what possibilities exist for shifting resources from one use to another, or to measure the contribution of different areas of the country, we are concerned with aspects, or components, of the national income.

Personal income

The income receipts of persons of the economy from all sources make up *personal income*. It is not a measure of production since it includes transfer payments and government interest, which are *not* a part of national income; and since it excludes social insurance contributions, corporate profits taxes, and undistributed corporate earnings, which *are* a part of national income.

But personal income has the decided advantage that it is the only one of the measures of national income or product for which monthly figures are available. Since its changes are ordinarily parallel to those of national income, it can

---

[13] *Survey of Current Business, National Income Supplement*, 1951, pp. 23-24.

generally be used as an index to the trend in national productive activity.

Disposable personal income

This is personal income minus personal income taxes and other personal fees and charges. It is our estimate of the purchasing power available to individuals from current production; and so it is the most significant total to use when we want to carry through a psychological inquiry relating the incomes of individuals to their consumption expenditures and their savings.

In general, of these five totals, it is national income that has the most use, followed by gross national product and disposable personal income.

Summary

Table 9 on p. 62 shows the relationships among the measures of production and income, with U. S. data for 1950.

The Earning and Spending of Income—Neglecting Government

We now revert to the curious equality we met toward the end of Chapter 1, between savings (by a particular definition) and investment (p. 38). This equality is worth considering closely because of the central place it has won in discussions of the cause and cure of unemployment and depression on the one hand, and inflation on the other. At first we review some basic concepts, reasoning, rather abstractly, as if government does not exist or is of negligible economic importance, and so can be neglected.

Expenditures for the production of the economy can be divided into two classes: expenditures for goods and services that are *not* used in any further production, and expenditures for goods that *are* used in future production. The former we call *consumption* goods and services (food, clothing, haircut,

TABLE 9

The Five Measures of Income and Production
(in billions of dollars)

	Disposable Personal Income	Personal Income	National Income	Net National Product	Gross National Product
1. Consumer purchases	193.6	193.6	193.6	193.6	193.6
2. Personal saving	10.7	10.7	10.7	10.7	10.7
3. Personal taxes, fees, etc.		20.5	20.5	20.5	20.5
4. *minus* government transfer payments and net interest, and business transfer payments*			−19.8	−19.8	−19.8
5. Contributions to social insurance funds			7.0	7.0	7.0
6. Corporate profits tax liability			18.6	18.6	18.6
7. Undistributed domestic and foreign corporate profits, adjusted for inventory valuation			8.5	8.5	8.5
8. Indirect business taxes and nontax charges				23.8	23.8
9. Business transfer payments,* current surplus minus subsidies of government enterprises and statistical discrepancy				−1.3	−1.3
10. Capital consumption allowances					21.2
Totals	204.3	224.7	239.0	261.5	282.6

* Business transfer payments are subtracted (item 4) as we move from disposable personal income to net national income. For these are part of personal income, but they do not measure and are not a part of national income. They are added in as we move from national income to net national product. For they must be covered by, and so are a part of, the receipts of businesses.

recreation equipment, and the like); the latter are *investment,* or *capital,* goods.

The only purpose of investment goods is to aid in the eventual production of consumption goods and services.

1. The largest proportion among investment goods is *fixed capital,* which consists of buildings and equipment of various sorts—drill presses, open-hearth furnaces, factory buildings, railroad engines and tracks, cement mixers, shovels, calculating machines, and the like.

2. An addition to inventories (stocks of raw materials or goods in process or finished products) is like an addition to fixed capital in that labor and other resources have gone into the inventories, and in that eventually the inventories will become available in some form as consumption goods and services. In both cases, labor and other resources have been employed, without obtaining any immediate increase in the quantity of consumer goods and services available.

3. Net foreign investment, which means approximately value of exports minus value of imports, is similar to home investment: we are using domestic resources to build up a claim on foreigners, which claim can in the future be transformed into consumption goods and services. The debt that the foreigner owes us can be turned eventually, for example, into imported woolens and wines. In somewhat the same fashion, a miller's inventory of wheat becomes transformed into flour, and finally into bread; and the railroad's locomotives become transformed, over their life span, into ton-miles of transportation.

Since we have divided all of production into the two divisions of consumption and investment, all the incomes earned in production must arise from these same two sources; from consumption expenditure and investment expenditure.

Income *equals* Consumption *plus* Investment.

Income can be disposed of in two ways: it is spent on consumption goods and services (this is the consumption expenditure we have already listed above), or else it is not spent on consumption goods. We call the part of income that is not spent on consumption *savings*. Hence,

Income *equals* Consumption *plus* Savings.

Since the national income is equal both to consumption plus investment, and to consumption plus savings, it must be that savings always equals the value of investment:

Savings *equals* Investment.

If we consider as investment the total production of investment goods in the course of any period plus net foreign investment, we have *gross investment*. Suppose that from this gross figure we subtract those investment goods which serve to replace other investment goods that have become worn out or obsolete. The remainder is *net investment*, the net addition to the economy's supply of investment goods resulting from the production of the year, plus net foreign investment.

Our reasoning to the effect that savings always equal investment holds whether we are speaking in terms of gross investment and gross savings, or in terms of net investment (gross investment minus investment goods that have become worn out and obsolete) and net savings (gross savings minus depreciation allowances).[14]

We can show this equality between savings and investment in a different way, reasoning in terms of net savings and net investment. Our savings over any period of time consist of the value of the additions we have made to our property during that time. Property takes three forms: money, securities, and physical goods. But money is either a security (the note of a bank or of the government), or a physical good (gold, silver, copper). We are left with only two categories. Securities, in turn, are debts owed by one person or institution to another, and for every dollar's asset in the form of a security that someone holds, someone else owes a dollar. Hence, *within*

---

[14] Gross or net investment, and gross or net savings, can have negative values as well as positive.

the economy, securities cancel out to zero. But if there has been trade with foreigners, and on balance the people of the economy are owed more (less) by foreigners, this portion of the securities does not cancel out.[15]

We are left with physical goods and the excess of exports over imports. Our net savings turn out to be (1) the value of the increase in the physical goods of the country—additions to plant and equipment, additions to inventories of goods, plus (2) any addition that may be made to claims on foreigners. But the sum of these two is what we have already called net investment.

The Earning and Spending of Income—Taking Account of Government

The simple equality between savings and investment that we have derived above is complicated by the existence of government taxation and government expenditure for output. We might, of course, add government expenditures to private (or non-government) consumption and investment expenditure, wherever they seem to fit best. Similarly, we might class government taxes together with savings, since taxes are like savings, a part of income not spent on consumption.

1. But we meet major difficulties when we try to make such a classification. With respect to government expenditure, we will not have much trouble with classifying public expenditure on park service, band concerts, and museum guards. This is clearly consumption. Also, it will be reasonable to classify expenditure on government buildings as investment. Department of Agriculture research reports are a service facilitating the production of (mainly) consumption goods and services by business. There are other fairly clear cases. But the bulk of government expenditure for output does not fit comfortably under any one heading. The services of night policemen on their beats are partly a protection to consumers, and partly

---

15 This reasoning follows in part that of J. R. Hicks, *Value and Capital*, Oxford, Clarendon Press, 1939, p. 182.

a protection to stores and factories (that is, a service facilitating production). The administration of justice, the maintenance of the army and navy, the activities of the State Department, the support of education—these are also partly services to consumers, partly public investment, and partly services rendered to private businesses. Therefore, it appears prudent to avoid the unsolvable question of how to classify government expenditures, and instead to list them as a separate item in total expenditure for output.

2. Furthermore, the motives of consumers who buy consumption goods and services and the motives of businessmen who mainly do the investing are different from the motives that lead government bodies to make given expenditures. Similarly, taxes are a compulsory drain on incomes, and differ in this respect from the voluntary savings of individuals and businesses. The logic behind the decisions is different. For this reason also it seems best to list government expenditures and taxes separately.

If we take account of government separately, the sources of earned income become private consumption expenditures, private investment expenditures, and government expenditures. The income so earned is disposed on consumption expenditures, savings, and taxes. Properly defined these include *all* the sources and *all* the uses of income. There is no room for a gap anywhere.

At this point some of us may have a sharp qualm. For in listing the sources of income as consumption, investment, and government expenditures, we have valued product in these same three classes. We have also identified above some of the product of government as services rendered to private business. Plainly there are many more examples than those we have listed. These are surely *intermediate products,* used up in producing final products, and therefore (pp. 47-48) not to be counted as a part of final product.

The objection is right. Part of government expenditure is for these intermediate services to business, and if we count

TABLE 10

THE SOURCES AND USES OF GROSS NATIONAL INCOME, 1950 *

(in billions of dollars)

Uses of Income	Sources of Income

Consumer purchases (6) 193.6	Consumer purchases (6) 193.6
	  Durable goods 29.2
	  (House furnishings and equipment, automobiles and accessories, etc.)
	  Nondurable goods 102.3
	  (Food, beverages, tobacco, shoes, magazines, etc.)
	  Services 62.1
	  (Transportation, recreation, medical care, etc.)

Gross private saving............ 40.3
  Personal saving (8 or 31) 10.7
  Gross business saving (32) 29.7
	Gross investment (35 or 39) 46.6
	  New construction (36 or 10c[1]) 22.1
	  Producers' durable equipment (36 or 10c[2]) 22.5
	  Change in business inventories (11 or 37) ... 4.3
	  Net foreign investment in the United States (26 or 38) .... —2.3

Taxes, including social security contributions; minus transfer payments, including net interest and subsidies........... 50.5
  Personal income taxes, fees, etc. (7 or 17) 20.5
  Corporate profits tax liability (13e [1] or 18) 18.6
  Indirect business taxes, liability, etc. (14a or 19) 23.8
  Social insurance contributions (20) 7.0
  minus government transfer payments (4a or 23a) †, including net interest (2c or 23b) and subsidies (14d or 23c) ... 19.3
Statistical discrepancy (14c or 34) .... —1.8
	Government purchases of goods and services (22) 42.5
	  Net Federal purchases... 22.8
	  State and local purchases 19.7

Gross National Expenditure..... 282.6	Gross National Product or Income 282.6

* *Survey of Current Business, National Income Supplement,* 1951, pp. 148, 149, 150, 151, 199. Final digits are rounded to the nearest number, and so subtotals may not add up exactly to totals.

† Business transfer payments do not appear in this table since they are subtracted ence in going from *personal income* (the sum of consumer purchases, personal income taxes, etc., and personal saving) to *national income,* and added in once in going from *national income* to *national product* (either net or gross). Hence the net contribution of business transfer payments to *gross national product* is zero.

all government expenditure as final product of the economy, we are exaggerating its contribution.[16]

However, there is an offset to, and an excuse for, this error. The final product of government is estimated too high. But the final product of business is by an equal amount measured too low. Businesses are not charged for the intermediate services of government rendered to them. These do not enter their costs, and hence do not enter value of their product.[17]

The figures for *total* national income or product are therefore not in error, the downward bias in the figure for business product just equalling the upward bias in the figure for government product. Current national product estimating assumes that the correction of these opposed errors is not worth the effort, in view of the desperate problem of classifying government expenditure into final and intermediate types.

Table 10 shows the U. S. Gross National Product for 1950, divided on the right into sources of income, or product (consumption, investment, government expenditures), and on the left into the uses of income (consumption, savings, taxes).

Since, as we have reasoned logically and shown (with adjustment for transfers and statistical discrepancy) in Table 10:

(1)	Consumption *plus* Savings *plus* Taxes	*equals*	Consumption *plus* Investment *plus* Government expenditure;

and since the *Consumption* on both sides of the equation is identically equal, then

(2)	Savings *plus* Taxes	*equals*	Investment *plus* Government expenditure.

---

16 This is aside from the question as to whether what the government *spends* on its services, no matter what they are used for, is a reasonable measure of the economic value of those services.

17 The profits and indirect taxes paid by business have no necessary relation either to the total of government services (the government may be running a deficit or surplus, and either a small or large part of tax revenue may come from direct consumer taxes), or to government services rendered to business. With only minor exceptions, taxes are best treated as transfer payments.

This can be put into the form

(3)
Savings
plus Taxes
minus Government
    expenditure
       equals   Investment.

Taxes minus *government expenditure* is the *government surplus*. Equation (3) therefore, is the relationship already worked out in the statistics of Table 5 (page 39), which ran, in summary form:

(in billions of dollars)

Personal saving 10.7	Gross investment 46.6
Gross business saving 29.7	
Government surplus 8.0	
Statistical discrepancy ....—1.8	
Gross private savings and government surplus 46.6	Gross investment 46.6

Or we could, with equal sense, modify equation (2), transferring *Taxes* to the right side. Then the relationship would read

(4)
        Savings   *equals*
Investment
plus Government Expenditures
minus Taxes;

or, *savings* equals *investment* plus *government deficit*. If, as in 1950, there is a government surplus, the "deficit" is entered as a negative figure. The figures for 1950 are:

(in billions of dollars)

Personal saving 10.7	Gross investment 46.6
Gross business saving 29.7	Government deficit ....—8.0
Statistical discrepancy ....—1.8	
Gross private saving 38.6	Government deficit 38.6

We will use this relationship in later reasoning on depression and inflation.

CHAPTER THREE

Fluctuations in the Real National Income:
The Problem of Index Numbers

THE NATIONAL INCOME ROSE GREATLY FROM 1939 TO 1950. BY Department of Commerce data, this rise was from 72.5 billion to 239.0 billion dollars, or to 330 per cent of the 1939 level. Variations in the national income have, of course, gone on continuously in the past. In 1933, output reached its low point of the great depression, 39.6 billion dollars; in 1929, it had been 87.4 billion dollars. In the short depression of 1921, the national income was 51.7, in 1920 it had been 69.5 billion dollars.

The national output consists, we have seen, of a vast collection of goods and services whose quantity is measured by the convenient common measure of money. This is much the best measure obtainable of the mass of unlike goods and services produced in the economy, but it introduces problems when we compare, as above, the national output of one year with that of another. If in the United States in 1950 prices generally had been 330 per cent of their level in 1939, then the real, or physical, output of goods and services would not have changed appreciably between the two years. But if prices had remained the same, then real output (or income) would have more than tripled.

The change in the figures for national income from year to year is, therefore, due in part to change in the quantities of goods and services produced (or, as we say, a difference in real, or physical, income), and in part to change in the prices of these goods and services. If we want to compare the real incomes (or outputs) of different years, we must try to eliminate the distortion introduced by changes in prices. Another kind of complication often appears: the kinds of goods and services produced in one year may differ from the kinds produced in other years in which we are interested. The problem of comparing the real incomes of different years therefore has three elements: (1) the *outputs* of individual goods and services, (2) the *prices* of goods and services, (3) the *kinds* of goods and services produced.

Simple production indexes

If the kinds of goods and services produced did not change greatly from year to year, and if we had data on the outputs of each kind, then it would be simple to average appropriately the changes in outputs. This gives us a production index without the need for taking price changes into account. The Federal Reserve's indexes of industrial production and certain measures of farm production and marketing are of this sort.

Even in this simplest case there is cause for some doubt. The greater the difference in output changes for individual goods, the less representative is any single measure, or index, of the general change in output. Suppose that output changes for different commodities are 200, 160, 20, 0,—20, and —60 per cent. A simple average of these changes is 50 per cent. But the truth about the changes lies rather in their diversities than in any single average figure. The average is not very representative, or typical. Despite generally increased production in World War II, we had in 1944 precious little gasoline for civilian use, no household refrigerators, and no radios or washing machines.

Measuring production
from value-of-production data

If we are trying to estimate changes in production from value-of-production data—for example, from data for the national income—we are compelled to follow a different procedure. We do not have physical-output data for much of the national income.

The data at our disposal are figures for value of national income in various years and figures on price changes. How can we solve the problem? The obvious strategy is to adjust the national income figures inversely to average price changes—to adjust national income figures downward in proportion as prices are high, to adjust them upward in proportion as prices are low.

But here again there are causes of doubt. The greater the differences in price movements for particular goods, the less representative is any single figure for the *average* price movement, which figure we must use when we try to eliminate the influence of price changes. Most prices in the United States moved up considerably during the recent war and postwar periods. At least four commodities had by late 1946 risen to over 430 per cent of their 1939 levels. But at the same time many commodities changed little, and at least 28 fell or did not change in price.[1] This wide price dispersion gives one reason for putting only moderate trust in measures of national production during World War II.

In addition, the kinds of goods and services produced are always changing to a greater or lesser extent, and we are compelled to make a tacit or explicit decision as to how many Ford-Ferguson tractors equal one M-4 tank. Or, if we are looking over a longer period, we must ask ourselves how many tallow candles equal one 40-watt electric bulb and how many surreys with fringed tops equal one Plymouth coupe.[2] Only a vague meaning attaches to a figure pretending to compare the na-

---

[1] R. C. Epstein, "Price Dispersion and Aggregative Analysis," *American Economic Review*, Vol. XXXVII (June, 1947), pp. 402-407.

[2] The same problem arises when comparison is attempted between the outputs or prices of two countries that produce unlike commodities. How many pounds of rice equal one bushel of wheat? How shall we value a thinly built cottage for use in the tropics, as compared to a stout New England house built to prevail against winter storms?

tional output of 1950 with that of 1800: the *kinds* of goods and services have changed too dramatically for us to be able to compare their *quantities*.

Indexes of output carry the clearest significance, we conclude, when they compare periods in which nearly the same types of goods and services are produced, when all types of output are changing in similar proportions, and when prices are changing in similar proportions. These conditions are usually met when indexes are constructed for the same country and for years not far apart. Output measures are then highly useful tools for indicating the productive performance of the economy.

The further we get away from such conditions, the more the significance of output comparisons is blurred. The figures can look plain but carry little meaning.

Constructing an Index of Output from National Income Data

The data that are available and that we can use in constructing an index of national output are the national income (value) figures for different years, and measures of relative prices.

We can best illustrate the construction of an output index by speaking in terms of one commodity. We assume we can obtain value, but not quantity, data for that commodity (in analogy with available national income data) for the years 1939 and 1950. Value is equal to price (P) times quantity (Q):

Value of output 1939 $= P$ 1939 $\times Q$ 1939.

Similarly for 1950:

Value of output 1950 $= P$ 1950 $\times Q$ 1950.

A comparison of the real income (or output) of the two years can be made by valuing the outputs of both years at the price of some one year. That one year (sometimes called the *base year*) might be 1939 or 1950, or an average of the prices of the two years, or even some third year. Usually little difference results in the final measure if the conditions of the years in question are similar. Suppose we use 1939 as our base year.

The outputs of 1939 and 1950 valued at the price of 1939 would be

$$\text{(1)} \qquad\qquad \text{(2)}$$
$$P\ 1939 \times Q\ 1939 \quad \text{and} \quad P\ 1939 \times Q\ 1950$$

This is the comparison that we want to make. The first of these figures, (1), is already given to us in the value of output for 1939. The other figure, (2), can be calculated. We have, in the figure for value of output in 1950, $P\ 1950 \times Q\ 1950$. If we can find a way to measure the ratio of prices of 1939 and 1950, we can calculate (2). For

$$\frac{P\ 1939}{P\ 1950} \times P\ 1950 \times Q\ 1950 = P\ 1939 \times Q\ 1950.$$

In the left side of the equation, the $P\ 1950$'s cancel out, leaving us the figure we want.

In strict analogy with this, we can construct an index of national output. Our national income (or output) data are value figures, giving us the sum of prices times quantities for each year. We also possess measures of average price changes in the whole economy.

The net national income of 1950, valued at prices of 1950, was 239.0 billion dollars. We want to calculate what the national income of 1950 would be worth, valued at prices of 1939. To make this adjustment, we should like, ideally, to have a price index of the constituents of national income (consumption, net investment, and government expenditure), each valued at factor prices just as national income is measured at factor prices. We lack such an index for these years. As a close substitute, we use an index of consumption goods (rather than all output), valued at market prices (rather than at the prices paid to factors).

Consumption goods prices rose by about 74.8 per cent between 1939 and 1950. Then the ratio of prices in the two years is 100 to 174.8. Our calculation is:

$$\frac{100}{174.8} \times 239.0 = 136.7$$

We estimate the national income for 1950, at 1939 prices, to be 136.7 billion dollars. The real national income (or output) increased (in 1939 prices) from 72.5 to 136.7 billion dollars, or by 89 per cent. If we set 1939 equal to 100 per cent, output increased from an index of 100 to 189.

We can summarize our calculations as follows:

IN BILLIONS OF DOLLARS

	1939	1950
Net national income (or output) (current prices) ...	72.5	239.0
Index of prices (1939 = 100)	100	174.8
Real national income (or output) (1939 prices)	72.5	136.7
Index of real income (1939 = 100)	100	189

We conclude that in order to get a comparison of quantities of real output we divide current values of output by the index of average prices. (Above, to obtain a measure of real output, we, in effect, divided 72.5 billion dollars by 1, and 239.0 billion dollars by 1.748.)

In these calculations, we have made use of an *index of prices*. Our next problem is to consider how a price index can be calculated.

Constructing an Index of Prices

Just as an output index is a measure of the average change that takes place in outputs, so a price index is a measure of the average change that takes place in prices. The difficulties we face in our calculation of a price index are these:

1. It is never possible to have in our index *all* the prices that exist in the country—prices in every hamlet, for every variety of good, and for every day of the year. Even when we want to construct an index for a particular class of goods, such as cost-of-living items or agricultural products or chemical products, it is seldom possible to get all the *relevant* price quotations that exist in the period of time with which we are concerned. We are forced to take a sample. The sample should be

as large as possible and it should be as representative as possible. The Bureau of Labor Statistics includes, in the calculation of its index of wholesale prices, quotations for 889 commodities taken from communities throughout the country.

2. The commodities produced in the economy and those appearing in our sample are not of equal importance. We must try to have them affect our final index in accordance with their relative importance—that is, we must *weight* them sensibly. As an example of the trouble we get into when we ignore weighting consider the following: Suppose that the price of wheat had doubled from 1939 to 1950 and that the price of wine had halved:

	1939	1950
Wheat (bushel)	$1.00	$2.00
Wine (quart)	1.00	0.50
Total	2.00	2.50
Price index, taking 1939 = 100	100	125

Our price index shows a rise of 25 per cent. . . . But suppose, instead of measuring wine by the quart, as above, we measured it by the gallon. Then our index is as follows:

	1939	1950
Wheat (bushel)	$1.00	$2.00
Wine (gallon)	4.00	2.00
Total	5.00	4.00
Price index, taking 1939 = 100	100	80

Something has gone wrong. There has been no change in the facts of the two situations, yet one index shows a price rise of 25 per cent, the other shows a price drop of 20 per cent. Our two calculations should lead to the same result, but they go marching off in opposite directions.

What has happened is that we have given different relative weights to the two commodities. Wine, whose price fell, was less important in the first calculation than in the second. The difference in the emphasis ascribed to wine was sufficient to alter the movement of the whole index.

The problem of weighting is present, explicitly or implicitly, whenever we construct an index. It is essential that it be solved consciously, with the best judgment that we can muster, not left to chance. In 1893, the Senate Committee on Finance presented a price index in which, among other items, wheat appeared once and pocketknives 25 times, because there happened to be prices obtainable for those varieties of knives. In consequence, price changes in pocketknives were given 25 times as much chance as price changes in wheat to influence the movement of the final price index—a result the compilers of the index certainly never intended.

The two problems of constructing price indexes that we have surveyed, sampling and weighting, are to some extent interrelated. The inclusion of a commodity in the sample implies that we judge that commodity to be of sufficient importance to be given some weight.[3]

We illustrate on page 78 the construction of a price index of the "cost of living." For the sake of simplicity only three commodities are included. Before calculating such an index, we must find out the typical budget, or basket of provisions, for which the consumer spends his income. The quantity of each item appearing in the basket determines the weight, or relative importance, we are giving to that item. We then calculate how the cost of that basket would have changed in one year (1939), as compared with some other year (1950).

In an economy like our own, where tastes of consumers and types of products change significantly as the years go by, indexes need to be brought up to date from time to time. The Bureau of Labor Statistics' Consumers' Price Index was revised in 1951 to take account of changes in the kinds of goods consumers were

---

[3] There are, in addition to these concerns, other technical and mathematical problems of calculation into which we do not go here, such as the choice of a base year or period; and whether the index should be constructed as a simple average, or average of reciprocals, or geometric mean

Commodity	1939			1950	
	Quantity (weight)	Price	Value	Price	Value
Potatoes ...	1 peck	$0.50	$0.50	$0.75	$0.75
Milk	4 quarts	.15	.60	.21	.84
Meat	2 pounds	.40	.80	.80	1.60
Total	....	....	1.90		3.19
Price Index (taking 1939 = 100) 100					168

buying. The last revision had been in 1941. Our rising standard of living in the decade meant that food and rent fell in importance in the average consumer's budget. Food had previously been given a weight of 41.6 per cent of total expenditure; in the new index its weight was 33.3 per cent. Rent fell from 13.8 per cent to 11.6 per cent. Additions to the index included television sets, frozen foods, canned baby food, cola drinks, men's rayon tropical suits, home permanents, velocipedes, and electric toasters.

Criticism of the Consumers' Price Index

The possible faults of a price index are illustrated by the charges levied in 1944 against the Bureau of Labor Statistics' Consumers' Price Index.[4] These charges were brought forward by the labor representatives of the 1943 President's Committee on the Cost of Living, and were generally supported by the national labor unions, A.F. of L. and C.I.O. The arguments of the unions for higher wages would have been strengthened by official acceptance of a cost-of-living index that rose steeply during World War II. The BLS index had risen 23.5 per cent between January, 1941 and December, 1943. The labor report charged that the average cost of living had in fact risen 43.5

---

4 Formerly called *Index of the Cost of Living of Wage Earners and Lower-Salaried Workers in Large Cities.*

per cent. The main faults of the BLS index, it was said, were its neglect to consider the following:

1. Underreporting of prices by stores and a large rise in prices of important goods not included in the index.
2. Disappearance of low grades of goods and deterioration in the quality of goods priced.
3. Large retail price increase in smaller cities not covered by the index.

These criticisms are, in effect, either that the prices collected were not a fair sample of the prices that actually existed for goods of equal quality, or that the weighting given to the collected prices became unrepresentative during the war years. A technical committee, with Wesley C. Mitchell as chairman, set up to investigate the charges, found that they had some, but very limited, validity. The Committee concluded that the BLS index should have risen in that period by 3 to 5 per cent more than it did, not by the 20 per cent argued for in the labor report.

CHAPTER FOUR

Production and Employment

THIS CHAPTER IS CONCERNED WITH THREE PROBLEMS: WHAT have been the changes in past years in total production in the United States; what have been the causes of these changes; and what are the prospects for increased production in the future? The Department of Commerce has issued estimates of the national income extending back to before World War I. The data are given in terms of current dollars—in other words, at the prices actually existing in the successive years. We can calculate an approximate measure for 1909—1950 of real or physical product (real income) by dividing each of the current national income figures by an index of its price level.

The Fluctuations of Production and Employment

The resulting measure of total production (Chart 1) shows a large rise during the years of World War I, a drop to a low in 1921, a continuous rise during the 1920's (save for the year 1924), until a maximum was reached in 1929. Thereafter, a drop was precipitous to the low of 1933, followed by a rapid increase to 1937. Output fell considerably in 1938, but rose thereafter to the unprecedented heights of World War II.

Usually, changes in employment parallel the changes in production. Over the course of the whole period of 40 years, however, production was rising relative to the quantity of employment—in other words, the *productivity* of the average worker was rising.

Production and Employment in the United States, 1909-1950

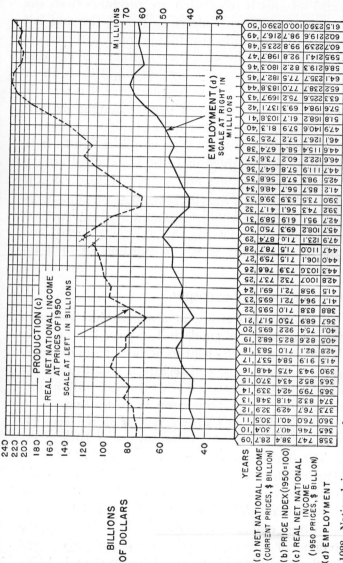

PRODUCTION (c)
REAL NET NATIONAL INCOME
AT PRICES OF 1950
SCALE AT LEFT IN BILLIONS

EMPLOYMENT (d)
SCALE AT RIGHT IN MILLIONS

BILLIONS OF DOLLARS

MILLIONS

(a) NET NATIONAL INCOME (CURRENT PRICES, $ BILLION)
(b) PRICE INDEX (1950=100)
(c) REAL NET NATIONAL INCOME (1950 PRICES, $ BILLION)
(d) EMPLOYMENT

YEARS

Sources: 1909-1928, National income and employment data from Basic Facts on Employment and Production. Senate Committee Print No. 4, 79th Congress, 1st Session, 1945, pp. 6 and 12. 1929-1950, income data, Survey of Current Business, National Income Supplement, 1951, p. 150; employment data, The Economic Report of the President, January, 1951, p. 181. Original calculations from the Department of Commerce and the Department of Labor. National income is the old series 1909-1928, and the new series thereafter. In 1929-1931, the new series averages 5 per cent higher than the old.

The price index, 1909-1939, is an implicit index derived from comparing national income in current dollars with national income in constant dollars, deflation being made on a product basis. From unpublished data of the Department of Commerce, used by permission. For 1940-1950, the price index is based on the Bureau of Labor Statistics Consumers' Price Index, adjusted, 1942-1946, in accord with the conclusions of the Mitchell Committee,

81

The only source from which we as members of the economy obtain goods and services is from what we produce—from the output of the economy. These abstract figures of rise and fall conceal millions of hopes fulfilled or disappointed with respect to consumption and employment. They represent a car that could or could not be bought; a house that could be built or could not be afforded; medicine and hospital care that was obtained or was not available; a suit of clothes bought or foregone; churches, jails, schools, or post offices built—or idle men who might have been producing these goods. The figures indicate the productivity that enabled us to be the central arsenal of munitions and other supplies and a crucial force in the winning of two world wars. They portray an expanding sense of well-being in numberless families because of the possession and enjoyment of goods previously beyond their reach; and they mirror in the 1930's the search of millions of men for work that did not exist.

Wartime output and peacetime output

Our achievement during wartime of a net product rising in 1944 to 183.8 billion dollars of goods and services is sometimes presented as a norm of what we ought to be producing in peacetime with the same labor force and technical conditions. For example, the 1944 total is contrasted with the 72.5 billion dollars of output of 1939. This comparison is misleading.

(1) For one thing, there was a price rise of 35 per cent between 1939 and 1944. If we valued the output of 1944 at the price level of 1939, the change is only from 72.5 to 136.1 billion dollars. (2) During the war years we were running our economy under forced draft, at a level we should not desire for ordinary peacetime years. (a) We attracted into the labor force nearly seven million emergency workers, old people on the verge of retirement or already retired, servicemen's wives, and boys and girls who would normally have been in school. Many of these people left the labor force with the conclusion of the war. (b) We increased our hours of work in manufacturing

from an average of 38 hours a week in 1939 to 45 in 1944. Some war plants adopted the 12-hour day, 7-day week. To retain these long hours would be to return to the standards of a quarter-century ago. (c) Some of our war production was attained at the expense of future output. We depleted our petroleum reserves, and dug deep into Lake Superior iron ore deposits. We also reduced specialized training for peactime pursuits; the postwar years have been handicapped by a deficiency of doctors, scientists, engineers, and teachers. (d) Beyond a certain point, increased production from an economy can be obtained only at the cost of multiplying controls. Over 134,000 directives, orders, and proclamations were issued during World War II by all divisions of the government. After V-J day, we did not tolerate for long the controls of the Office of Price Administration, War Production Board, War Manpower Commission, and other authorities.

The upward trend of the long run

Within this rather short period that we are surveying, the fluctuations in output associated with prosperity and depression (with high and low employment) stand out conspicuously. We note the high points of 1917, 1929, 1937, and 1944; and the low points of 1921, 1933, and 1938. For still shorter periods (say for 1929–1937, or 1937–1943, or 1918–1924), the dominant importance of output fluctuations correlated with employment changes is unmistakable.

Over the whole period, there is a clear tendency for output to rise. If we should stop our series with 1938 or 1939 (eliminating the boom years of World War II), the rising trend would be much less emphatic, because the great depression of the 1930's would then come at the end of our series. But even so, a line drawn through the average of the output figures would slope upward.

Estimates covering a longer period of time also show a strong upward trend, although the figures become less reliable in the earlier years, and, as we have seen before, there is obstinate difficulty in comparing periods far apart, when *kinds* of goods produced are much different. The *qualitative* difference between the outputs of 1870 and the outputs of today is just as important as the *quantitative* difference that alone is measured by an index number: in 1870 there were no radios, plastics, telephones, synthetic textiles, automobiles, hard-surfaced roads, electric motors, mechanical refrigerators, or airplanes.

If, however, we can neglect this qualitative difference, or hold it in the back of our minds, we see that the Kuznets series, 1879—1938 (Chart 2) portrays a doubling of the *real* national income every 20 years, or a yearly rate of increase of nearly 3.5 per cent. The last two points on the figure, lower than the trend, give emphatic evidence of the wastage of resources in idleness during the great depression of the 1930's.

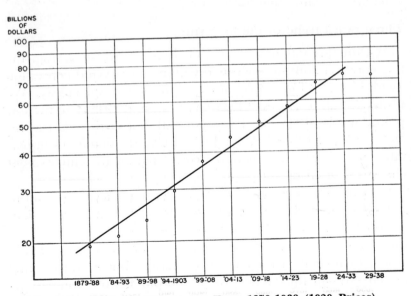

Chart 2. National Income per Year, 1879-1938 (1929 Prices).

Source. Simon S. Kuznets, *National Income, a Summary of Findings.* National Bureau of Economics Research. New York, 1946, p. 32. In order to minimize error originating from scantier and less accurate data of the past, averages are presented for overlapping 10-year periods.

Or if we stay with Department of Commerce data: in 1909 national income (1950 prices) was 75 billion dollars; by 1929, 123 billion dollars; by 1950, production was 239 billion dollars; by 1970, if the trend continues, it will be about 430 billions.

The Productivity of Labor

Production per capita is a measure of the real income available to the average income receiver in the economy. For some purposes it is more useful to look to average output per employed worker, or the *productivity of labor*. The productivity of labor is usually measured in terms of product per worker per year, or product per man-hour. Chart 3 below portrays the over-all productivity of labor per man-hour in the United States, 1850—1940.

The series shows a rise in output per man-hour from 17.3 cents in 1850 to 74 cents in 1940 (at 1940 prices), more than four times the 1850 level. The average increase per decade was 18 per cent, or 1.7 per cent a year. The rates of increase varied

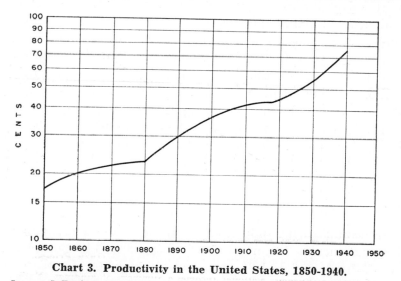

Chart 3. Productivity in the United States, 1850-1940.

Source: J. Frederic Dewhurst and Associates, *America's Needs and Resources.* New York: Twentieth Century Fund, 1947, p. 25. Chart is in terms of cents per man-hour, 1940 prices.

considerably from decade to decade, from a 3.3 per cent rise 1870—1880, to almost 42 per cent 1930—1940. If the past average rate of increase continues, production per man-hour will be 103.4 cents by 1960.[1]

Productivity is crucially important in measuring the performance of the economy. Usually it isn't dramatic, like depression and unemployment. We hardly notice a 1 per cent or 3 ½ per cent rise in output per worker per year. But over the course of a generation or more it is the trend of productivity that is overwhelmingly significant in fixing our material welfare—the quantity of ships and shoes and sealing wax at our disposal.

Increased productivity may come from (1) increased skill and effort of the average worker. (People often wrongly assume that this is the only source.) If increased skill and effort emerge naturally out of better techniques, quicker minds, or better training, there can be no objection. But what of the girl in the shirt industry who sews the topstitch on the collar and must speed up her effort until she works on two to three thousand shirts a day? Increasing rates of work, above all in monotonous and highly specialized tasks, lead eventually to physical and psychological breakdown and are not evidence of economic progress. (2) Increased productivity may also originate from better supplies of raw material, better plant organization, and more and better equipment. These facilities give the employee more to work with, and so raise his output.

The general evidence is that higher productivity in the United States has not come from harder work or faster rates of work, but from the other sources—increased skill and better supplies, organization, and equipment.

Manufacturing

In manufacturing industries (Chart 4) production per man-hour has increased nearly steadily since 1909. The rate of increase—between 3 and 3½ per cent a year—is greater than in

1 J. Frederic Dewhurst and Associates, *America's Needs and Resources*, pp. 22, 23. New York: Twentieth Century Fund, 1947.

any other major sector of the economy. By 1939 output per man-hour was more than two and a half times larger than in 1909. Increased scientific and technical knowledge is the main cause.

The greatest increases in productivity took place in new industries. Volume of production was increasing rapidly in these fields, giving opportunity, with larger scale, for better organization and better processes. Also improvements in technical devices occur most rapidly in new machines and processes. Once the ice is broken with the new development, minor improvements follow easily. Up to 1939 productivity increases were as follows in certain relatively new areas: [2]

Product	Rise in Output (per man-hour)	Years
Rayon	400%	1923-1939
Industrial chemicals	over 300	1919-1939
Automobiles	180	1919-1939
Petroleum refining	290	1919-1939
Rubber tires and tubes	325	1921-1939

The areas where productivity did not rise rapidly were generally those whose output did not expand—among them, leather, furniture, lumber, and food processing. Unchanging technical methods in these areas were both cause and effect of output's not expanding.

The measurement of productivity changes during World War II is difficult because of drastic changes in types of products from those of peacetime, and further changes and improvements during the war years. But in the fields where the type of product remained nearly unchanged, output per man-hour generally rose where total output was rising and fell where total output was falling (because of wartime restrictions). Once again the explanation partly lies in the chance of making use of more effective equipment, processes, and skills as output rose, and partly in the concentration of technical research on production problems of expanding fields.

---

[2] Bureau of Labor Statistics data from the *Monthly Labor Review*, Vol. XLIII (December, 1946), pp. 893-917. The following pages draw heavily on this study.

In war industries where product remained unchanged for a number of months and hence productivity can be measured, the record is magnificent. Huge output was wanted, and custommaking gave way to mass production. Liberty ships slid down the ways by the hundreds: man-hours required per ship dropped 55 per cent between December, 1941 and December, 1944. Manhour requirements for Victory ships dropped 50 per cent, and for destroyer escorts 45 per cent, in a 10-month interval. In aircraft the shift was drastic from producing in small quantities at

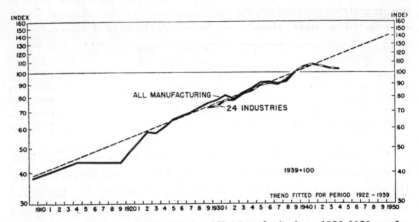

Chart 4. Output per Man-Hour, All Manufacturing, 1909-1939, and 24 Selected Non-Munitions Manufacturing Industries, 1929-1944.

Source: Department of Labor, Bureau of Labor Statistics, *Basic Facts on Employment and Production.* Washington: Government Printing Office, 1945, p. 7. It is difficult to compare productivity of "munitions" industries in wartime with their peacetime record because of the drastic change that takes place in the types of goods produced. Hence, during the later years, 24 non-munitions industries are represented separately.

the buyer's order to producing by thousands according to standard design. Labor-saving devices were multiplied—jigs, special tools, assembly line production—which would not have paid if only a few planes were to be built; jobs were broken down into small steps so that little training was needed; and people who had hardly seen a plane before developed high effectiveness.

Productivity of airframes rose 160 per cent in three years—as much advance as in the best ten years of the automobile industry.

Outside the war industries, the record is equally remarkable, if we take into account the troubles of the time. Supplies were scarce and hard to get, wartime government regulations had to be complied with, and skilled labor was being drafted away. There were extra costs in finding new labor: emergency workers had to be hired, from dislocated communities, in a seller's market for labor. As a whole these nonmunitions manufacturing industries showed an average productivity rise of some 7 per cent in 1939—1941, then a moderate decline of 4 per cent by 1944. There were general increases between 1944 and 1945. Some industries made remarkable gains:

Productivity per man-hour	1945, compared with 1939
Boots and shoes	up 11%
Bread and other bakery goods	26
Glass Products	21
Hosiery	38
Ice Cream	53
Paints and varnishes	20
Rayon and allied products	51
Cigars	33
Woolen and worsted goods	18

In nearly all these industries where the effectiveness of work increased, output rose also—economies could be achieved with greater scale. Conversely, in industries where productivity fell— for example, cement, clay construction products, newspaper and periodical printing, all down 11 per cent in productivity—total output was usually also declining because of wartime restrictions.

Mining

Production per man-hour in mining has risen during the last 20 years at the rate of 3 per cent per year, almost as rapidly as in manufacturing. Continuous improvement in mining practices has more than offset depletion of the richest ores and difficulty in reaching ores. In bituminous coal mining, 60 per cent of underground production was cut by machine in 1919, 88 per cent in 1939. The loading of coal by machine rose from 1 per cent of underground production in 1924 to 31 per cent in 1939, and 53 per cent in 1944. Strip and open-cut mining (surface soil is laid aside and ores dug out with steam shovels), which gets out far more ore per man-hour than underground mining, has been growing more common in coal, iron ore, and nonferrous mining. Better recovery processes in nonferrous mining have made economical the utilization of accessible low-grade ores.

Productivity increased more rapidly than usual around 1931 when lowered total output discouraged the working of any but the richest ore bodies. During World War II the need for working low-grade ores decreased productivity in lead and zinc mining and in certain other nonferrous metal-mining industries. Other mining industries maintained productivity at a high level by postponing development work, which for the time being returns *no* product. Labor supply was an urgent problem in nonferrous metal mining. Wage increases were granted by the War Labor Board in 1942 to attract men into the work; in the same year there was a "freeze" to prevent skilled men from drifting away into other jobs; and, finally, skilled miners in the nonferrous field were furloughed from the armed forces. Under wartime priorities, new equipment continued to be installed from 1941 to 1945; new drilling and ore-handling devices in underground metal mines, loading machines and conveyors in underground coal mines and in open workings, larger low-swung trucks, belt conveyors, and improved excavators.

The largest wartime rise in productivity—over 25 per cent between 1939 and 1945—took place in crude petroleum and natural gas extraction. But the simple measure of productivity is misleading. The rise was due mainly to a drop in new well-drilling. One can always raise current productivity in this way— at the expense of future productivity.

Railroad transportation

Productivity in railroad transportation is measured in terms of passenger mileage and freight ton-mileage per man-hour of labor. The rate of increase from 1919 to 1939 was nearly 3 per cent a year, a little lower than in manufacturing and mining. More powerful engines and better roadbeds made possible longer trains and faster schedules. More durable rails and ties cut the labor needed for construction and maintenance, and roadbed construction methods grew more efficient.

From 1939 to 1944 man-hour output rose almost 50 per cent. The main cause was fuller loading of cars. A considerable rise in the average load requires from the railroads only slightly more work—a little more maintenance work, perhaps a little more bookkeeping. Postponement of some maintenance work, in the face of war shortages of men and materials, also contributed to higher productivity, though at the cost of more maintenance work in postwar years.

Agriculture

Agricultural productivity (Chart 5) varies from year to year, but the long-run trend has been upward at the rate of 1.2 per cent a year, considerably less than the rate of increase for manufacturing, mining, and railroading.

The upward trend reflects the combined influence of more and better equipment and better farm methods. Some farm practices in the United States today are scarcely different from those of Egypt in remote centuries before Christ; over half of all farm work is done by hand. But farming is growing increasingly mechanized. There is more mechanical power on United States farms today than in all its factories—over 3 million tractors and 35 million other machines. The farmer now utilizes better varieties of plants and animals (hybrid corn, disease resistant types of wheat, improved breeds of cattle), better insecticides and new chemical weed-killers, and more effective methods of soil cultivation (crop rotation, contour plowing, scientific fertilization).

The fluctuations in agricultural productivity year by year are considerable. One main cause is varying weather conditions, which are unpredictable from season to season and do not average out even over scores of years. A second is the flight, in depression times, of unemployed city workers into unproductive subsistence farming, and their migration from the farm back into urban occupations in time of prosperity. The farmers who remain on the farm in good times as well as bad are on the average the more productive group. Hence productivity in agriculture is more closely correlated with employment opportunities in the nation than with total output of agricultural commodities.

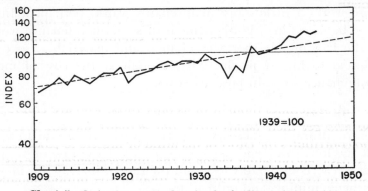

Chart 5. Output per Worker in Agriculture, 1909-1946.

Source: Data from Department of Labor, Bureau of Labor Statistics, *Basic Facts on Employment and Production.* Washington: Government Printing Office, 1945, p. 10; and L. J. Ducoff and M. J. Hagood, "Trends in Agricultural Employment," *Monthly Labor Review,* Vol. LXV (December, 1947), pp. 649-653.

Farm productivity rose 25 per cent during wartime, 1939—1944. The weather was good, and farm workers put in more hours of work. But less farm equipment was bought than in prewar years because of government restrictions on its production. On net balance there is evidence of "concealed unemployment" in the 1930's: farmers were producing less than they could. After 1939 effort was greater under the combined incentives of higher prices, government guarantees, and patriotism.

The prospects for increased productivity

No one who looks over this record of remarkable peacetime advances in productivity and of spectacular wartime performance can think of the United States economy as essentially static and unprogressive. Yet we more often than not hear arguments implying that technical change is a minor phenomenon in the economy, or suggesting that the chief problem is that of sharing a fixed output more equally. Economists themselves are often extravagantly preoccupied with the logic of a static economy. But the most significant characteristic of our economy is economic growth—rising total output and rising productivity—and its central problems arise in the causes and implications of this growth.

Is the record going to continue? Are the fruits of our manual and mental work going to keep on swelling in quantity and quality? (Work, we remember, includes not only ditch-digging, farming, and house-building, but also the labors of the Attorney General, of scientists, teachers, and business managers. "Workers" are sometimes thought of as only those who are employees and who get their hands dirty, but actually include everyone who contributes the effort of his mind or muscle to production.)

A basic encouraging factor is the unprecedentedly heavy investment by private businesses—a total of 184 billion dollars in the five years 1946 through 1950. The expenditure is proof that quantity and quality of industrial equipment is rapidly increasing, and this will have its effect on output per man-hour.

Many specific advances during World War II and afterward give promise of rapidly rising productivity in the years to come. For one thing, *new machines* were introduced. In the aircraft industry a new high-speed milling machine designed for the rapid shaping of awkward aluminum parts reduced job time to one-fortieth of its previous amount. In the Pratt and Whitney aircraft engine plant, a monster machine of wartime worked on 20 cylinder heads at one time. It bored, counterbored, and faced intake- and exhaust-valve guide holes, and bored intake-valve seats. The two men required to operate it replaced 30.

Among *new methods* introduced is an expanding use of electronic devices that can sort and count, judge temperatures (as in the furnaces of steel mills), evaluate color far more accurately than the human eye (in textile mills), switch off the power if one of 500 threads breaks (in weaving), and so forth. Most of the labor displaced by these sensitive devices is routine and monotonous. Resistance welding, which fuses parts by electrical resistance rather than by the use of any added filler metal, has been a striking time saver. In the spot-welding of aluminum sheets in aircraft construction, one machine can make 100 welds a minute: the prewar record was 100 rivets per man per hour.

The following other developments are hopeful: expansion of assembly-line production; increased use of special metals, including steel alloys and aluminum and magnesium; increasing use of continuous flow production methods (rather than production by batches) in the chemical industry; better materials-handling machines; and growing use of remarkable calculating and measuring machines.

In agriculture a major mechanical revolution is under way, speeded by the great rise in agricultural incomes during World War II. Farmers can repair, replace, and modernize their equipment as they could not during what was to them the depressed 1920's and the yet more dismal 1930's. In 1948 farmers owned 3.3 million tractors; in 1929 only .8 million. The number of combines rose nearly 14 times in the same period. The tractor has put on rubber tires, and so become faster and more flexible. Hydraulic controls and tools mounted directly on the tractor make it a versatile device for lifting, scooping, sawing wood, moving earth, and many other functions. Cotton pickers and corn pickers are coming into wide use. A new corn picker shreds the corn in the field, so that it is delivered to the barn, ready for the silo, untouched by human hands. Machines for thinning and harvesting sugar beets are likely to spread. An air-driven hoe device is being used experimentally in California—five or more hoes can be powered from one central air compresser moving slowly through the field. New kinds of cultivators that pulverize the soil in one operation are challenging the traditional mold-board plow. A new type of barn automatically feeds hay down to cattle, saving nearly all the labor formerly needed. Many other new devices are on the way. Some of them will earn their keep and spread into general use.

Small farms cannot afford the overhead costs of much mechanical equipment, which necessarily lies idle in the barn most of the time. One solution is for the farmer to cultivate more land. In 1930 the average United States farm was of 155 acres; in 1940, 174 acres; by 1945, 195 acres. But machines tailor-made to the needs of the small farm are currently being advertised. Livestock and fruit farms remain the least mechanized: the human skill and judgment required in these lines have not been found in machines.[3]

Mechanization is only one road to higher farm productivity. Progress will continue in better breeding practices, better plant varieties (promising in the near future as much as a 50 per cent jump in production of many vegetables, field grains, and alfalfa), further checking of erosion, and tighter chemical controls of plant diseases, insects, and weeds.

Recent improvements in tools and techniques are beginning to show decisive results. Production per acre of major crops fell from 1867 to 1937. Since then there has been a sharp rise. Good weather, we must admit, is part of the explanation, but only part. From 1937 to 1948, production of cotton per acre rose 43 per cent, of corn and wheat 23 per cent, of potatoes 17 per cent, and of oats 35 per cent.

In American industry generally, a continuously larger share of our effort has gone into research. Expenditures for research have roughly doubled every ten years from 1900 to 1939—twice the rate of increase of the national income. World War II raised research efforts into new magnitudes. The government invested heavily in war research projects—for example, radar, jet

---

[3] "The Machine and the Farm," *Fortune*, Vol. XXXVIII, No. 4 (October, 1948), pp. 97 ff.

and rocket propulsion, guided missiles, and atomic energy—whose spectacular results advertised the treasure to be found. In postwar years the volume of Atomic Energy Commission research and government war research has no peacetime precedent. Most large private businesses are also planning on, or are under way with, expanded research activities. Total governmental and private expenditures on research in 1947 reached $1.2 billions, greater than the expenditures of the peak of the war, three times those of 1940, seven times those of 1930.[4]

All this evidence is highly optimistic. But it is not conclusive. There are intangible factors involved that elude positive prediction, among them the morale of employees and the initiative of business managers. Productivity in the British coal mines fell steadily for ten years from the middle 1930's on, despite increased mechanization, doubled wages during the war, and extended social insurance. The chief cause was apparently low morale—resentment against the social conditions and working life of the miner. In the United States the strikes and other causes of low productivity in early 1946 reflected in part our desire to take some time off after the continuous pressure of wartime. Many of us wanted to go fishing or simply to loaf awhile.

But even though we take the most pessimistic view possible of the prospects in the United States, there is no reason to expect any cessation of our remarkable long-range increase in productivity. It rests with us to determine whether the fruits of increased productivity will be taken in a combination of increased total production and increased leisure, or whether a part or all of these advantages will be wasted in unemployment.

The optimum rate of technical progress

New machines, new methods of organization, new raw materials, and new products are not introduced without their cost to the society. One element is the economic cost: old equipment and processes are reduced in value or made worthless by

---

[4] *Ibid.*, p. 108.

the introduction of the new. The improvement is socially desirable only when its advantage compensates for this loss; and not then, in fact, unless the improvement is definitive enough so that it will not in turn become obsolete in the near future.[5] Often these considerations mean that the improvement ought to be introduced rather slowly, as it gives decisive evidence of its value, and as the older equipment gradually wears out.

A second kind of cost of progress, which does not enter into the bookkeeping of firms, is the human cost. Technical improvements often make obsolete the skills of workers, forcing them into less skilled occupations with lower pay, or forcing them to undergo retraining and perhaps to move to new locations. The linotype, following its introduction in the 1890's, made obsolete the skills of hand typesetters. The Owens automatic bottle machine replaced skilled hand blowers. The continuous rolling mill introduced into the steel industry during the 1920's enabled a single mill to turn out with 125 men a quantity of sheet steel formerly produced by 4500 men in 96 mills. The community as a whole is more productive and has a higher real income in consequence of the technical advance; but individual workmen often find the same change a disadvantage or even a lifelong tragedy.

The economy can minimize this human cost by establishing retraining programs and by facilitating the movement of labor from surplus areas to areas where its skills are needed. But it cannot altogether eliminate the human costs of progress. The existence of such cost indicates that the optimum rate of technical progress is not the rate that is best from an economic point of view only, but a somewhat lower rate. At this lower rate, the less rapid increase of real income is compensated for by decreased human costs.

---

[5] A competitor will introduce an improvement in production if it has any margin of advantage over older methods (that is, if average costs are lower). A monopolist requires a more decisive advantage such that (in the simplest case where output remains unchanged) total costs with the improvement are less than running costs (total variable costs) with the old method.

CHAPTER FIVE

Production and Prices

THE LEVEL OF TOTAL PRODUCTION AND THE RATE OF CHANGE of that level have a systematic relationship to the average price level of an economy.

Wholesale and Retail Prices

We plot in Chart 6 the data of the Bureau of Labor Statistics for wholesale and for retail prices, together with the series we have used before for net production in the United States. Wholesale prices are those paid by businessmen for commodities bought in quantity; retail prices are those that retail sellers charge for consumers' commodities. (But the indexes do not measure the prices of the *same* goods at different stages of the productive process, as we might ideally desire. The prices are not only for different stages, but also for different commodities.) Wholesale prices show a greater percentage variation than retail prices: they rise higher and fall lower. One cause is the greater extent of rigid (unchanging or slowly changing) pricing in manufacturing, transportation, and the retail trades, whose charges make up the difference between wholesale and final retail prices. This rigidity is explained by monopolistic or conventional pricing in the given fields. A change in demand for retail goods forces price changes back upon the more nearly competitive suppliers of basic wholesale goods—farmers, and other raw material producers—rather than upon retailers, transporters, or manufacturers of finished products.

Chart 6. Production, Retail Prices, and Wholesale Prices in the United States, 1909-1950.

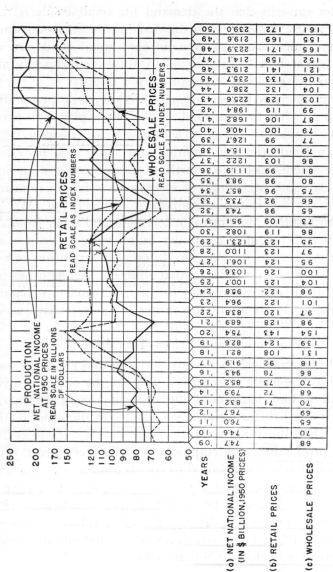

PRODUCTION
NET NATIONAL INCOME
AT 1950 PRICES
READ SCALE IN BILLIONS
OF DOLLARS

RETAIL PRICES
READ SCALE AS INDEX NUMBERS

WHOLESALE PRICES
READ SCALE AS INDEX NUMBERS

YEARS	(a) NET NATIONAL INCOME (IN $ BILLION, 1950 PRICES)	(b) RETAIL PRICES	(c) WHOLESALE PRICES
'50	239.0	172	191
'49	219.6	169	155
'48	223.9	171	165
'47	214.1	159	152
'46	219.3	141	121
'45	235.7	133	106
'44	238.7	132	104
'43	225.6	129	103
'42	198.4	119	99
'41	168.2	106	87
'40	140.6	100	79
'39	126.7	99	77
'38	115.4	101	79
'37	122.2	103	86
'36	111.9	99	81
'35	98.3	98	80
'34	85.7	96	75
'33	73.5	92	66
'32	74.3	98	65
'31	95.1	109	73
'30	108.2	119	86
'29	123.1	123	95
'28	110.0	123	97
'27	106.1	124	95
'26	103.6	126	100
'25	100.7	125	104
'24	95.8	122-	96
'23	96.4	122	101
'22	83.8	120	97
'21	68.9	128	98
'20	75.4	143	154
'19	82.6	124	139
'18	72.8	108	131
'17	61.9	92	118
'16	94.3	78	98
'15	85.2	73	70
'14	79.9	72	68
'13	83.2	71	70
'12	76.7		69
'11	76.0		65
'10	74.6		70
'09	74.7		68

Sources: Production data (net national income at 1950 prices) from Chart 1, p. 81. Retail prices are the "Consumers' Price Index," from *Basic Facts on Employment and Production,* Senate Committee Print No. 4, 79th Congress, 1st Session, 1945, p. 16; and *Economic Report of the President,* January, 1951, p. 193. For 1941-1946, the index is corrected in accord with the conclusions of the Mitchell Committee. It is calculated on the basis of 1935-1939 = 100, and all figures are rounded to the nearest whole number. Wholesale prices are from the same sources, pp. 17 and 194 respectively. 1926 = 100, and figures are rounded to the nearest whole number.

Another cause is that the demand for retail goods is relatively stable as compared with the demand for goods at wholesale, where fluctuations of demand for capital goods are extreme. We eat bread fairly regularly through prosperity and depression, but steel is a prince-or-pauper industry

Retail prices were higher compared to wholesale prices after 1920 than they had been in 1914–1920. The explanation partly lies in the particular causes of a drastic price collapse, 1920–1921, in agricultural commodities and other raw materials. Another element lies in the growth, in goods near consumption, of more elaborate packaging, of increased services in retailing, and of other aspects of monopolistic competition. We no longer, for example, buy our crackers, salt, and sugar from the grocer's barrel, but in boxes under brand names; and perhaps the store delivers to us. But the different composition of our two indexes—the circumstance that different commodities are included in the one rather than in the other—makes it hazardous to reason closely about the causes of their relative movements.

Production and Prices—Description

How do prices change as production falls and rises? We look especially at wholesale prices, since they are the more sensitive. In general we find that production and prices move together, a rise in the one being associated with a rise in the other, and a fall with a fall. But the correlation is not nearly so close as that between production and employment. The very great price rise of World War I continued to its maximum *after* the war. Prices broke, and dropped abruptly during the short depression of 1921. They rose a bit as output increased toward 1925 or 1926, and then fell a little even though production kept on increasing to 1929. The movements of production and prices agree more closely after 1929 than before.

How We Should Expect Prices to Behave as Production Changes

The prices of *individual* commodities are determined by the influence of supply and demand Neglecting the complications introduced by monopolistic policies as distinct from those of competition, we can reason as follows: (1) If the quantity of goods supplied to the market increases (or if demand for them decreases), prices tend to fall. If potatoes are harvested in abundance some year, consumers will be persuaded to buy them up only if their price drops below its previous level. (2) If, instead, the quantity demanded increases (or if supply decreases), prices tend to rise. If the public becomes convinced of the merits of those washing machines that wash, rinse, and dry clothing automatically, the manufacturers of the machines realize that they can charge higher prices for them and still sell a large volume.

In the short run, when it is difficult to introduce new resources into a field, a rise in prices owing to an increase in demand leads to only a moderate rise in output. In the longer run, factories are expanded and new factories built in such a field, and as supply on the market grows, prices fall below their previous level. The manufacturer of our automatic washing machine soon finds, to his sorrow, other manufacturers entering into competition with him. They develop or obtain the use of effective designs and set up the necessary machinery. Eventually as supply increases, producers are forced to lower their prices in order to sell their outputs.

In the converse case of a drop in prices due to a fall in demand, individual producers (seeking the maximum profit possible under the new conditions) decrease their supply on the market. As time goes on, some of the producers shift over into more attractive fields—perhaps by the hard road of bankruptcy—and output declines further. Prices then rise somewhat from their previous level.

We can describe both of these situations by saying that supply is less *elastic* (that is, output responds less to a given change in price) in the short run than in the long run.

Prices of individual goods, then, are determined by the conditions of supply and demand. We are now concerned with explaining average prices—that is, prices of all goods and services in the economy. Nevertheless, the basic explanation remains the same: supply and demand conditions still determine average prices over the whole economy. But now we need to speak of supply *as a whole* and demand *as a whole*.

An increase of demand when much unemployment exists

Suppose that a large percentage of labor and other resources in the economy is unemployed. (In 1932 and 1933 about one-quarter of the working force was unemployed.) Prices are sagging downward, especially in the more purely competitive fields of agriculture and raw material production. In some areas where there is much monopolistic insulation from competition and where labor unions have been able to maintain their wage rates, prices are falling little or not at all.

In this situation, suppose that businessmen suddenly find that they can sell more of their products. Total money demand has increased. The increased demand might have originated in several possible sources. It might have come from consumers' deciding to save less and spend more for consumption goods: they might even have drawn on their past savings. It might have come from businessmen's decisions to buy more investment goods in the form of buildings, equipment, or inventories of raw materials. It might have come from more government spending for war- or peacetime purposes. Finally, the increased demand might have originated in more buying by foreigners, perhaps in anticipation of war abroad or because of crop failure.

Since there is heavy unemployment, it is easy for employers to hire more resources at approximately current prices: unemployed labor is abundant, hours can be lengthened for people who are working part-time, raw materials can be obtained readily, and plants running at only a fraction of capacity can expand quickly.

Some employers may, as they expand their output, find that their efficiency of production is diminishing, but this is not likely if they had been operating their plants at relatively low volume. Usually firms will find average efficiency rising as they expand output of their plants toward planned capacity and can make increasing use of mass production methods.

Taking into account both these influences—prices of labor and other resources, and efficiency of production—we should not expect average costs to rise with rising output. As an over-all result, since output (supply) can be expanded readily without higher costs, prices are not apt to rise appreciably. The effect of the increased demand will be almost entirely to increase output, hardly at all to increase prices.

We can find illustrations of this in the periods of the past when unemployment was greatest. In the years 1921–1922 when unemployment was 11 and 7 per cent, respectively, of the working force, output rose considerably while wholesale prices were almost constant. In the years 1933–1937 when 25 to 14 per cent of the working force was unemployed and in 1938–1940 when unemployment varied between 19 and 15 per cent, output rose considerably while prices rose moderately or even fell a bit. (Unemployment of labor is an approximate, but useful, indication of idle equipment and abundant raw materials.)

An increase of demand when there is moderate unemployment

Suppose there is only moderate unemployment of labor and other resources and that total demand increases. Some firms will still be able to expand readily if they happen to be in localities where more unemployed labor is available than is true generally, if they have idle equipment or can readily intensify the use of their equipment, and if they have easy access to more raw materials.

Other firms, however (since unemployed resources are rather scarce), will find it necessary to pay higher prices to obtain more labor or more raw materials: they must bid them away from other firms who are also in the market to buy them. Many firms will find efficiency diminishing as they try to force a larger output out of a given factory, office, farm, or mine. They are overloading the plant, pushing it beyond the point of maximum efficiency. Since the costs of these two groups of firms are higher with larger output, they will not increase their output unless they are induced to do so by the offer of higher prices. Finally, some firms, who feel themselves insulated against inroads of competition, will be encouraged by the increased demand to raise their prices.

Hence, if demand increases in an economy where there is moderate unemployment of resources, output will rise: unemployed resources will be put to work, and those already employed will be used more intensively. And prices will rise also.

In the somewhat longer run (as we have seen above), prices are apt to recede from the point reached shortly after demand increased. For one reason, resources will flow into competitive fields where output is especially short and prices are especially high. Capital equipment will be built and installed in such businesses; mineral resources will be surveyed further and mines extended; and workers will train themselves for occupations where wage offers are relatively high. For a second reason, imitators are apt to encroach on fields where monopolies have kept prices especially high.

In Chart 6, such periods when unemployment was moderate, and demand, output, and prices were all increasing, appear in 1914–1915, 1922–1923, and 1940–1941. (Wartime controls, and their after effects, blur the picture during and following the War.)

An increase of demand when there is already full employment

Suppose there is approximately full employment of all resources of the economy: all the labor force is at work and many people are working overtime. We are making as full use as is reasonably possible of the natural resources and capital equipment of the nation. And then demand increases still further.

The only possible effect is for prices to rise sharply. In fact, they will rise in the same proportion as money demand increases. If demand rises by 20 per cent, prices must rise by 20 per cent. Output cannot rise appreciably if we are already making full use of all our productive resources; and people can spend more money on the output of the economy only if that output is sold at higher prices. Manufacturers, retailers, and farmers, faced with the opportunities of boom times, raise prices with pleasure. They can sell their entire output at higher prices. And employees, both in and outside labor unions, find demand for their services urgent and are able to win higher wage rates.

Graphic representation of the relation between total production and prices

Chart 7 summarizes what we have just said. The chart portrays only average changes: it blurs details, in which our special interest will sometimes lie. We assume that the efficiency with which the economy utilizes resources remains about the same during the period of expansion. Hence, we can plot the movement of production and employment together: when employment rises, production rises in the same proportion.[1]

Prices are charted on the left, from a low level at 0 to a very high level as we move upward. Output and employment are at a very low level at 0, increase to the right until all resources are employed (output is, therefore, at a maximum) at F.

As demand increases from a very moderate quantity, we should expect production and employment to increase much, prices little. As demand increases further, the effect is more and more on prices, less on production and employment. Finally, at full employment of resources, production can increase no further, and any increase of aggregate demand will increase prices only.

---

[1] Efficiency will, however, diminish (output rises by a smaller proportion than employment of resources) if the productive equipment of the economy becomes overloaded, or kinds of products are changing rapidly, or the effort or hours of labor diminish. This divergence is one cause of higher prices as full employment is approached.

The effect of a drop in total demand

A drop in demand means that businessmen cannot find buyers for current output at current prices. The volume of production, prices, or both, must drop. There is some asymmetry between our former case of increasing demand and this case of declining demand: whereas businessmen are glad to see prices rise and wage earners are glad to see wage rates rise, both resist so far as they can the fall of prices and wage rates. Often, the resistance is bitter, accompanied by rising social antagonism.

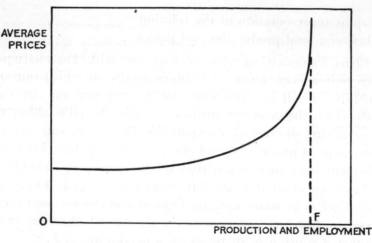

**Chart 7. The Price Level and the Level of Production
and Employment.**

Prices, therefore, tend to be more flexible in an upward, than in a downward, direction. England had little success in the attempt to deflate prices during 1925–1930; nor had France any greater success through the middle 1930's. The German effort in 1930–1932 heightened social conflict and helped pave the way for the Nazis.[2]

---

[2] Australia, on the other hand, furnishes an exception. There, in 1932, a 25 per cent cut in wages was accomplished successfully. The United States in 1929-1932 went through a wholly unintended drastic price drop, paralleled only by Germany: wholesale prices here fell 32 per cent and retail prices 20 per cent. We do not want the experience again, if we can avoid it.

As demand drops, businessmen who have some degree of monopolistic power try to maintain their prices and reduce output instead. Labor unions try to maintain their standard rates. But just as businessmen may give confidential discounts, employees may, in fact, accept less pay then they are officially supposed to get by union rules. Farm groups, coal-mine associations, and others descend on Washington in pursuit of special legislation to maintain their prices.

The greater the amount of unemployment of resources, however, the more difficult it is to maintain the prices of the past boom period. Prices drop the most in those areas where there is the greatest proportion of competitive, as opposed to monopolistic or administered, pricing, and where there is the greatest proportion of unemployed labor, business managers, capital equipment, and natural resources. These productive resources, or their owners, are willing to accept lower rates of return in order not to remain unemployed. And so the level of prices of the whole group is forced downward.

CHAPTER SIX

The Main Constituents of Total Production

AT THE TIME THE UNITED STATES BECAME INDEPENDENT, agriculture was by far the dominant industry. Such manufacturing as there was seemed to Alexander Hamilton a "vast scene of household industry." The picture has changed much since then.

The Long Trend for Major Industries

It is convenient, following Colin Clark, to divide production into three main divisions: primary industry, consisting of agriculture, forestry and fishing; secondary industry, covering manufacturing, mining, and building; and tertiary industry, consisting of commerce, transportation, communication, and services. We do not have trustworthy estimates of output going back many decades into the past, but it is possible to measure the relative importance of these industries by numbers of employees as far back as 1820 (Table 11).

The fall in the per cent of the work force in primary industry is found in all countries where productivity in primary industry is rising. As average output grows, a smaller proportion of our energies needs to be put into this area, which produces goods for which demand is rather quickly sated as supply increases. The average person in the United States was eating about the same volume of food just before World War

TABLE 11

PERCENTAGE OF WORKING POPULATION IN VARIOUS INDUSTRIES, 1820-1950 *

	Primary Agriculture Forestry Fishing %	Secondary Mining Manufacturing Building %	Tertiary Commerce Transport Communication Services %
1820	72.3	12.3	15.3
1840	68.8	14.9	16.1
1860	60.2	19.9	19.8
1880	49.4	25.5	25.0
1900	37.4	29.0	33.5
1920	26.7	33.2	40.0
1940	22.9	31.3	45.7
1950	14.6	35.0	50.4

* For the years 1820-1920, Colin Clark, *Conditions of Economic Progress*, London: Macmillan, 1940, p. 185, From census data presented by Whelpton, in *Journal of American Statistical Society*, Vol. XXI, p. 339. For 1940 and 1950, *The Economic Report of the President*, January, 1951, pp. 181, 182. The data for these years exclude unemployed persons, and proprietors and self-employed persons in secondary and tertiary industries.

II as he had in 1870, but was buying five times as much manufactured products. During this period, the number of farmers increased only 60 per cent, whereas the number of factory workers rose about 400 per cent.

How are people moved, as agricultural efficiency grows, from the farm into urban kinds of production? They could be ordered to go, but not even Soviet Russia has found compulsion practicable in this matter. The alternative is that they be induced to go, by less attractive conditions in agriculture than in expanding industries. This inducement results naturally from sharply falling prices of farm products as farm output rises.[1] For the United States, in 1949, the average incomes of

---

[1] Agricultural products face in general an inelastic demand—a given percentage rise in output can be sold only at a greater percentage fall in prices, so that total receipts fall. This is the reflection in market demand of the relatively quick satiation of consumers with farm products as their quantity increases. . . . Non-financial incentives are, of course, also relevant to choice of occupation: Many people like the gregarious working and living conditions of the city better than rural life.

people engaged in primary, secondary, and tertiary industries were as follows:

Primary	Secondary	Tertiary *
$2393	$4184	$4029

* Calculated from the *Survey of Current Business*, July, 1950, pp. 15 and 23. The figures are based on net national income created in the three sectors; that is, net value of production at factor prices.

But men change their occupations with reluctance: noneconomic ties and the risks of taking a leap into different work are a drag on migration into remunerative and expanding occupations. Many of us simply follow in our fathers' footsteps. Others interpret the long-run decline of an old industry as merely temporary bad times.

And the tendency of migration away from agriculture to raise rural incomes relative to urban incomes is opposed by the circumstance that so many more children are born in the country than in the city. The rural reproduction rate in the United States is about double the rate of large cities.[2]

Paradoxically, agriculture would be relatively prosperous in an economy in which farm efficiency of production is stagnant or falling. In progressive areas of the world, farm incomes have remained relatively low over the generations, and so persuaded a rising proportion of the work force to go into nonfarm occupations. The method in the long run of raising farm incomes relative to urban incomes is *not* by subsidizing farmers, whether by a parity program or other device. This leads toward a larger output of farm products, relative to urban products, than would exist otherwise, and so to continued depression in relative farm incomes. An effective social policy of raising relative farm incomes would increase the mobility of farm labor; that is, would

[2] Rural net reproduction rates vary typically between 1 and 1.8; those of large cities between .5 and .7. Among the extremes are Graham County, Arizona (1.833), and New York City (.475). A net reproduction rate of 1.0 means that the population is, in the long run, tending just to maintain itself, not counting immigration or emigration. (Data from the Bureau of the Census, in *Current Population Reports*, Series P-20, March 24, 1950.)

make it easier (through training programs, job placement services, and other devices) for farm people to move into urban
occupations.

Short-Run Changes in Output of Particular Industries

Table 12 ranks 10 industries approximately in order, from
those, during the great depression, in which prices moved least
flexibly as demand fell and rose, to those in which prices moved
most flexibly.

TABLE 12

PRICES AND OUTPUTS BY INDUSTRIES, 1929-1932-1937 *

| Industry Group | Percentage Drop 1929-32 | | | | Percentage Rise 1932-37 | | | |
	Total De-mand	Prices	Out-put	Elas-ticity of Supply	Total De-mand	Prices	Out-put	Elas-ticity of Supply
1. Motor vehicles ..	77%	12%	74%	6.2	66%	2%	64%	32.0
2. Agricultural implements ...	86	14	84	6.0	101	9	84	7.6
3. Iron and steel ..	80	16	76	4.8	100	20	67	3.4
4. Cement	62	16	55	3.4	44	20	24	1.2
5. Auto tires	56	25	42	1.7	57	27	24	0.9
6. Leather products.	45	33	18	0.6	64	29	27	0.9
7. Petroleum products	47	36	17	0.5	66	21	37	1.8
8. Textile products .	56	39	28	0.7	54	24	24	1.0
9. Food products ...	45	39	10	0.3	23	24	−1	−0.04
10. Agricultural commodities ..	55	54	1	0.02	47	36	8	0.2

* The percentage changes in prices and output are from the National Resources Committee, *Structure of the American Economy*. Washington: Government Printing Office,
1939; Vol. 1, Table XXII, p. 386. The figures for percentage change in demand are
approximate, being calculated from the given price and output data. Elasticity of supply
is calculated. The original sources of data are the Bureau of Labor Statistics index of
wholesale prices, and Federal Reserve Board indexes of output. Percentage changes are
calculated on 1929 as a base.
By 1937 total real output had about recovered to the level of 1929 (the round figures
in billion dollars are (1929) 109, (1932) 66, and (1937) 109. Current money value
of net output had not recovered (the corresponding figures in billion dollars are 87,
42, and 74).

The effect of a drop in demand is least on price and most on
output in those industries (motor vehicles, agricultural imple-

ments, cement, iron and steel) in which the monopolistic, or administered price, element is strong—that is, where products are not standardized and where a large share of output comes from a few firms. Such policy tends to dominate the selling of goods whose production requires much manufacturing, and which are ready or nearly ready for sale to the ultimate consumer. The price of bread at retail, for example, tends to change little when demand changes; the price of wholesale bread tends to vary more; the price of flour is still more sensitive; and the price of wheat is most sensitive of all.

Among the more purely competitive industries where the effect of the demand declines is mainly on price (in our list, agricultural and food products, and textiles) are those that supply raw materials, nondurable goods, and standardized commodities in general.

Parallel results usually occur when demand is increasing. Where the monopolistic, or administered price, element is strong, the main effect is on output, and prices rise only moderately. Where the competitive element is strong, output tends to rise less, prices more. It is often casually argued that monopolistic industries hike prices upward enthusiastically when demand revives. The facts are to the contrary. Prices are inflexible in that area both in downswing and upswing.

Elasticity of supply

We have calculated in Table 12 what we have called, rather loosely, the *elasticity of supply* of each industry over the periods indicated. We use this as our measure of flexibility of prices— that is, of how much on the average output changes when we have a small change in prices. Elasticity of supply is defined as

$$\frac{\text{percentage change in quantity}}{\text{percentage change in price}}$$

For example, the average elasticity of supply for motor vehicles in 1929–1932 is 74/12, or 6.2.

If, when there is a 1 per cent change in price, quantity of output changes by more than 1 per cent, supply is called *elastic*. If, when there is a 1 per cent change in price, quantity changes by less than 1 per cent, supply is said to be *inelastic*. With one exception supply for the first five industries in both decline and revival is elastic: prices change relatively little, output relatively much. The supply of the last five industries is, with two exceptions, inelastic—above all for food products and agricultural commodities where output changes little but prices fluctuate widely.

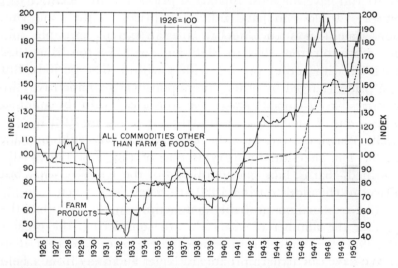

Chart 8. Wholesale Agricultural and Industrial Prices, 1926 = 100.

Source: Department of Labor, Bureau of Labor Statistics, *Basic Facts on Employment and Production.* Washington: Government Printing Office, 1945, p. 18; and *Survey of Current Business,* p. S-5 in various issues.

It should be noticed as we look to these elasticities of supply that "other things were *not* constant." For example, when demand dropped for agricultural implements, it is not true that demand for motor vehicles remained constant. Demand was, at this time, declining for all commodities. If demand for motor

vehicles and other commodities had been maintained, some of
the resources used in agricultural-implement production would
have transferred to the production of motor vehicles and other
goods; and output of agricultural implements would have
dropped still more.

Long-run elasticity of supply

The dates that we have been surveying are for short periods
only—three years of decline in demand, five years of rise of
demand. It is by no means sure that the industries which in the
short run have the most inflexible prices (greatest elasticity of
supply) would also have inflexible prices in the long run.
Sometimes that is true. Steel rails, as an extreme example, sold
for $28 a ton from 1901 to 1916, and for $43 a ton from 1922
to 1932, with output varying widely within these periods. But
the prices charged by other "monopolistically competitive" industries have changed greatly over the decades. In the automobile industry the jalopy we bought for $2000 in 1920 had by
1939 been improved into the effective car we could buy for
$900. The chemical industry is one of the most tightly dis-
ciplined—that is, most monopolistic—of the United States, but
prices of chemicals during 1920–1939 fell 54 per cent.

The explanation probably lies mainly in the fact that the
greater the number of years we are considering, the greater
the flow of resources into a field where prices are kept high
relative to costs (where profits are large) and away from a field
where costs are rising and demand shrinking. Eventually, as
businessmen set up to produce substitutes in a field or migrate
away from it, the changed output of the industry has its effect
on prices. We can repeat a previous conclusion: In all industries, monopolistically competitive as well as nearly purely
competitive, supply is more elastic in the long run than in the
short run.

Both particular industries and the whole economy are subject to other major influences on supply. Techniques and organization in a progressive economy improve as the years go

by. Hence from any fixed quantity of resources a larger output is produced. Production per worker, per unit of equipment, and per acre of land rises.

Such improvements in techniques can have decided effects during the course of only a few years. They are overwhelmingly important, in a progressive economy like our own, over the course of scores of years and of centuries.

Also, the work force grows or declines, and its average skill and effort change. New natural resources may be discovered and technical changes may cause existing resources to be revalued; or resources may be depleted. The quantity of capital equipment used in production can increase or decline. The zeal and effectiveness of management can change.

All these influences are at work and affect supply in the long run. If supply increases, and demand remains unchanged, then prices will fall.

War experience—expansion of output in particular industries

During our World War II experience, the incentive of price rises toward getting an increased supply from industry was, outside of agriculture and other special fields, of secondary importance. The price of steel plate and glass plate had not, after 52 months of war, risen at all, but output had multiplied greatly. The price of pig iron rose only 15 per cent over a period when the output of alloy steels was rising 433 per cent.[3] The main explanation of increased production in war industries and essential civilian supply industries lay in the controls of the War Production Board and the effective cooperation of industry with those controls. The essential measures were those of priorities and allocations, which channeled supplies of raw materials to the most essential industries. Other measures checked the building up of inventories of raw material in the ware-

---

3 Output of 1944 compared with that of 1938. Data from Senate Hearings on Extension of the Price Control Act, p. 1567, and Third Annual Report of the Truman Committee. Quoted in S. E. Harris, *Price and Related Controls*, pp. 277-279. New York: McGraw-Hill, 1945.

houses of individual plants, mobilized idle supplies, and encouraged conservation procedures—such as standardization of end products and elimination of frills.

The situation in 1941 of sample companies in lead mining illustrates the diversity of obstacles to expansion, and the diversity of possibilities of expansion. The information was given in response to inquiries made by the Truman Committee.

1. Federal Mining and Smelting, and American Mining and Smelting: "A 1-cent increase in price would increase production 10 to 20 per cent in 6 months."
2. Combined Metals Reduction Co.: "Price increase would not result in higher production because we are now working all marginal ore bodies."
3. Shattuck Denn Mining Corp.: "Higher price would increase ore from small mines sent to our mill. Our own mine now operating to capacity."
4. Silver King Coalition Mines Co.: "Mining of submarginal ores will be discontinued unless price rises."
5. Dayrock Mining Co.: "By spending $20,000, we would increase production within 30 days by 2 per cent. Within 90 days, the maximum increase could be 40 per cent, at an expense of $75,000."
6. Sherman Lead Co.: "By spending $50,000 we would increase production within 60 days by 50 per cent. The mine now is being operated at its greatest economic rate of production. Any increase in output will involve an increase in cost and a lesser return to stockholders. . . . To achieve a substantial fraction of 50 per cent possible increase, sixth- and seventh-day weekly operation is required. Such overtime at time and one half [will cause] production under present prices to be obtained at a loss."
7. Shenandoah-Dives Mining Co.: "An adequate price increase would add 5 per cent to output within 90 days; and would increase production at least 20 per cent with additional development calculated."
8. Triumph Mining Co.: "No material increase possible with price increase until new tunnel and mill are completed." [4]

4 Special (Truman) Committee Investigating the National Defense Program, Report No. 480, Part 5, pp. 216–219.

Changes in Demand

In Table 12, the changes in total expenditure (demand) vary considerably from one group of commodities to another. In 1929—1932 while the total expenditure on agricultural implements was dropping by 86 per cent, demand for food products and leather products was declining by only 45 per cent. In the five following years, while demand doubled for iron and steel and agricultural implements, it rose by about a half for textiles and agricultural commodities, and by only a quarter for food products.

Part of the explanation clearly lies in the rigid prices of the former commodities in both periods. If prices of a good do not drop in depression, buyers tend to shift away from buying that good. They may buy more of other goods whose prices have dropped greatly. In revival, buyers tend to buy more of those goods whose prices rise little.

But this is often an incomplete explanation. Will a man who is discouraged from buying steel *I*-beams by their high price be encouraged thereby to stock up on wheat? It seems doubtful. The shift of demand from one commodity to another is only one element in explaining changing expenditures on those particular commodities. The other element is that total demand for all commodities was declining in 1929—1932 and rising in 1932—1937. The following chapters are concerned with this basic problem of changes in total demand.

CHAPTER SEVEN

The Cost of Unemployment and
the Aim of Full Employment

IN THE LAST SEVERAL DECADES, THERE HAVE BEEN WIDE VARIA-tions in the degree to which we have utilized the resources of the nation. In many of these years, production could have been increased considerably if we had made effective use of more of our resources.

The Cost of Unemployment

Over the years 1930—1939, an average of 18 per cent of our working force was unemployed, or nearly one man in five (Chart 9). Suppose we had instead enjoyed reasonably full employment. How much would our output have increased? We might argue (*a*) that it would have increased by less than the proportion of the newly employed to those previously employed, because the unemployed, with many exceptions, were those who were less effective and less regular.

(*b*) On the other hand, there was much part-time employment among those who are listed as employed—people working half a day instead of a whole day, or three or four days a week only. Also there was much *concealed unemployment*. This we define as *bad allocation of labor* due to general unemployment[1] in the society—the employment of people in tasks requiring less skill and ability than those for which they are

---

[1] See p. 129.

fitted. Many a mechanic sought refuge from depression on a subsistence farm, and lawyers and scholars operated filling stations. In addition, through fear of unemployment, men slow down their work in time of depression; and unions sometimes stipulate for "make-work" rules—for full crews, stand-by musicians, maximum width of paint brushes, or a limit on the number of bricks to be laid a day.

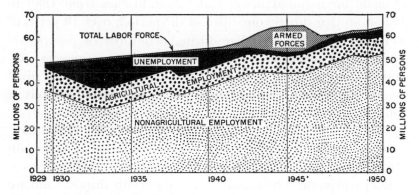

Chart 9. Estimates of the Labor Force, Employment, and Unemployment in the United States, 1929-1950.

Source: The Economic Report of the President, January, 1949, p. 105; January, 1951, p. 181.

The latter effects are dominant. Output could have risen by considerably more than the proportion that "full employment" would have borne to actual employment in the 1930's. Employment could have risen to nearly 49 millions, instead of the decade average of 42 millions, or by 16 per cent. But production could have risen by 48 per cent.

This estimate is based on 1929 and 1947 data. We calculate a full employment output for each of these years, and then what output would have been in the 1930's assuming a steady growth at full employment levels. From this we subtract actual production. The difference is 470 billion dollars of net production, at 1950 prices.[2] This immense volume of goods and services—what we did not produce in the 1930's, but could have produced had we employed our resources fully—is nearly four times the total production of 1937, and about double the booming output of 1944.

The unemployment data for the preceding several decades are less reliable; also they do not take account of part-time unemployment and of concealed unemployment. One careful estimate for manufacturing and like industries from 1889 to 1926 finds that during one-third of the period, over 10 per cent were unemployed, and that during two-thirds of the period more than 7 per cent were unemployed.[3] At no time was unemployment as heavy as in the 1930's. Still earlier in the nineteenth century the United States suffered prolonged periods of bad times (pp. 215-217).

To the extent that, at higher levels of output, we should have used up resources that are not perishable and that are available to us in limited quantity, the loss through unemployment is not permanent. The resources remain at our disposal and we will utilize them at some future date.

But labor time gone to waste is gone forever: its output is irretrievably lost. Time is our ultimate scarce resource.

In addition to the plain loss of time, there is an inevitable deterioration of skills, as men are away from their trades for months and years, and perhaps are forced to take other, lower-rated jobs:

---

[2] The net national income of 1929, at 1950 prices, was $123.1 billions. 96.9% of the work force was employed. We assume (see p. 133) that at reasonably full employment 5% of the work force would, on the average, be out of work owing to personal or frictional causes. Hence full employment output in 1929 was $120.8 billions. Similarly, in 1947 actual production was $214.1 billions at 1950 prices, with 96.5% of the work force employed; and full employment output was $210.7 billions. If the yearly increase in output had been a constant amount from 1929 to 1947, production would have totaled $1483 billions in the 1930's, as compared with the actual $1013 billions—an increase of 46.5%.

[3] Data of Paul Douglas, for manufacturing, transportation, construction, and mining. Unemployment is usually more severe in these than in average occupations.

I was an apprentice engineer and during the depression [1931] I was laid off. I got the offer of my job back but I was working then as a labourer and getting 30 s. a week. I just couldn't go back to my apprentice's wage of 15 s. I'm sorry now that I didn't.[4]

I have given up all hope of getting back to . . . my original work. I feel very keenly the loss of my trade union positions and the pity I receive from people who knew me. I feel sometimes like a hunted animal whose holes have been stopped up.[5]

Training for trades and professions shrinks during depression. Young people are discouraged from beginning a period of apprenticeship or schooling that will lead only to unemployment. One may as well be unemployed without the training. Union policies reflect the opposition both of unions as a whole, and of their unemployed members in particular, to starting new apprentices when skilled men of long service are out of work. In union contracts with employers, the proportion of apprentices to skilled workmen is often specified. Of a sample of union contracts negotiated before 1929, 12 per cent specified one or fewer apprentices to 10 skilled workmen, but 41 per cent specified this among contracts dated 1935–1940.[6] Diminished training means that the working population has a lower average level of skill, and hence that the economy will be less productive in the future owing to the lessened effectiveness of labor.

We have not yet mentioned what is probably the most important of all the losses brought about through unemployment. This is the psychological cost, the cost in morale. A person who wants and cannot find an employee suffers inconvenience. A person who wants and cannot find a job suffers disaster—not only lack of income with the privation and train of petty and major humiliations which that may involve, but also a verdict

---

[4] *Disinherited Youth,* a survey made by the Carnegie United Kingdom Trustees during 1936-1939, p. 13. Quoted in Sir William Beveridge, *Full Employment in a Free Society,* p. 246. New York: W. W. Norton, 1945.

[5] By an unmarried mechanic, in *Memoirs of the Unemployed,* p. 154. London: Gollancz, 1934.

[6] Sumner H. Slichter, *Union Policies and Industrial Management,* p. 36. Washington: Brookings, 1941.

that he has within him no contribution that the economy values. Once he is convinced that he is "no good," then the verdict becomes in large measure true: he is not likely to show the effort and confidence that are the first requisites of success. Even if there is adequate unemployment insurance, idleness demoralizes.

Beyond the unemployed themselves are their families, who are blocked from their chance of living rounded and expanding lives, constrained within a narrowing circle of humiliations and privations. It takes an unusual person to overcome so hostile an environment. All too generally there is a deepening sense of frustration and bitterness.

Any long spell of unemployment leaves you with little to be proud of and much to be ashamed of. Our child is still too young to realize that it is her mother who works. We carefully keep her from knowing it. . . . You have no life when you have no work; there are so many things you cannot do and so few that you may. . . . It is the work we want as much as the money.[7]

When Mr. C. lost his job at Winchester's, his wife was successful in getting a job there, and he did the housework. He did not mind until the neighbors made fun of him. They saw him working outside the house. He and she have never quarreled over the housework, but she felt very badly when she saw how miserable he was, and when she is home she protects him from the criticism of the neighbors by making certain that he engages in no domestic duties at which they will see him.[8]

Even if Mr. Leventhal gets a job on WPA again . . . he will work just to keep the family going. They will have no opportunity to save and build up any security for their old age. With the employment situation in his trade what it is, there is little likelihood of his finding a job in private industry. Mrs. Leventhal says that she worries a great deal about her children's future.[9]

My chief trouble is monotony of a long spell of unemployment. We are willing to forego replacements in the home, even new

---

[7] By a skilled wire drawer, in *Memoirs of the Unemployed*, pp. 180-181. London: Gollancz, 1934.

[8] E. W. Bakke, *Citizens Without Work*, p. 183. New Haven: Yale University, 1940.

[9] Eli Ginzberg and Associates, *The Unemployed*, p. 135. New York: Harpers, 1943.

clothes, although our present ones cannot last much longer. But monotonous and insufficient food and having nothing to do . . . kill a man's interest in life. . . . Perhaps I miss cigarettes most and I hate being chained to home most. There is no substitute for work.[10]

The Meaning of Full Employment

What is meant by the phrase "full employment"? We look first to employment of resources other than labor—natural resources and capital equipment. Ought we to set as a goal that every vein of coal should be mined, every deposit of copper or lead exploited, every acre of land cultivated, every machine and every tool put to use? We know as a matter of common sense that such an objective would be foolish.

"It doesn't pay" to work the poorest ores; some land isn't worth cultivating; it's best to junk worn-out or obsolete machinery.

Such submarginal resources will not return a product that covers the cost of the other factors used with them.[11] We shall get a larger product by using those other factors more intensively on better quality resources. It is sensible to leave thin and inaccessible strata of coal unmined and obtain our coal from richer deposits closer to market. If 100 men plus equipment can extract 90,000 tons of coal per year from poor deposits, but if these men and the equipment can produce 180,-000 tons per year from available richer veins, the first deposits can justifiably be left unworked. Likewise, it is sensible to leave barren and distant farm lands uncultivated, and instead get our agricultural supplies from the richest lands close to markets. It is reasonable for a society to junk equipment in good working order if new, more efficient equipment appears that can produce a greater output from a given input of labor and other

---

10 By a skilled millwright, in *Memoirs of the Unemployed*, p. 105.

11 The cost of those factors (more exactly, their *opportunity cost*) will be measured by the returns they earn in the best available other uses. Hence, their returns from being employed on submarginal resources will by definition not cover their cost.

resources (including in input the resources required for building the new machines).

If, therefore, we rank in order the resources of the society other than labor, from the best to the poorest, we always come to a margin below which it is not worth while to use them. Idleness of such poor, or submarginal, resources is not a token that the economy is ineffective in utilizing its factors.

Does the same reasoning hold for labor? As we go down the scale from people who, from a combination of professional and psychological qualities, are very effective, to those who are less and less so, we come eventually to those who are so inefficient and unreliable that their contribution to production is not equal to a minimum wage. That people are so incompetent is often avoidable, and no other investment of the economy is so well justified as that effective toward diminishing disease, nurturing physical vigor and mental balance, and increasing the skills of the population. Nevertheless, seriously handicapped people are among the population. Should such people be left unemployed?

Our social ethics, from religious and other motives, requires that we aim at maintaining a decent minimum standard of life for all members of the population, whether or not they are able to contribute effectively to the social product. The cost of maintaining the individual is hence a fixed cost from the point of view of the whole economy. This cost continues whether or not the individual works and so is not relevant to the question of whether or not he should be at work.

The issue then becomes whether the workers in question can, in some job or other, add *anything* to the output of the economy. The answer is nearly always "Yes." The blind man who weaves baskets, the man who wipes windshields at the filling station, and the man who picks up papers in the park with his spiked stick, all add something to the social output. If we consider in addition the educational value of congenial work toward better skills and its therapeutic value toward better psychological adjustment, we must conclude that there are few among even the drastically handicapped who would not be of greater use to the society at work than idle. Almost all of us can through our work make *some* contribution to the general good.

When is a person unemployed?

Some persons are idle without being unemployed. A man living on interest from his investments is not said to be one of the unemployed. We do not consider as unemployed people who are on vacation, or ill, or disabled, or going to school. Neither are housewives to be considered unemployed. These people are not in "gainful work" *voluntarily:* they are unable to carry on gainful work or else do not want a job.

Our concern is not with these, but with the *involuntarily* unemployed: people able to work and wanting work, but still without jobs. But just as *able to work* is subject to a wide range of doubt, so also is *wanting to work.* Wanting work is a matter of degree, varying in accordance with many influences: the pay rate; type and location of a job in question; working conditions; family responsibilities; other income available to the family; state of indebtedness; the difficulty, expense, and embarrassment involved in getting a job; and so forth. There are blurred edges to the concept of "unemployed" and possibility of varying classifications.

We might look at a particular case: Suppose a skilled mechanic who had been working at $1.50 an hour is offered work in his trade at 75 cents an hour. If he refuses to take the job, shall we consider him a loafer, voluntarily idle? Suppose our mechanic is offered a job as soda clerk. If he refuses to give up the trade in which he has been trained and perhaps spent years of work, to accept relatively unskilled work, shall we consider him lazy and not an honest member of the unemployed? Suppose he is offered a job, acceptable in itself but 30 miles away from his home? Shall we insist that he move himself and his family, if he has one; or commute by bus or train two or more hours a day, or perhaps buy a car?

The decision as to whether or not a person is unemployed is, therefore, difficult to make in many borderline cases. The rule of reason must apply. If he is able to work, is seeking work, and is not offered any job at all, we will certainly call him unemployed. And even though he is offered a job, if the offer seems unreasonable in view of the circumstances, we will still call him unemployed—that is, involuntarily unemployed, not merely an idler.[12]

The concepts of unemployment set up by states or by unions administering unemployment benefits may easily go astray in special cases. Certain Indians in northern Michigan are accustomed to act as guides during the summer, and hunt and fish during the winter. In the winters of the 1930's, they fell under the legal classification of "unemployed," and gladly accepted unemployment benefits. The story is told also of two farmers in Germany whose sons worked for them. One day they became aware of the opportunity offered by the law. Each hired the other's son, and then after a time fired him. The sons went back to work for their own fathers as before; but they now by legal definition were unemployed and so entitled to draw benefits. Rules defining unemployment evidently must be carefully drawn to minimize undesired inclusions or exclusions.

The total work force

The number of persons unemployed is the difference between the total work force and the total of employed persons. The total work force is not necessarily any fixed proportion of the total population. In recent years, the work force has increased by more than the total population because the production increase has been concentrated in the 20-to-24-year, productive, age groups. Nor, in any given year, is the work force a fixed number of persons. Over 5 million persons in the

---

12 There are social scientists who have declared that a man is not unemployed if there is any job available at any rate of pay, anywhere in the society. Such a viewpoint defines away the problems involved.

United States are undecided as to whether or not to look for jobs. Many of the workers who are auxiliary earners for the family fall into this classification. If the main income earner of the family loses his job or takes a pay cut more of these people will want jobs; the labor force increases. Professor Slichter estimates that about 10 million families in the United States, or one in three, have more than one income earner. Another marginal group is to be found among the 2 million young people who enter work in normal years. Many among these must make a doubtful decision whether to take a job or continue in school a bit longer. And also many of the 2 million people above the age of 65 who are working must make close decisions on whether to retire or keep on working a year or so longer.[13]

More of these hesitant people will be attracted into looking for jobs and accepting jobs if there are job opportunities available where pay rates are attractive, where hours of work are convenient (especially important for housewives), where work is clean and light, and location close at hand. Improvement in working conditions therefore tends to increase the size of the work force.

An increase in the number of jobs *available* has a twofold influence: on the one hand, it induces people to look for work who previously considered their chances too poor to justify the fatigue, embarrassment, and expense of job-hunting. On the other hand, some people withdraw from the labor force when the primary earner of the family obtains a job or gets an increase in wages. A change in the demand for labor, therefore, causes off-setting movements both into and out of the labor force.[14]

---

13 Estimates of Sumner H. Slichter, "More Job Givers Wanted," *Fortune*, Vol. XXXIV (October, 1945), p. 160.

14 The argument we have given in the above two paragraphs can be reversed. We have said that the numbers and kinds of jobs available *help to determine* the numbers (and kinds) of persons in the work force. It is no less true that the numbers and kinds of jobs employers are willing to offer *depend on* the numbers and kinds of workers available.

As a consequence of these influences, the labor force has a decidedly varying total and is composed in part of different individuals from month to month. In the course of a year, some 10 to 15 million persons join the work force at least temporarily; hence, if the work force averages 60 million, some 70 to 75 million people have been at work during at least part of the year. Seasonal fluctuations are wide: 3 to 5 million more people are usually in the work force in midsummer than in midwinter. In January, 1950, the civilian work force was 62.8 million, in August 66.2 million—a difference of 3.4 million. Because of offsetting movements into and out of the work force over the cycle, the seasonal variations are larger than the cyclical variations.

Employment estimates and unused productive capacity

The best sources that we have for employment and unemployment data are the Census returns of 1940, 1930, and before; and the current *Monthly Report on the Labor Force,* also of the Census Bureau.[15] The monthly surveys obtain their data from a carefully stratified sample of the whole population—about 25,000 households in 123 counties throughout the nation. But all estimates have their particular deficiencies. The monthly reports understate the amount of unused labor power in the country.

---

[15] In the monthly surveys, the labor force is defined to include all persons in the population of age 14 or over who report themselves:

(1) At work on a private or government job, including the self-employed and unpaid family workers;

(2) With a job but not at work because of vacation, illness, labor disputes, bad weather, or temporary layoffs with definite instructions to return within 30 days of layoff;

(3) Not at work but actively seeking work;

(4) Not at work and not actively seeking work because of indefinite layoff or one lasting longer than 30 days, temporary illness, or the belief that no work is available in the community or in their line of work.

Individuals listed under (1) or (2) are classified as "employed," those listed under (3) or (4) as "unemployed." All other persons over 14 are classified as "not in the labor force"—mainly housewives, students, and those too old or otherwise unable to work. Social Science Research Council, *Labor Force Definition and Measurement.* Bulletin 56 (Washington, 1947), pp. 10-11.

1. They include as employed those people who worked only part time. Some of the farmers, businessmen, and professional men listed as employed hardly worked at all, but were included because of their status—that is, because they had a business at which they *might* be working. Many of the part-time employed would like to work more if acceptable jobs could be obtained without too difficult a search. Part-time work has become in our economy a main institutional device to alleviate the pressure of unemployment.

2. Some of the potential workers are not classified in the work force at all. These are people who are not at work and not actively seeking work, but who would try to find jobs if the search were not so arduous, or if jobs with better wages and working conditions were available. This group is not important in boom times, but it is in time of depression.

3. Concealed unemployment—the employment of people where they are less productive than in the jobs they could obtain if there were "full employment" (p. 130) —is necessarily omitted from the statistics.

There is a counterinfluence in that some people withdraw from the labor force when conditions improve, but this is a minor factor compared with those given above.

Kinds of unemployment

What types of unemployment exist in our society? We exclude from our count of the total work force those people who are "unemployable" by reason of drastic physical or mental handicap, though this, too, is a relative term. During World War II when demand for labor was intense, ways were found to fit the blind, the deaf, and those otherwise handicapped into jobs suiting their abilities. They were usually, in the stimulus of being found useful and needed in the society, exceptionally effective in those special jobs.

However, in the labor force as usually defined are people who, though not obviously handicapped, are so in fact. They are of limited mechanical ability or general intelligence, "hard to get along with," unreliable, spiritless or lazy, or given over-much to drink. These marginal workers add up to 2 per cent or more of the work force;[16] and though they are useful in casual and emergency work, they will be unemployed much of the time.

In addition there is *frictional unemployment*. Some industries are seasonal. Farming, canning, lumbering, construction, the Christmas trades, and so forth, reach their seasons of maximum output and then contract during the remainder of the year. Others, like the buggy and silk industries, decline over a number of years and so release workers. A certain proportion of people are always, for one reason or another, leaving their jobs and seeking work elsewhere. Even in good times a person unemployed for any reason is likely to take a week or several weeks before finding an acceptable new job. If a declining industry in one locality leaves a surplus of workers unemployed or in low-paying and subsistence work, months or even years may pass before they gradually migrate to take jobs elsewhere or until new industries appear in the vicinity of their homes.

People are very reluctant to move far from their homes. Save in the highly skilled brackets, labor flows far more readily from one occupation to another than from one location to another. If a shipbuilding plant is expanding and offering high wages, many a local clerk, barber, and janitor will take a job there; but usually not many, even of those in ship construction trades, will move themselves and their families to the plant from a long distance away.

This frictional unemployment, arising from the fact that the right man is not in the right place at the right time, can be separated logically from *general unemployment*, which is widespread unemployment over most of the area of the economy and in most occupations. The chief concern of these chapters is the problem of general unemployment.

16 Estimate of Sumner H. Slichter, in *Problems of Definition and Measurement of Employment.*

Acceptable full employment

By *full employment* we mean that business sales of goods and services plus the output of government have reached approximately the nation's capacity to produce.

The basic determinant of the nation's capacity to produce is its labor supply: this is the fundamental datum on which estimates of maximum production must be based.[17] If there is much unemployment, the economy could produce more. If, on the other hand, the nation is making use of all the labor force reasonably available, with adequate incentives and with appropriate allocation of all resources including labor, then the economy is running at its maximum capacity.

We do not, however, mean by full employment that potential sales of goods and services are so high (that is, money outlay is so great) that there are always more vacant jobs than unemployed men. If money outlay for goods and services were so large that this was usually true, inflationary pressures to raise wages and prices would be tremendous. Unions and individuals could easily obtain higher wages or their equivalent in better ratings. Raw materials producers and farmers would find the prices of their products booming; and even administered-price industries (where prices tend to be rigid) would find incentive and opportunity to keep edging their prices upward. Average efficiency of production would decline as firms pushed their plants beyond planned capacity. Furthermore, with such extremely heavy demand it would be difficult for firms to go bankrupt. If the least effective businesses are not weeded out by bankruptcy, the average effectiveness with which the economy uses its resources falls—another cause for higher prices.

There is even a possibility—if unions press strongly for

---

17 This is obviously true in the short run when all the factors that affect labor's productivity (natural resources, capital instruments, techniques) are approximately fixed. It is true even in the long run if we are thinking of the maximum that could be produced in view of given consumption needs. But it is, of course, also true that if we had more resources, more capital instruments, or better techniques, production would be larger from a given labor force.

higher wages, and administered-price businesses follow inflationary pricing policies—that prices would tend to rise sharply
when employment, viewed from the standpoints of potential
output and the human costs of unemployment, is still unbear-
ably low.

When strong inflationary pressures exist, the government can
sit on the lid of prices only precariously. We know from war
and postwar experience how quickly pressure builds up against
the maintenance of price ceilings. The situation is unstable. It
is especially unstable in a democracy: legislators want to get
re-elected as much as employees and businessmen want to have
higher incomes.

Nor is price control the only sort of control needed. When
prices are held down in competitive industries, demand is
greater than supply;[18] and for important articles of consumption, the government will be forced, in the interest of fair
distribution, to institute a rationing system. To minimize frictional unemployment (and also to ease the problem of price
control) the government may order production carried on in,
and raw materials allocated to, areas where there is available
labor. The mobility of labor may need to be encouraged, and
perhaps the direction of demand channeled toward those products for which productive capacity is available.

Briefly, beyond a certain point increased production and
employment can be gained only at the cost of multiplying government controls.

In the United States it is the prevailing opinion that government controls ought to be minimized as far as possible in view
of other major aims. With respect to prices, we should like
them to be kept down by the competition of businessmen for
more sales, rather than by a permanent OPA; and businessmen

---

18 This is not necessarily true in monopolistically competitive areas. The
experience of the Office of Price Administration in World War II, as well as
theoretical reasoning, indicates that monopolistically competitive firms may be
willing to supply larger quantities at going prices.

will compete for more sales only if they are not producing at their full capacity—that is, if a margin of unemployed resources is available.

To the extent, therefore, that we want to minimize direct government controls over economic life, we will desire less than the level of employment that is associated with strong upward pressure on prices and the resulting need for much government control. Our aim is to choose the best compromise possible amidst our objectives—high production and employment, stable prices or no more than moderate price rises, and minimum direct government controls.

Where is this "best" level of employment? We follow a middle-of-the-road judgment, and define acceptable full employment to mean that *about 5 per cent of the work force would on the average be out of work.*

This implies, in a labor force of 60 million, normal unemployment of about 3 million. This 3 million is *not* a hard core of chronically unemployed and miserable people. It is a shifting group, composed mostly of people out of work for a few days or weeks between jobs. If the people who are, for some reason or other, out of work should on the average require one month before finding another job, in the course of a year 36 millions of the working force will change from one job to another. (This total of 36 million includes a good deal of double-counting, since some people will change jobs more than once.)

Such job-shifting is necessary if men are to have freedom to change work when they like and is required also in part by variations of demand and of supply and the consequent decline and rise of individual firms and industries.

There is nothing sacred about such a figure. If a person dislikes and fears considerably the continuance or extension of government controls, he may consider a larger figure for unemployment acceptable. *Fortune* magazine has suggested 7 per cent, or over 4 million unemployed in a work force of 60 million.[19] If a person does not fear the extension of government controls, is inclined to think they would be efficient, and is humanely concerned with the psychological cost of even temporary unemployment to the individuals concerned, he will prefer a small figure. Lord Beveridge considers 3 per cent an adequate allowance for unavoidable unemployment.[20]

Under the extreme pressure of wartime, the British were, in fact, able to reduce the numbers of unemployed to less than ½ of 1 per cent of the total civilian work force. In the United States during wartime unemployment reached a minimum of 8/10 of 1 per cent.[21] During most of World War II, it ran between 2 and 5 per cent. In 1947, a year of inflation, it was 3.4 per cent.

What would the attainment of continuing full employment mean in the lives of the citizens of the United States? There would be, of course, a larger output for all of us to share. But other effects would probably be deeper and more important. Men would still lose their jobs occasionally, but they would be assured of finding a new one soon and certainly before their unemployment compensation had run out. Not only would continuing unemployment be gone, but the haunting fear of it would also be gone, and this latter would probably be the greater boon to human welfare. Today each employer and employee knows that he may be impoverished by a general collapse of the economy in which the individual is nearly helpless.

Unemployment has proved to be, in recent years, our most important economic problem.

---

19 "Transition to Peace: Business in A.D. 194Q," Vol. XXIX (January, 1944), pp. 84 ff.

20 *Full Employment in a Free Society*, pp. 127-129. New York: W. W. Norton, 1945.

21 This was in October, 1944.

CHAPTER EIGHT

What Causes Changes in Employment?

THE MAINTENANCE OF HIGH EMPLOYMENT AND PRODUCTION requires policies on: (1) total expenditure for goods and services, (2) the location of industry and the mobility of labor, and (3) the level of prices.

Total Expenditure

Expenditure means the spending of money for goods and services produced by the economy. But individuals do not spend for the sake of spending, nor ought they. "Expenditure" means prudent spending for the sake of obtaining wanted goods and services. It is convenient when we are looking at influences on the volume of expenditure for goods and services to talk in terms of *gross* expenditure, which is made for, and equals, *gross* production (Chapters 1 and 2). We have already divided gross expenditure for goods and services into three divisions.

1. Consumers' expenditures for currently produced goods and services. This is a part of output that is *not* used in any further production—shirts, haircuts, lamb chops, theater plays, passenger automobiles, and the like.

2. Expenditures by business for investment goods, which is a part of output that *is* used in future production—steel rails, office and factory buildings, bottling machines, inventories of cotton fabrics, and so forth.

3. Expenditures of government for currently produced goods and services.

135

Expenditure in the private economy for consumption and investment goods, plus government expenditure for goods and services, *may* be of the volume and direction that purchase the production of the economy at its effective full capacity. At this point there is what we call full employment and in addition (we assume temporarily) a fairly stable price level. But total expenditure may instead, in certain areas or over the whole economy, be excessive, leading to a continuing upward spiral of prices. Or it may be unduly low, leading to low production, heavy unemployment, and sagging prices.

Our primary problem, therefore, is to investigate the causes determining total expenditure. We consider, first, influences determining the total sales of consumption goods and services and investment goods to private individuals and businesses. Our basic conclusion will be that the volume of expenditure on consumption is a passive element, depending mainly on the level of income received in the economy; and that investment is, in the private economy, the active source of change in the level of income. It is evident in advance that there are inter-relations between these two: that increased investment provides increased incomes for persons working on new plant and equipment and, hence, the means for higher consumption; and that, conversely, any change in consumption gives cause to business-men to increase or decrease their rate of investment. The third and last of the constituents of total expenditure for goods and services is that of government. Chapters 9, 10, and 11 consider these three kinds of spending. Chapter 12 studies resulting fluctuations in production and employment.

If total expenditure in the economy is inadequate to evoke acceptably high employment, what can be done to increase it? In Chapter 13 we survey certain doubtful suggestions for increasing total expenditure. Chapter 14 considers certain basic issues of policy.

Chapters 15 and 16 are concerned with a number of means of stimulating private consumption and investment.

The expenditure of government for goods and services has

not, except during war or periods of heavy defense expenditure, been a large part of total expenditure, nor has it been in significant degree determined in volume or direction from the point of view of its effect on total employment and production. In both respects, the future is likely to differ from the past. The intake of money into government from taxes and loans is, of course, an equally important concern with governmental expenditures, because taxes and loans influence private expenditures on consumption and investment. If, despite measures to encourage them, private consumption and investment remain inadequate, the government budget (its revenues and expenditures) can be utilized to increase total expenditure in the economy (Chapter 17).

The Price Level; Inflation

Increases of private or public expenditures can lead to sharp price rises in particular areas or occupations, where supply is especially short compared to demand, while unemployment is still heavy elsewhere. An increase in the hiring of labor in Massachusetts will not diminish unemployment much in California, and a road-building program may not do much to alleviate unemployment in the local textile industry. This implies that the direction of expenditure, labor mobility, and the location of industry are concerns of public policy (Chapter 18).

If total money expenditures expand still further, the scarcities multiply and price rises become general throughout the economy. (In fact it is possible, with expansive wage-demand policies by unions and pricing policies by monopolistic business, that prices may tend to rise steeply when there is still much unemployment.) Efforts to increase production and employment by increasing expenditure will, beyond some point, be increasingly frustrated by a succession of price rises. The level of prices is, therefore, a relevant matter for our consideration (Chapter 19).

The continued central economic problem of many nations during the postwar years has not been deficient, but excess, expenditure. Inflation—that is, continued, serious increase in the general price level—has raged about the world, disrupting production and nurturing social hatreds. Inflation is the consequence of continued excess of expenditure for output, over the value of output at existing prices. We consider the background of recent inflations, what happens during inflation, and the cure (Chapter 20).

CHAPTER NINE

Consumption Expenditure

OCCASIONALLY PEOPLE HAVE TRIED TO EXPLAIN THE DEPRES-
sion of the 1930's on the ground that at long last the United
States' economy had been able to produce more than enough
for all of us. "It is a glorious thing to contemplate," runs one
conclusion, "that we can at long last produce more than we care
to consume." It is certain that this explanation of unemployment and lowered production is wrong. We did not have men
idle because we produced more than we wanted to consume.
The average weekly income per person in 1928 was about
$13.40, not a munificent figure. By 1932 it had fallen to $6.20.[1]

The United States has the highest standard of living in the
world. But judged by very moderate criteria, there is much
evidence that we are not as well off as we should like to be, and
as we can be. One piece of evidence is that at every income
level the amount spent for consumption increases when income increases.[2] In other words, we should like to consume
more if we could afford to. The bar to increased consumption
is not that people have run out of wants, but that they have
run out of money.

But, some may argue, the criterion of wants is a doubtful
one; perhaps we want more than is good for us. Then we can
bring up more objective evidence. Life expectancy is rather
closely correlated with real income. In a survey of infant mor-

---

[1] In money terms. The fall in money income was cushioned by a fall in prices:
the 1932 weekly income bought a quantity of goods and services that would have
been worth, at 1929 prices, about $7.80.

[2] See p. 143, Chart 10.

tality following 23,000 births in 8 cities, deaths occurred at the rate of 52 per thousand in homes averaging less than one person per room, and at the rate of 136 per thousand in homes averaging two or more persons per room.[3] Of 1077 tuberculosis cases in Hartford, Connecticut, over a five-year period, more than half were in a slum district covering less than a tenth of the city area. In Cincinnati, 1929–1931, deaths from four common children's diseases averaged 127 per 100,000 in the poorest homes, and 29 per 100,000 in the best homes.[4] Life expectancy among Negroes, whose incomes are low compared to those of whites, is about 8 years less than the average for the white population. In all of these cases, other elements than income alone are correlated with life expectancy—degree of knowledge of sanitation, inherent physical resistance, specific housing deficiencies, and so forth—but income level is one basically important element.

During World War II Selective Service found, of 22 million men examined, 9 million unfit for general military duty. Among the unfit, Selective Service estimated that one-sixth had defects that could still be rather easily remedied. The defects of many of the remainder could have been remedied earlier or avoided altogether had there been adequate health care from birth. Better food, housing, and medical attention would have been vitally useful.

The over-all food supply of the United States is adequate, though among low-income groups there remain acute deficiencies. The diets of 25 to 30 per cent of nonfarm families, and of 10 to 25 per cent of farm families in 1935–1936 were rated "very poor" by the standard of the National Research Council.[5] The American public as a whole consumes less milk,

---

3 Children's Bureau, U. S. Department of Labor, *Causal Factors in Infant Mortality*. Washington: Government Printing Office, 1925.

4 Rollo H. Britten, "The Relation between Housing and Health," *Public Health Reports*, Vol. XLIX (November 2, 1934), pp. 1301–1313.

5 The budgetary data are from the Consumer Purchase study of 1935–36. See on this general subject, Frank R. Garfield, "Markets and Living Standards," *Postwar Economic Studies*, No. 1, Board of Governors, Federal Reserve System, 1945, from which some of the above data are taken.

fruit, and vegetables than dietitians would recommend, and too much sugar, cereals, and meat.

With respect to housing, our situation has been chronically bad. A survey in 1935 estimated that 11 million houses (36 per cent of the total) were substandard. At least three-quarters of farm houses were without conveniences of any sort. In New York City alone, there were 290,000 rooms without windows to the outside, and far more rooms that opened only on air shafts or alleys. The 1940 Census found nearly one-quarter of all dwellings in need of repairs whose neglect threatened the safety of the occupants, and another quarter in need of minor essential repairs. With the cessation of most civilian building during wartime, the housing situation worsened further and was highly critical at the end of the war with respect both to quantity and quality. In 1949 nearly 9 million city homes were substandard, defined as needing major repairs, lacking private baths, or in bad neighborhoods. At the end of the 1940's some 30 million of us in the United States—not counting those on the farm—were living in places below moderate standards of health, safety, or convenience. During the period 1947—1951, urban and farm houses built, plus conversion of existing buildings to create additional living quarters, added not far from an extraordinary 1,500,000 dwelling units a year. Side by side with this we can put the normal increase in number of families (about 500,000 a year), plus the abnormal increase in families implied by the high postwar marriage rate, plus some undoubling of couples living with relatives. On net balance we are gaining on our housing shortage. But the over-all shortage will still be with us for years to come, and in addition there are local emergency needs of the post-Korea defense program.

In medicine we have made immense progress in the past century, nearly doubling our average life expectancy. But there is still much to do. On an average day there are about 7 million people in this country so disabled by sickness or injuries that they cannot carry on their usual tasks. Of these, nearly half would otherwise have been working or looking for work. Every year about 40 times as many working days are lost because of sickness or injury as were lost annually through strikes in the 10 years before World War II—a figure worth looking at as partial evidence on the relative importance of health and labor problems.

Our medical facilities are badly distributed: the poor have more sickness and get less medical care, and people who live in rural areas have less attention than those in the cities. Fifteen million people live in counties that have either no hospital or none that meets minimum standards of professional associations; and forty million people live in communities lacking full-time public health service. We have nearly conquered typhoid fever, smallpox, and diphtheria, but much remains to be done with respect to maternal and infant mortality, tuberculosis, venereal disease, cancer, and mental illness. Our progress in the past century and a half is most impressive, but this progress is encouragement toward further advance rather than excuse for resting on our oars.

Some of these problems of the level of consumption can best be met by private expenditures; some can best be met by government expenditure. In either case they indicate that unemployment is not caused by "producing too much."

Consumption Expenditure by Income Groups
Particular channels of consumption expenditure

The most elaborate study ever made of consumer expenditure in the United States is that of the Natural Resources Committee for 1935–1936. The data are subject to some criticism but are without question substantially correct. All consumers together, in 1935–1936, spent on the average nearly two-thirds of their consumption outlay for the basic essentials of food, clothing, and shelter. The following are the exact percentages for three main channels of expenditure.

Food, clothing, and housing 63%

Household operation and furnishings, and automobile expenditures 21

Medical and personal care, education, reading, tobacco, transportation other than automobiles, recreation, and other items 16

Consumers with higher incomes buy more than those with low incomes in every single one of the above 14 subdivisions of total consumer expenditure. There is no indication, in broad

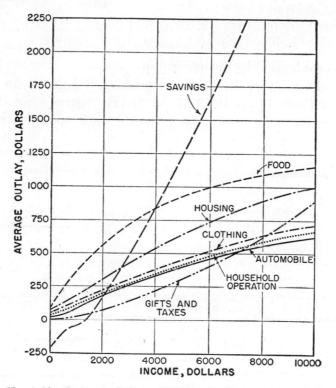

Chart 10. Average Outlay of Nation's Consumer Units for Major Categories of Disbursements at Different Income Levels, 1935-1936.

Source: National Resources Committee, *Consumer Expenditure in the United States.* Washington: Government Printing Office, 1939, p. 38.

classes of goods and services, of any surfeit of wants (Chart 10).[6]

But as incomes rise, with prices of consumer goods not greatly different, the percentage increases of expenditure in different lines are not equal. An increase of average incomes by a given percentage implies an increase of expenditure on food of less than that percentage, and an increase of expenditure by more than that percentage on travel, furnishings, clothing, and education. But even with respect to food, which by National Resources Committee estimate shows the least rise in expenditure with rising income, expenditure would increase by 44 per cent with a rise of 56 per cent in the incomes of consumers.

Total consumption by income groups

An annual survey of consumer finances, conducted for the Board of Governors of the Federal Reserve System since 1946, covers by means of careful sampling the entire population of

TABLE 13

THE SPENDING AND SAVING OF FAMILIES THAT POOL THEIR INCOMES
TO MEET MAJOR EXPENDITURES, 1948 *

	Income Range	Median Income	Per Cent of Total Income of Each Group Going Into:			
			Federal income tax	Consumer spending	Saving	Total
Highest fifth of families.	over $4,500	$6,000	13	73	14	100
Second	$3,200-4,500	3,750	6	88	6	100
Third	$2,400-3,200	2,840	5	92	3	100
Fourth	$1,500-2,400	2,000	4	98	—2	100
Lowest fifth	under $1,500	860	1	129	—31	100

* "1949 Survey of Consumer Finances," *Federal Reserve Bulletin*, Vol. XXV (July, 1949), Table 7; Vol. XXXVI (January, 1950), Tables 3, 15. The details of the percentages may not add up exactly to 100 because of rounding of final digits.

6 There might, however, be a drop for particular "inferior" goods, such as potatoes, corn pone, and margarine, as people move up into higher-income brackets. That is, they prefer to fulfill these kinds of wants by buying more expensive types of commodities or services.

the United States living in private households. Table 13 presents data from their study for 1948. In this table, savings increase as incomes rise in per cent of income, and hence still more emphatically in number of dollars.

But it is possible for *the quantity* of savings to increase out of higher incomes without savings making up an increasing *percentage* of income. Suppose that a person with a $2000 income saves $200, and that a person with a $4000 income saves $300. Savings were 10 per cent of income in the first case, 7½ per cent of income in the second case—a smaller percentage, but the dollars of savings increased. The assertion that quantity of savings rises as the income bracket rises is a more conservative statement than to argue that the percentage of income saved rises as income rises. The data that we have support the latter, and stronger, assertion.

The Relation of Consumption to Income— The Consumption Function

The relation between consumption and income is given the general name of "the consumption function." Suppose that some person receives an income of $3000 and that he spends $2700 on consumption. His

$$\frac{\text{total consumption}}{\text{total income}}$$

or, as it is called, his *average propensity to consume,* is $2700/$3000, or 9/10.

Suppose that his income rises to $3010 and his consumption to $2705. Then out of a change of $10 in his income, he spends a changed amount of $5 on consumption. The proportion

$$\frac{\text{change in consumption}}{\text{change in income}}$$

where the change is small, is the *marginal propensity to consume*. The marginal propensity to consume of our subject is, therefore, $5/$10, or ½.

It is possible similarly to calculate the average and marginal propensities to consume for the whole economy. The name "propensity to consume" is not a happy one. These propensities refer, not to tendencies or desires only, but to actions carried out by people when they receive a given income or a given addition to income. The relation between consumer expenditure and income given by the propensity to consume is analogous to the relation between quantity of a good bought and its price.

The Volume of Total Consumption and Total Saving

We have briefly described above how consumer expenditures vary as we move along the scale from poorer to richer income groups.

We now progress to a topic that can be easily confused with the above but is, in fact, distinctly different. Suppose the total national income of the United States changes. Many individuals and families will shift from one income level to another —a higher or a lower—and we should expect their consumption expenditures and their savings to vary in some resulting fashion. The way in which total consumption and total savings vary depends on (*a*) the distribution of income of the United States at the old and new levels of national income, and (*b*) how the people who shift from one income level to another alter their expenditures.

Budget Evidence on Consumption and Saving

Basic information on the relation of consumer spending to income must come from budget studies. Our primary purpose is usually to predict future levels of consumer spending when income changes. If we simply carry forward the relationships we find today between total income and total consumption, we are assuming that all the other factors that influence consumer spending aside from current income—degree of inequality of income distribution, quantity of accumulated savings, expectation of price and income changes, availability of specific goods, and the like—will have the same importance, and in the same direction, as today. This simple trust is apt to make for errors in estimate, as it did when estimates of postwar consumption by both government and private agencies nearly all went far astray.

We must look as closely as we can at the psychology of the individual family spending unit and then adjust as best we can for all the expected other conditions, in addition to income levels, that will in the future affect consumer spending. There is a temptation to do the easy thing and trust in a high mathematical correlation between consumption and income for some brief period of the past—current Commerce data go back only to 1929 and cover a peculiar span dominated by deep depression and high war boom. But this is a temptation to error.

We list below the influences on consumer spending that appear most strategic.

The level of current income

The data shown above indicate, as we have seen, that higher income is usually associated with both higher consumer spending and higher savings. In fact, savings rise so rapidly, when income grows, as to make up a higher percentage of income.

Effect of a change in income

The evidence is conclusive in budget studies that people whose incomes have fallen try to maintain their old standard of living, and in the effort to do so, cut their savings down toward zero or even spend more than their incomes (through borrowing or drawing on past savings). For example the 1947 Federal Reserve survey finds: [7]

---

[7] "1947 Survey of Consumer Finances," *Federal Reserve Bulletin*, Vol. XXXIII (August, 1947), p. 958.

TABLE 14

EFFECT OF A CHANGE IN INCOME ON SAVINGS

1946 income compared to that of 1945	All family units	"Large" savers	Medium savers	"Small" savers
1946 income larger by 25% or more	100%	28%	44%	28%
No substantial change in income...	100	27	52	21
1946 income smaller by 25% or more	100	19	38	43

Those whose incomes had fallen included fewer large savers and more small savers than the other groups.

There is much reason to believe that the previous year of highest income—even if it had been 3 or 5 or 7 years back—will have continuing strong influence on consumer spending and saving. High-income groups find it fairly easy to cut savings in order to maintain consumption. Among low-income groups, major drops in income are usually the result of unemployment. Some people are, at any given time during depression, just beginning a long spell of unemployment. These must adjust their consumption to a drop in income from something near the peak level. Most people obtain work at least part of the time, and so the influence on their living habits of incomes close to the full employment level does not wear off.[8]

It is not certain from the data above or from a 1942 survey of the Bureau of Labor Statistics that families whose incomes have risen spend appreciably less than families of the same income level whose incomes have remained stable.

We conclude from this that, for the whole economy, consumer spending will be higher and personal savings lower at any given national income level if the national income has fallen from a previous peak, than if the national income had been rising or stable.

[8] Franco Modigliani, "Fluctuations in the Saving-Income Ratio," *Studies in Income and Wealth*. New York: National Bureau of Economic Research, 1949, Vol. II, pp. 384–388; James S. Duesenberry, "Income-Consumption Relations," in *Income, Employment and Public Policy*, pp. 54–81. New York: W. W. Norton, 1948.

Effect of a change in other people's incomes

How are we affected by the spending of others with whom we come in contact? If we live among people whose incomes and spending are high compared to ours, will we spend more out of a given income than if we were living among people whose incomes and spending are comparatively low?

The answer is "Yes"—from budget data,[9] as well as from human psychology. It is basically misleading, in a country of high living standards like the United States, to think of consumer spending as being fixed by the need of people for elementary requirements of life: for food, clothes, and shelter from wind and too much weather. We are social beings, profoundly moved by our need for status and social respect; and one way of seeking these is through spending in reputable ways. Our spending is stimulated if we associate with people whose patterns of living constantly suggest to us attractive goods and services we have not so far afforded. Our spending is depressed if we associate with people whose expenditure habits are more modest than our own.

This has an important implication with respect to redistribution of income. It is often argued that taxing the rich and subsidizing the poor—and so diminishing inequality of income— would raise consumer spending. This is probably untrue. The argument rests on the belief that the *marginal* propensity to consume of the rich is sharply lower than that of the poor, so that a dollar taken from the rich cuts their consumption less than it adds to the consumption of the poor. But it appears in fact that there is little difference between these marginal propensities[10] so that if peoples' habits of consumption remain the same, for given incomes, after as before the redistribution, consumer spending will not be raised very much. But people's

---

[9] James S. Duesenberry, *Income, Saving, and the Theory of Consumer Behavior*, pp. 48–54. Cambridge: Harvard Press, 1949.

[10] Harold Lubell, "Effects of Redistribution of Income on Consumers' Expenditures," *American Economic Review*, Vol. XXXVII (March, 1947), pp. 157–170; and his "Correction," in *American Economic Review*, Vol. XXXVII (December, 1947), p. 930.

habits of consumption would not remain the same. If there are fewer Joneses to keep up with—fewer people of conspicuously higher spending—average consumer spending would be generally less at any level of income below the top incomes. (And investment spending would be cut, to the extent investors are discouraged by heavy taxes on high incomes.)

Special Influences on Total Consumption

1. A fairly close relationship existed between total consumption and total income in the 1920's and 1930's (p. 154). But during World War II consumption was much smaller compared to income than it had been before. The 1942—1944 figures run 16 per cent less than we should have expected from the simple evidence of prewar data. The explanation is plain enough. The War Production Board did not permit the manufacture of the kinds and quantities of consumer goods we should have liked to buy. Also some of us patriotically saved more (for war bonds), and so bought less consumer goods than we normally would.

2. Two causes immediately after World War II worked to increase consumption relative to income. One of them arose from the decline or complete stoppage during wartime of the production of durable consumer goods—automobiles, washing machines, radios, and most goods containing metal. There was, therefore, an unusually heavy demand for these goods for several years after the war. We have not been buying to make up for all additional durable goods that we did without during the war—the man who was accustomed in the 1930's to buying a new car every year didn't buy five new cars as soon as he could get them—but we have bought more than usual.

3. A second factor causing higher consumption in the postwar years is that savings of individuals rose during wartime. The total in the form of cash, deposits, and federal securities in mid-1945 was 141 billion dollars, nearly three times higher than it had been in 1939. The possession of a backlog of savings, by giving people a sense of security against future needs,

encourages spending out of current income, even though the savings themselves are not spent.

4. The data of the recent past give cause for further doubt concerning the closeness with which we may always expect to predict consumption from knowing income. Spending for durable consumer goods behaves in a volatile fashion, more like investment spending of businesses than like the spending of consumers for nondurable consumer goods. Durable goods are usually defined, following Kuznets, as those averaging a useful life of more than three years. Consumer durable goods are such products as furniture, automobiles, refrigerators, and radios.

One element in the explanation is that we often buy these goods on credit; hence, their purchase is less closely bound to the level of disposable income than is the buying of other consumer goods. Another element is that durability means *postponability*: we can postpone buying them if we feel pessimistic about our future prospects, or speed up our buying if we are hopeful. We can make the rattling old-fashioned icebox do for another year or we can turn it in for a new one now.

This significant behavior of spending for durable consumption goods is concealed in the figures for total consumption-spending, since the former makes up only 10 to 15 per cent of the latter. It suggests that spending for durable consumption goods is not simply an automatic resultant of changes in consumer incomes, but has a vitality of its own depending on consumer expectations. Therefore it ought to be included among the causes of changes in total expenditure, and so among the causes of changes in employment and output. Some economists prefer, therefore, to regard changes in output and employment as a resultant of changes in private spending for all kinds of durable goods, both consumer and business.[11] At the least,

---

11 The objection against doing this is greater difficulty in calculating the statistics and greater awkwardness in interpretation. In other words, the objection is practical, rather than fundamental.

durable goods are a peculiar class of consumer goods having a dynamics of their own.

Although durable consumer goods make up only a small part of total consumer expenditure, they do cover a large part of total expenditure for durable goods. Household goods and passenger automobiles made up 36 per cent of total durable goods in the period from 1919 to 1939, the remaining 64 per cent being producers' durable goods. If we include residences, the proportion of consumer durable goods rises to 51 per cent.[12]

5. Is the level of interest rates an important influence on consumption? In the past, it was usual to argue that changes in interest rates would, through their *incentive* effect, cause differences in consumption spending—or, one could say instead, changes in saving, since savings are disposable income *minus* consumption. A rise in interest rates was supposed to decrease consumption (increase savings) through offering people the reward of a higher return on their savings. A fall in interest rates was supposed to increase consumption (decrease savings). There are many reasons why people save—provision for a rainy day, to get a house or a car, to gain prestige in the community, to secure the interest or dividends obtainable on their savings, or because they can't think what else to do with their incomes! Interest is only one of these incentives. Furthermore, its influence may work in reverse for some people and discourage savings, because if one wants to obtain a given income in the future from his savings, he will need to save *less* if the interest rate is high. On net balance, it is not thought today that interest rate changes have, through their incentive effect, any significant influence on consumption.

But interest rate changes may, in a different way, influence consumption. Interest returns go mainly to the higher-income groups, who do the bulk of the saving. In 1935, of incomes under $5000, 14 per cent came from property sources, among which interest is a large element; of incomes over $5000, 47 per

---

12 Terborgh's data, summarized in the *Cleveland Trust Company Bulletin*, April 15, 1940.

cent came from property sources.[13] The percentage of income originating in property sources, including interest, rises consistently as we ascend the income scale. Hence a rise in interest rates will affect consumer spending by shifting income from interest payers (mainly low-income groups) to income receivers (mainly high-income groups). The effects on consumption are those associated with greater inequality of income (pp. 149-150).

However ordinary changes of 1 or 2 per cent in interest rates are not likely to have any large effect on consumption (or savings) through this income effect. And such effect as does exist will be realized gradually over the course of months and years as old loans are paid off and funds are re-lent at the new rates.

The Savings of Corporations

We have reasoned so far as if individual consumers were the only units in the economy that make decisions as to whether to consume or to save their incomes. But business corporations also make similar decisions. When their incomes are low, they pay out in costs and in dividends more than their incomes—that is, their savings are negative. United States corporations "dissaved" in every year of the period 1930–1938. In 1932 they actually paid out 6 billion dollars more than their earnings. When, on the other hand, the incomes of corporate business rise to rather high levels, their savings become appreciable. In 1950 net corporate savings amounted to 13.6 billion dollars.[14]

Corporation savings are also influenced by factors correlated

---

[13] *Concentration and Composition of Individual Incomes, 1918–1937.* TNEC Monograph No. 4 (Washington, 1941), p. 48; Henry Wallich, "The Changing Significance of the Interest Rate," *American Economic Review*, Vol. XXXVI (December, 1946), p. 771.

[14] *Survey of Current Business*, Vol. XXIX (July, 1949), p. 11. The data given are for net corporate savings, but on a gross basis (adding depreciation reserves), the same conclusion usually holds. For certain strategic years, the net figures run:

IN BILLIONS OF DOLLARS

	1929	1932	1933	1939	1941	1944	1950
Net national income	87.4	41.7	39.6	72.5	103.8	182.4	239.0
Net corporate savings	2.6	—6.0	—2.4	1.2	4.9	6.1	13.6

with their past incomes and the amount of their past savings (net surplus).

The Evidence from National Income Statistics

1. Annual data, 1921-1950

In Chart 11 are portrayed the savings of individuals during the years 1929—1950. Income is taken to be the income actually disposable by individuals.[15] From this we subtract what indi-

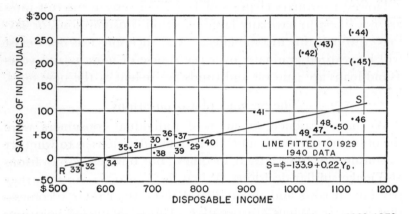

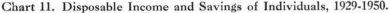

Chart 11. Disposable Income and Savings of Individuals, 1929-1950.

Source: Department of Commerce, new series, real per capita data; in dollars at 1946 prices. *Survey of Current Business* (July, 1949), p. 10; (February, 1951), p. 9. Deflation by means of the Consumers' Price Index of the Department of Labor (*The Economic Report of the President*, January, 1949, p. 104; January, 1951, p. 193), adjusted in accord with the conclusions of the Mitchell Committee.

viduals spend on consumer goods. The remainder is their saving out of disposable income. The original data are corrected for price changes (since a rise in money income counts for little if prices rise equally) and are put on a per capita basis (since individuals are not, on the average, better off when national

---

15 The national income, which is the income created by the services rendered by individuals or by their property, is subject to one addition (transfer payments, for which no service is rendered), and three deductions (savings retained by corporations out of income, social-security contributions, and income taxes paid by individuals and corporations) before we have a figure for disposable income.

income rises if the population is growing equally fast, or faster). Hence, we compare *real per capita* income with *real per capita* savings.[16] The line *RS* is drawn to show the average relationship between savings and disposable income, 1929 to 1940: a rise in income of 1 dollar meant in that period a rise of about 22 cents in savings, and a fall of 1 dollar meant ordinarily a fall of about 22 cents in savings.

Chart 12 is another convenient way of showing the relationship between disposable income, savings of individuals, and their consumption expenditures. The only change is that here consumption is plotted against income. Since income minus consumption equals savings, no new information is given: this is simply an alternative way of presenting the data given in Chart 11.

The 45-degree line *OB* is drawn to show how consumption would vary if all of income were spent for consumption: at $500 of per capita disposable income, $500 is spent for consumption; at $600 of income, $600 is consumed, and so forth.

The line *RS* is, as before, drawn to show the actual *average* relationship for the years 1929–1940. The distance between any point on *RS* and the point just above it on *OB* measures the amount of individual saving. For example, at a disposable income per capita of $700, the expected value of consumption would be $680. Saving, therefore, would be $20.

On this chart, as on the previous one, we see savings becoming considerably smaller when income declines. The average propensity of individuals to consume,

$$\frac{\text{total consumption}}{\text{total income}}$$

therefore can vary, depending on level of income. It is largest at low levels of income: in 1933 it was $563/550, or 102 per cent. At higher levels of income, it becomes progressively small-

---

[16] Data are of the Department of Commerce. To obtain "real" figures for disposable income and savings, the original current figures are divided by a series based on the Bureau of Labor Statistics consumers' price index.

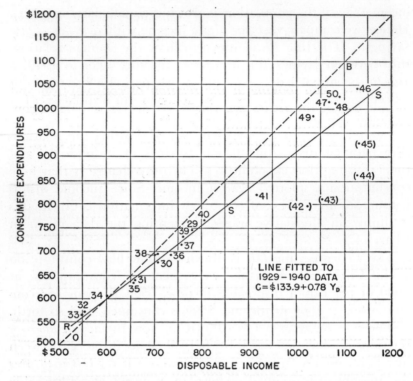

Chart 12. Disposable Income and Consumer Expenditures, 1929-1950.

Source: See Chart 11. Real per capita data; in dollars at 1946 prices.

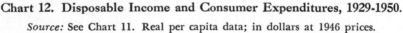

er: in 1940 it was $768/807, or 95 per cent. The marginal propensity to consume,

$$\frac{\text{change in consumption}}{\text{change in income}}$$

seems to be about the same for all levels of income (in other words, *RS* is a straight line). An increase in consumption expenditure of about 78 cents occurs when disposable income rises by 1 dollar—that is, the marginal propensity to consume in this period was typically 78 per cent. (This must, of course, agree with the previous figure of 22 cents of added savings when disposable income rises by 1 dollar.)

But, for reasons we have in part seen, these data do not give a close prediction of spending and saving in the postwar years.

2. Long-run stability

We have been looking at the relation of consumption and income during the 1920's and 1930's. We also have data of considerable reliability extending as far back as 1879.[17] It is a significant fact that averages of such data by decades, 1879–1928, show that 85 to 90 per cent of total income was consumed in *every* decade. As time passed and our average real income grew, our consumption grew also. Our average real income approximately doubled during the early 1880's and the 1920's; and our rising wants for automobiles, refrigerators, plumbing, radios, and the like have kept pace nearly exactly with the rising production of the economy.

—Not that there is any element of chance about this rise in consumption; rather, what we dare admit that we want rises with rising income. We want savings too, since we want to be able to buy things in the future. Normally we remain in uneasy balance, wondering whether we can justifiably squeeze a few more dollars out of savings to put into consumption or whether we ought instead to contract consumption a bit and so heap up a little more savings against future wants. We spend as much as we can. Mark Twain had the psychology of the situation right when, the story goes, he defined the cost of living as "All you've got, and then some."

3. Short-run instability

It is possible to find in, or construct from, Department of Commerce information, figures for consumer spending and income by three-month periods running back as far as 1935. Such quarterly data show a high degree of variability.[18] No formula

---

[17] Simon S. Kuznets, *Uses of National Income in Peace and War.* National Bureau of Economic Research, Occasional Paper 6 (New York, 1942), pp. 30–35.
[18] Robert V. Rosa, "Use of the Consumption Function in Short Run Forecasting," *Review of Economics and Statistics,* Vol. XXX (May, 1948), pp. 91–105.

at present calculated or likely to be calculated, seems likely to be able to predict their surprises. Within the years 1935–1950, but excluding the war, there were three times when consumer spending and disposable income actually moved in opposite directions—one increased and the other decreased.

Many short-run influences can be pointed out as probably guilty in contributing to this variability—consumer expectations about employment, income, and price changes; changes in quantity of liquid assets, changes in tax rates, tax refunds, veterans' bonus payments, and the like.

Summary

What, finally, do we know about the relation of consumption to income? We know (1) that the long-run relation, over the decades, is a fairly stable one—by Kuznets' data, consumption is regularly 85 to 90 per cent of income. (2) We know that there is great instability, unpredictable from any mathematical formula, in the short-run, quarter by quarter, relation of consumption to income. (3) Savings tend to fall in time of depression, in dollars and in percentage of income; and they tend to rise in time of revival, both in dollars and percentage-wise. Our data on consumption and income are too rough, and the period for which we have information too peculiar for us yet to be able to predict for a given year in the future, still less for a given quarter.

The most useful formulas that we have so far, attempting to relate consumption (or savings) and income, are those of Modigliani and Duesenberry. The Duesenberry formula mainly rests on two generalizations from experience: first, that in the long run an individual's spending depends on his place in the community's income distribution—that is, on the degree to which he has incentive to emulate the consumption of others. This means that if the degree of income inequality does not change much in the long run, the average propensity to consume will not change much either. Second, that during a period of depression, consumers try to maintain their standard of living, and so consume higher proportions of income.[19]

But the Duesenberry formula does not include other influences that may at times be crucial, nor can it predict short-run relationships adequately.

Secular "Underconsumption"?

We have seen that consumption has kept increasing through the decades as income has increased, so that the proportion of consumption to income has remained approximately constant. This evidence casts doubt on the contention that we will be, over future years, faced with the problem of persistent underconsumption—if we understand this to mean a lowered proportion of consumption to given incomes. It appears plausible that in the future, as in the past, people will increase their consumption when increased incomes make it possible. We will return to this general matter later (pp. 224ff).

[19] The formula runs, in real capita data, new Commerce series:

$$\text{Savings in any year} = \text{Income of that year} \times \left(.25 \; \frac{\text{Income of that year}}{\text{Income of previous year of highest income}} - .196\right)$$

CHAPTER TEN

Investment Expenditure

THE TOTAL OF PRIVATE, THAT IS, NONGOVERNMENT, EXPENDI-ture on output in any year can be divided into private spending for consumption goods and services and private spending for investment goods. As we have seen, private spending on consumption is ordinarily, though not always, a result rather than a cause of changes in income. We now try to explain why and how private spending on investment varies from year to year.

Kinds of Investment (or Capital Formation)

When we speak of private *investment,* or *capital formation,* as related to the national output and to employment, we do not, of course, mean *financial,* or *monetary,* investment, which is the purchase of stocks, or bonds, or already built houses, and so forth, because the money we spend for these may simply pass from our account or pocket into someone else's account or pocket, and not lead to any increased production in the economy.

We mean by investment, *real investment* in the private economy—the purchase by businesses and individuals of newly produced capital goods. These include (1) Producer's capital goods: (*a*) The buildings and equipment of all sorts of business enterprises—manufacturing, mining, agriculture, transportation, financial institutions, and wholesale and retail selling. (*b*) The stocks or inventories of raw materials, or semifinished or finished products held by these enterprises.

(2) Consumer's capital goods, in which we include only residences.

(3) The net foreign balance. This is the excess of buying by foreigners in this country over our buying from them, adjusted for gifts. It is, as we have already seen, in two respects like the other kinds of private investment above, and so is usually classified with them: it represents spending for goods and services, with no *immediate* increase resulting in the flow of consumption goods within the economy; and it also represents the building up of a claim that can in the future be turned into consumption goods and services.

Part of government expenditure is, of course, also for such investment goods, but here we will mostly confine our attention to private investment. We can speak either in terms of gross investment, meaning the total of these capital goods produced in a period of time, say a year; or we can talk of net investment, which is gross investment minus the depreciation of existing capital goods, and hence measures the change in the quantity of capital goods in the economy.

The Incentive to Invest—The Marginal Efficiency of Capital and the Rate of Interest

Producers' real investment means the buying of newly produced buildings, equipment, and inventories of goods. Why should businessmen buy such property, and so cause them to be produced? The simple reason is that they hope to add to their incomes. This motive holds also for a part of consumer's real investment: residence construction by speculative builders. But house construction ordered by the ultimate owner is not carried on for profit. In the reasoning immediately below, we are concerned with that dominant part of private investment carried on by business firms.

The businessman who is considering investing must weigh advantage against disadvantage. On the negative side, as a deterrent to buying, there is the sinking of money into buildings, equipment, and inventories. Of course, the businessman expects to get his funds back some day through sale of the property or of finished products, but in the meanwhile the money is "tied up." If the businessman borrows from some outside source, he must pay interest on the funds. Equally, if he uses his own funds, he loses the interest he might gain through lending. In either case, the deterrent is measured by the *interest* on the funds invested. This is the cost of the investment.

On the positive side, as incentive to buying an asset, is the gross profit prospect throughout the life span of the asset. If a person buys a house for investment, he expects to get a return (rent, plus selling price if it is sold again) which will pay taxes and other costs of operation, pay back the original cost, and leave over some residual besides. Such a residual, figured as a proportion of the cost of the asset, is the *rate of return over cost,* or as it is more often called lately, the *marginal efficiency of capital.*[1]

A businessman will want to buy those assets whose marginal efficiencies are greatest relative to the interest rate, because expected net profit from the assets is the difference between their marginal efficiency and the interest rate. If the marginal efficiency of an asset is 7 per cent and the cost of borrowing money is 5 per cent, a 2 per cent net profit is obtainable.

New investment means in the main an increase in the quantity of plant and equipment. More plant and equipment means, in turn, the possibility of (1) getting a previously attainable output at lower cost, (2) increasing output, which would otherwise be impossible, *or* (3) getting a more desired

---

1 More exactly, since capital assets may last a considerable period of time, the marginal efficiency of capital is the rate of discount that would make the present value of the net returns from a marginal asset over all its useful life just equal to its cost. We can calculate it as follows: Suppose the house costs $10,000 to build, and that we expect to keep it three years, getting in a net rent of $1000 each year, and to sell it at the end of the third year for about $9000:

$$\$10,000 = \frac{\$1000}{(1+R)} + \frac{\$1000}{(1+R)^2} + \frac{\$10,000}{(1+R)^3},$$

where R is the marginal efficiency of the investment, and comes out to be nearly 7 per cent.

type of output. But suppose that plant and other productive facilities are generally modern and efficient, and that of these facilities, a large proportion is idle because of deficient demand. Then there is little room for new investment—that is, few capital goods exist whose marginal efficiencies exceed the interest rate. Businessmen will not buy, and the capital goods will not be produced.

Clearly it is not the current returns from capital assets that determine the marginal efficiency of capital, but the *expected future returns*. Current returns might be large to businessmen generally (as in 1929), but if the future prospects appear glum, they will not invest. Or current returns might be miserably low, but if future prospects seem rosy, businessmen will invest.

We conclude that the quantity of investment is determined by the marginal efficiency of capital and the interest rate. The higher the marginal efficiency relative to interest, the more investment will be carried on. The lower the marginal efficiency relative to interest, the less investment will be carried on. It is possible that the outlook for returns is so glum to businessmen, and hence so little production of capital goods is carried on, that over the whole economy capital equipment wears out faster than it is replaced—that is, net investment is negative.

Influences on the marginal efficiency of capital

Suppose a businessman is considering buying a ribbon light-bulb machine or a spot welding machine; or is considering building a new open-hearth furnace or adding a wing to the plant; or buying three new dump trucks, a carload of coal, or a ton of 26-gauge sheet metal. What influences the net returns he may expect from his purchase?

The net returns expected from a capital good are the difference between its prospective yield over its whole life span and its cost. Any influence that pushes up yield or pushes down cost will increase the net returns—that is, raise the marginal efficiency of capital.

1. A major cause of higher marginal efficiency of capital is

effective *innovation*. A businessman innovates when he introduces new products, utilizes new production methods, develops a new source of raw material, opens up a new market, or sets up a new organization of his industry. In all these cases, it is the *new* that should be emphasized—doing something different from what was known and practiced in the industry. In many businesses the surest way to keep out of bankruptcy is to keep constantly a jump ahead of the other fellow, to be constantly improving or innovating. If a businessman has an effective innovation at his disposal, he is justified in expanding plant and equipment even though the national income is at low ebb and conditions in his trade are miserable. Firms were expanding in production of stainless steel, of plastics, and of synthetic textiles even in the pit of the 1930 depression.

2. Another basic influence is to be found in expected demand conditions. For many commodities, the level of local or national income is the strategic determinant of how much will be sold. General Motors, in estimating demand for their cars in an ordinary peacetime year, finds this to be true. Their price policy is not in doubt. The prices of their cars will be kept in the usual relationship to those of their close competitors, Ford and Chrysler. The chief determinant of how many they will sell is the incomes of consumers.

For long-run types of investment, present demand is not of much importance compared to demand expected in the rather remote future, and demand in that future may be determined mainly by expected population change. United States railroads in the nineteenth century expanded their tracks into areas where the existing numbers of people could use only a fraction of the transportation service provided. But the population, it was optimistically thought, would grow so enormously as to more than make up for any current extravagance in track-laying. The crossroads settlement would be a county seat, the village would be a great city, and all would be well. So also with the laying of water mains, sewage systems, and roads, the building of power lines, and the extension of telephone communication. These may be determined mainly by expectations of demand a decade or more in the future, and not by today's demand.

In still other cases, the demand of buyers may be altered by effective advertising or by an innovation elsewhere in the economy. Or a shift of custom or taste may be expanding (or contracting) demand for particular goods; or expected conditions of wartime may improve or worsen the prospects of a particular good. We can sell more of our new dentifrice if we proclaim its merits on the radio and in the newspaper. Sheet-steel producers can expand if the auto industry is selling more cars or if war demand expands the market for steel products. And if women begin to wear hats like Hedy Lamarr's and we can produce them, we are encouraged to stock up on materials and buy new stitching machines.

In all of these cases, a heavy demand may lead to rising prices (rather than to larger sales at current prices). Needless to say, the expectation of rising prices also will raise the expected yield from capital goods.

3. A third influence on marginal efficiency of capital is the rate of investment currently going on in the relevant field. If the demand for machines or raw materials of a given type rises sharply, the pressure on the facilities available for producing them will be considerable, and costs of production are likely to rise in the overburdened factories. A rise in the price of the machine or material will diminish its marginal efficiency, because expected returns are now smaller relative to this price.

4. The greater the quantity of any particular kind of capital good already in existence (assuming some given quantity of labor and other cooperating resources), the more the potential or actual supply of its products. Hence the lower will be their price and the less the yield to be expected from an additional unit of that kind of capital good. If there is already a large supply of trucks or of store buildings in our town, we are to that extent discouraged from setting up in the trucking business or from building more stores.

5. There is an intangible influence—the state of business confidence—which businessmen themselves are inclined to think very important and which economists have come to emphasize increasingly. None of us can foresee clearly the future worth of an office building, a special lathe, silver-mining equipment, a bottle-making machine, or a display counter. We have little or no grounds for judgment as to the worth of these capital goods 7, 10, 15, or more years in the future—if they will then be in existence at all. Should we buy them—that is, invest? Because of this substantial ignorance of the future, the degree of general optimism or pessimism in the business community is a chief determinant of the volume of investment.

This same ignorance of the future leads firms to include in their calculations of the marginal efficiency of assets a heavy allowance for adverse events. Some large companies will not make an investment unless they expect "it will pay itself out" in two or three years, even though the asset lasts much longer. During wartime our government encouraged firms to invest in capital equipment for war production by permitting them to depreciate it over the course of five years, even though much of the equipment might still be valuable for peacetime uses.

The general optimism or pessimism of the community with respect to prices on the Stock Exchange also profoundly affects the amount of new investment that goes on. Suppose buyers and sellers of stocks on the Exchange are pessimistic about the future, and value at a low level the shares of certain corporations. A businessman who wishes to expand his plant and equipment (that is, he is confident about the future of his own business) would be foolish to have new plant and equipment built, if he can buy up at a low price the controlling shares of a business already possessing the needed kind of plant and equipment. The pessimism of the exchange has caused *real investment* sharply to decrease.

Alternatively, suppose that investors on the Exchange are optimistic about the future, and stocks can be easily sold at high figures. A corporation may now be induced to spend on investment projects what would be ordinarily extravagant sums, if the requisite money can be obtained immediately and at a profit by selling stocks or bonds on the Exchange. Real investment is, therefore, boomed by the optimism of the market.

But the judgment of people who buy and sell on the Stock Exchange is often unsound. Many or most of them have made no adequate study either of short-run or long-run prospects of firms (even if any evidence for this latter is available). Furthermore, the bulk of more expert professional buying and selling in the market is done by people who do not care very much what the earnings of particular companies are likely to be over the course of the next few months or years. What they worry about is whether particular stocks will rise or fall in price in the next few days or weeks. In other words, they are concerned with predicting average market opinion of the near future, not with estimating the long-run real value of securities.

In summary, investment is influenced profoundly by the state of business confidence. Not only does general business optimism or pessimism have a direct effect on the volume of investment, it also has an indirect effect through changes in the prices of securities on the Stock Exchange. These price changes, in turn, reflect in large part the opinions of persons whose knowledge of long-run values is slight, or whose interest lies in forecasting *short-run* swings of prices.

6. Finally, there is the important matter of taxation. The only significant way to figure expected returns from investment projects is to figure them *after taxes*. Costs are raised and revenues are lowered by excise, sales, and similar taxes. The incomes earned by individuals and by corporations have come to be subject to very high rates of taxation. During wartime rates rose to about 23 per cent on the lowest taxable incomes, and to about 90 per cent on the highest taxable incomes (above $200,000) of individuals. All but the smallest corporations paid 40 per cent tax on their incomes, and in addition, an excess-

profits tax of 95 per cent.[2] The rates have been lowered since, and then raised again. Taxes remain a crucial influence on the net returns to be expected from investment.

All together we have surveyed six influences on the marginal efficiency of capital: (1) innovatory changes, (2) expected demand conditions, (3) the rate at which investments is currently going on, (4) the quantity of capital goods of relevant types already in existence, (5) the state of business confidence, and (6) tax rates.

The rate of interest

Interest is a deterrent to investment since it is a cost that businessmen must pay when they invest. The higher interest rates are, the sharper the deterrent. But when interest rates fall toward zero, investment is not always increased. A businessman will not invest if, in the best opportunity open to him, he expects to lose 20 per cent, even though interest were zero. Interest, therefore, has a one-sided effect: if the rate of interest rises extremely high—to 10 or 30 per cent a year—investment will certainly be choked off. But lowering the rate of interest to zero will not necessarily stimulate investment.

Interest is a payment made to lenders, a payment that induces them to give up their command over ready cash and accept, instead, a security or promise of repayment in the future. The higher the interest rate (assuming a given pattern of expectations about market conditions), the more money will be given up in loans by potential lenders of money; the lower the interest rate, the more will potential lenders be inclined to hold to cash in hope of a better chance turning up later.

If the banking system, perhaps as a consequence of Treasury and Federal Reserve policies, is flooding the country with cash, then the desire of individuals and institutions to "invest in cash" will increasingly be satiated. They will tend eventually

---

[2] There was an over-all limitation on the proportion of income to be taxed away, and 10 per cent of the excess-profits tax was to be credited against postwar tax obligations.

to lend out increasing amounts at low interest rates rather than to keep on expanding their holdings of cash, and so continue to keep on losing the interest that is obtainable. Even so, as our experience of the 1930's indicates, fear of higher rates can be for years an important influence on the decisions of potential lenders.

Also, a general expectation of low interest rates will tend to bring about their realization by increasing the willingness of holders of cash to lend. The Treasury and Federal Reserve, by conspicuously standing ready to lend at low rates on strategic securities—in other words, by standing ready to buy these securities at high prices—can diminish the fear of rising rates, and so help to bring about low rates.

It is possible for the Treasury and Federal Reserve between them to push interest rates downward even in a time of unexampled demand for loans. Average rates on United States Government securities fell from 2.3 per cent in 1942 to 1.9 per cent in 1944, despite an immense increase in borrowing for war purposes. Between the 1920's and 1930's interest rates on all kinds of loans decreased. Loans by banks to their customers fell from a level averaging about 5 per cent in the middle of the 1920's to between 2 and 3 per cent in the late 1930's. This fall reflected in part government monetary policies. In part it reflected outside influences that increased the ability of the banking system to lend at a time when demand for loans from trustworthy borrowers was at low ebb.

How important is the rate of interest?

A low rate of interest, we have said, is a stimulant to investment since it reduces the cost of the funds that businessmen must use in investment. A high rate is a discouragement to investment. But *how important* an influence is the interest rate?

The marginal efficiency of capital, or the gross profit expectation of businessmen, does not reflect only slow changes in the productivity of capital. It is, we remember, an *expectation* and so varies not only with the facts of the objective situation, but also with the confidence of the business manager. When the flow of investment spending is abruptly shriveled at the onset of depression, the explanation appears to be a general collapse of the marginal efficiency of capital, not a change in the interest rate. Suppose, as is easily possible, the marginal efficiency of investment falls to negative levels: businessmen expect to lose money even on the best possibilities open to them. To offset the gloomy sentiments of business mangers, one would have to charge negative rates to persuade them to invest—that is, subsidize them by letting them pay back less than they originally borrowed. This might conceivably be done, but it means loss to the lender, and so could not be done by any private banking system.

The marginal efficiency of new investment to a businessman is likely to vary widely, from perhaps 100 per cent per year or more in the warmth of optimism about a new process, new synthetic, or new market down to minus 30 per cent from the *best* investment open, in the gloom of deep depression. (On the average human beings are probably more hopeful than events bear out. More has been invested in prospecting for gold in our West and in Alaska than has been taken out of productive mines.)

For short-run investments in inventories and machinery the calculations of businessmen are likely to be rough and ready. If a safe margin is not obtainable on inventories and if machinery is not expected to pay for itself in three or four years, the investment will not be undertaken. A fluctuation of interest rates within the ranges we have experienced in recent decades, say 6 to 2 per cent, is of secondary importance. For long-run investments, such as buildings, public utilities, ships, and railroads, where interest might be expected to bulk more largely in the mind of the businessman (since the interest will have to be paid over many years), the effect of varying rates is still likely to be moderate because of the dominating effect of the uncertainties of the future.

Statistical studies carried on by Professor Tinbergen for the period 1919–1932 in the United States indicate that the influence of interest rates was very small on changes in inventories and other short-term investments. The influence of interest rates on long-term investment was found moderate, "the influence of profits and, in the case of residential building, of the shortage and abundance of houses being much larger."[3]

What we have said minimizes, but does not deny, the influence of the interest rate. Some hesitant decisions will be influenced favorably toward investing by a fall in interest rates, and some will be influenced unfavorably by a rise in interest rates.

Investment in the Interwar Years

We now look at the actual investment carried on in the United States during the 1920's and 1930's. We can use estimates either for gross investment (total outlay for business plant and equipment, for housing, inventories, and net-exports) or for net investment (the former, minus an allowance for depreciation, depletion, obsolescence, and so forth).

However, our present concern is to look in some detail at the chief constituents of investment. Gross investment figures are the basic data that are collected (in other words, statistics on the output of capital goods). Net investment is calculated only as a residual, after subtracting estimates for depreciation. Since depreciation allowances are subject to wide error, it is best to use the more reliable figures for gross investment. Total gross investment and four main subdivisions are shown in Chart 13.

Total gross investment is plainly a highly variable thing. The changes by billions of current dollars and by percentages between successive major peaks and valleys are given below, the year 1920 being taken as starting point:

	1921	1929	1932	1937	1938	1941	1943	1948
Billions of dollars ..	—9.3	+6.6	—5.5	+10.4	—4.1	+12.0	—16.0	+41.1
Percentages	—50	+72	—33	+945	—36	+162	—82	+1174.

3 Jan Tinbergen, *Business Cycles in the United States of America*, p. 184. Geneva: League of Nations, Economic Intelligence Series, 1939.

With these we can compare the changes for the same years in consumption expenditures:

	1921	1929	1932	1937	1938	1941	1943	1948
Billions of dollars	−7.0	+26.1	−29.6	+17.9	−2.6	+17.7	+20.0	+75.6
Percentages	−17	+48	−38	+36	−4	+27	+24	+74

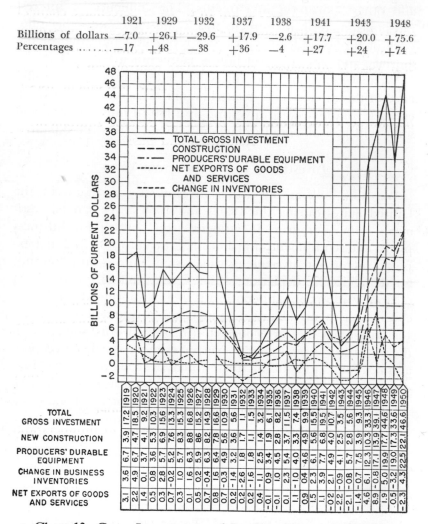

Chart 13. Gross Investment and Its Constituents, 1919-1950.

Source: Data for 1919-1928 from Federal Reserve Board, Department of Commerce, Bureau of Labor Statistics, *Basic Facts on Employment and Production.* Washington: Government Printing Office, 1945, p. 12. Data for 1929-1945 from *Survey of Current Business,* Vol. XXIX (July, 1949), p. 10; for 1946-1950, Vol. XXXI, *National Income Supplement,* 1951, p. 150.

Changes in consumption, by billions of dollars, are usually larger than changes in investment, but often not much larger, and for several years not at all. In terms of percentage changes, the evidence is that usually percentage changes in investment are far greater than percentage changes in consumption. (The year 1943 is anomalous, since wartime controls cut drastically the volume of resources going into private investment uses.)

Of the four constituents of total investment, the most important are construction and producers' durable equipment.

1. Construction, both residential and business, has over the past hundred years gone through fairly regularly recurring periods of high and low activity. The building "cycle" has varied from 13 to 22 years, averaging a bit over 17 years.

Why should building have these fluctuations? Two important reasons are (a) the long life of buildings and (b) the slowness with which builders and suppliers of construction equipment respond to growing scarcity or abundance of buildings. Suppose that construction has been proceeding at a rather high level and that buildings are rather plentiful. Vacancies appear in business structures, apartments, and houses. Rents and the prices of buildings gradually decline. But some time is required to convince builders, through their persisting losses, that the business has taken a chronic turn for the worse, and that they should enter other lines of work.

As time goes on, buildings gradually grow older, become obsolete, fit new needs badly. Families increase in numbers and (in recent decades) shrink in average size, and demand quarters adapted to their needs. But if building contractors are few, some time is required before new entrepreneurs are convinced that building prospects have taken a continued turn for the better, and that they have a good chance of success in entering or returning to the field. Some time is required, too, before skilled men can be trained or assembled, and new or used equipment collected. The main influence on residence building, concludes Tinbergen's survey for the United States, is the relative abundance or scarcity of houses some four years back.

There are other elements in the explanation of building fluctuations. Among these elements are innovations in transportation (the canal, the railroad, the automobile), which have redistributed industry and population; contractions of civilian building during wartime (especially during World Wars I and II), which have left behind a backlog of deferred demand; and the drops during depression in incomes of consumers, which force them to postpone buying new homes.[4]

The 1920's were a high, and the 1930's a low, period of the building cycle. This is true both for construction of business plants and for residence construction. If we take averages for the periods 1921—1929, and 1930—1938, we find the former dropped 50 per cent, the latter 74 per cent.[5] Just as construction sustained employment and the level of total production by its own high level in the 1920's, so it deepened the depression by its collapse in the 1930's.[6]

2. Investment in producers' durable equipment bulks about as large, on the average, as construction. From the decade of the 1920's to the decade of the 1930's, investment in business

---

[4] Interest rates have not been an important influence on the *fluctuations* of building. Mortgage interest rates have been very rigid over the past. Even a drastic drop in the interest rate from 6 to 3 per cent would, in a sample case, reduce the yearly payment for interest and on the principal only from $422 to $310. If we add taxes and insurance, the yearly total cost drops only from $579 to $467. (For a $6000 house in Queens, New York City, on which a $5400 FHA loan is amortized over 25 years.) C. D. Long, *Building Cycles and the Theory of Investment*. Princeton: Princeton University, 1940, pp. 26–30.

Also, for longer-term investments, like building, the importance of the risk element grows more rapidly than does the importance of the interest charge. J. R. Hicks, *Value and Capital*, p. 226. Oxford: Clarendon Press, 1939.

[5] Kuznets' data.

[6] Public construction (not included in the above private investment) is remarkably constant over these years, varying between extremes of 1.4 and 3.5 billion dollars annually. Contrary to general opinion, it was very little larger in the 1930's than in the 1920's: the increase averages 5 per cent. It was only after 1933 that federal government expenditure for construction (both direct and through federal aid to state and local units) expanded to large dimensions. Decline in state and local construction over the 1930's almost compensates for the increase that took place in federal construction.

equipment dropped only about one-fifth, whereas investment in plant construction was dropping one-half.

If we should add together business investment in plant construction (excluding residence construction for consumers) and in equipment, we have a total that usually is larger than all the other elements of private investment put together. Investment in business plant and equipment was still dominantly important all through the 1930's when, it is sometimes argued, the government was spending heavily for construction and other purposes.

3. Inventory accumulation rises and falls sharply over a period some three to four years in length as businessmen expect price rises or increased demand or fear the reverse. Years of maximum increase of these stocks of raw materials and semifinished and finished goods are 1920, 1923, 1926, 1929, 1937, 1941, 1946, and 1948. Years of lowest inventory accumulation are 1921, 1924, 1928, 1932, 1938, 1943, 1947, and 1949. Difference in spending for inventories from year to year may be 3 or 4 billion dollars or more.

Apparently, changes in spending for inventories are the main explanation of the minor fluctuations in output and employment that we have experienced at intervals of generally three or four years: perhaps (counting peak to peak) 1920, 1923, 1926, 1929, 1934, and 1937. (The distortions of heavy defense and war expenditures by government followed hard after 1939.)

A boom that rests upon inventory accumulation in any important degree (1923, 1929, and 1937) is one that promises to collapse promptly, because businessmen cannot continue indefinitely to pile up rapidly increasing stocks of materials and finished products. When they stop increasing their inventories (unless rising consumption spending or other spending takes up the slack), the boom is over. Conversely, when inventories are shrinking rapidly, as in 1932, there is promise that times will soon be better when businessmen decide not to reduce their stocks further or decide to increase them from a low level.

4. Our last kind of private investment is net exports of goods and services, or "net foreign investment." In ordinary peacetime years it is of slight significance in explaining the fluctuations of total investment. If we block out years immediately affected by war, we note that at the most (1938) it contributed 1.1 billion dollars, or 1.3 per cent, of gross national expenditure; and at the least (1936) diminished gross national expenditure by 0.1 billion dolars, or 0.1 of 1 per cent. On the other hand, during and after wars foreign trade can have an appreciable influence on national expenditures. In 1919 and 1947 net exports contributed about 4 per cent to gross national expenditure

Foreign trade is normally a help toward greater efficiency of production: it extends the advantages of specialization to a world-wide scale. Also, the United States critically needs a few special commodity imports. And of course, sudden shifts in the volume and types of exports and imports will have strategic and dislocating effects even in peacetime. But this country is not significantly dependent on foreign trade for the maintenance of employment—despite conventional left-wing allegations, and sometimes arguments from the right, that capitalism cannot live without exports.

CHAPTER ELEVEN

Government Expenditure

THE TOTAL AMOUNT OF EMPLOYMENT AND PRODUCTION IN AN economy is dependent on the total amount of spending for goods and services produced. In fact, the total incomes received *are* the total spendings in the economy: you can't have income without spending. We have discussed consumer expenditure for goods and services, and private investment expenditures. We now come to the third and last kind of expenditure for output—the expenditures of government for goods and services.[1] When we add these three elements together, we have the total expenditure for goods and services produced in the economy, and have in the same figure valued total national income and total national production.

The Trend of Expenditures for Goods and Services, 1909-1950

Chart 14 shows the three sources of income over 1909—1950, together with their total, gross national product or income. Consumer expenditures are much the largest of the three, usually about two-thirds of the total, and present a fairly close relationship to gross income. Private investment, or capital forma-

---

[1] "Government" includes federal, state, and local governments; but "government expenditure for goods and services" excludes that part of government expenditure that is not for currently produced goods and services: relief payments, veterans' allowances, food stamps, pensions, loans, payments from social-security funds, and purchase of existing assets.

tion, shows the pronounced variability that our reasoning has led us to expect.

Government expenditures include state and local expenditures, as well as federal expenditures. The over-all trend of government expenditures is upward within the interwar period at roughly the same rate as the national income. But this trend conceals sharp divergences within the individual units of government.

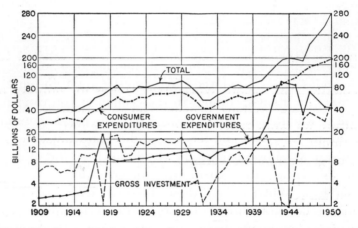

Chart 14. Gross National Product and Its Constituents, 1919-1950.

Source: Data through 1928 from Department of Labor, Bureau of Labor Statistics, *Basic Facts on Employment and Production.* Washington: Government Printing Office, 19/5, p. 13; for 1929-1950, *Survey of Current Business, National Income Supplement,* 1951, p. 150.

Local expenditures (which are larger than state expenditures) varied approximately in accord with the level of gross production. Expenditures rose continuously during the 1920's to a peak in 1929. They fell to 1933, and thereafter rose somewhat to a level about three-quarters of the 1929 peak. State expenditures, on the other hand, expanded consistently throughout the period. In no year of the 1930's did state expenditures fall below the level of 1929, though there was a modest and temporary decline below the levels reached in 1931 and 1932. The largest item in state and local expenditures taken together is for schools—about a quarter of the total in 1941. Some of the next most important expenditures are for highways, welfare, general administration, police and fire, and health and hospitals.

Federal expenditures, in contrast to both the above, have followed a pattern generally counter to that of production and employment in the economy. Following World War I federal expenditures declined sharply to a low point in 1923. Afterward they rose moderately to 1932, dropped somewhat for one year, and then rose more rapidly into the later 1930's and the war period. Except in the late 1930's and during World War II, federal expenditures were smaller than the total of local and state expenditures. The major item in federal government expenditures just before World War II was for military purposes, including veterans' benefits. Aid to agriculture and expenditure for work relief were also large, followed by outlays to maintain the civilian divisions of the government and to carry on general public works.[2]

The ability of state and local governments to spend in excess of their tax revenues is sharply limited, in contrast with that of the federal government. The capacity of the former to borrow is restricted in accord with their long-run ability to obtain tax revenue from the sometimes scanty local resources. Often they have inherited bad credit standing from past bad administrations. More important are legal prohibitions and restrictions that may impose arbitrary limits on the use of government credit. Futhermore, the federal government has the considerable advantage of control of the currency and credit system of the nation.

How the United States met the problem of unemployment, 1930-1940

In addition to certain specific measures that we shall consider later, a government has two general means of combatting

---

[2] Certain of these items are transfer payments and so do not enter into the national product.

depression and unemployment: monetary policy, and fiscal policy.

1. Monetary policy is concerned with the supply of money in the economy. In the 1920's there was rather general confidence among economists and government officials that monetary policy was sufficient to control the business cycle. Attention was centered mainly on the movement of prices: if prices threatened to rise drastically in the boom, it was argued that the Treasury and Federal Reserve should raise the interest rate through their powers, and so discourage businessmen from borrowing and investing. If one could only cut the top off the boom, then a succeeding depression would be avoided or mitigated. Conversely, in time of threatened depression, the interest rate should be lowered to encourage investment.

We have reasoned that a lower interest rate (even if interest rates on all kinds of loans could be controlled by the monetary authorities, which they cannot) is an inadequate stimulus to greater investment. This is the current view, and emerges out of the experience of the 1930's as well as from abstract reasoning.

When the recession got under way in 1929 and 1930, the Federal Reserve followed the orthodox prescription and lowered its discount rate sharply, from 6 per cent in 1929 to below 2 per cent in 1931. The rates on other kinds of loans also fell in these first years, but, with the exception of bankers' acceptances, not so sharply. More important, government bonds were bought by the Federal Reserve on the open market in some quantity in early 1930 in the effort to increase the quantity of money at the disposal of individuals, businesses, and banks. These measures were too weak to withstand the contractionary process under way of canceling debt, reduction of bank loans, and shrinkage of the money supply. By 1933 the quantity of money had dropped 25 per cent below its 1929 level. But of course this does not imply that a monetary policy that succeeded in maintaining the supply of money would have averted a depression, though it doubtless would have made the depression less severe.

During the 1930's interest rates continued to fall. The rates charged by banks in large cities on loans to customers fell from 6 per cent in 1929 to between 3 and 2½ per cent in 1935 and afterward. Bankers' acceptances fell from their general level of 3 to 5 per cent in the 1920's to less than 1 per cent. Treasury bills, close to 5 per cent in 1929, fell also to less than 1 per cent, with three-month bills attaining 1/100 of 1 per cent. Good quality corporate bonds fell from their range of 4½ to 6 per cent in the 1920's to under 3 per cent by the end of the 1930's.

Such a fall in interest rates had never been experienced before in this or any other country. It was the policy of our monetary authorities to drive down interest rates, but it is not likely that they would themselves have had the courage to push their policy so far. There were outside factors involved.

Interest rates, like other prices, fall when there is excess supply, an excess of money available for lending at the current rate over the quantity of money which is wanted for borrowing at that rate. The great increase in money supply during the 1930's gradually came to satisfy the anxiety of people and institutions to "invest in cash" for the sake of security. They became increasingly willing to lend at lower interest rates. The swollen supply of available money flowed partly from (a) action of the monetary authorities—open-market operations and other policies of the Federal Reserve that increased the reserves of member banks, and so made them able to lend. In part, it came also from (b) an increased legal rate of issuance of silver certificates, and from (c) the huge inflow of gold (about 15 billion dollars by the beginning of World War II) which increased bank reserves, and so made banks more able to lend. Finally, (d) there were the funds supplied by lending agencies of the federal government, especially the RFC, which by the end of the decade had loaned or invested 13.5 billion dollars.[3] These agencies increased the supply of funds, and so tended to depress interest rates for kinds of loans whose rates the Federal Reserve could not directly affect.

This large supply of funds available can be contrasted with the meager demand for investment funds from glum business- men and apprehensive potential home builders. Excess re- serves, which measure the unused lending power of banks, rose to peaks of 5 billion dollars at the end of 1935, and 7 billion dollars at the end of 1940, as interest rates fell.

Though such a thoroughgoing test of "easy money" had no precedent, the recovery record was not very satisfactory. We did experience a rapid, but uneven, recovery from the pit of the depression in 1932—1933 up to 1937. But in that year (when interest rates had fallen to a level much lower than in 1932) we suffered a sharp setback, and thereafter, to the de- fense and war periods, endured a level of some 8 to 10 millions of unemployed. In so far as our subsequent employment ex- perience can be said to be the result of "easy money," it was not very encouraging.

2. The use of federal government revenues and expenditures as an anti-depression weapon was not a measure first thought out carefully, then applied. We did not "plan it that way." The Hoover administration, in office until 1933, wanted to bal- ance the budget—that is, make tax and other revenues at least equal to expenditure; and it made efforts to economize to that end. But as the national income dropped by one-half from 1929 to 1932, the revenues of the federal government also de- clined by about the same proportion. In addition, growing necessary relief expenditures offset the attempted economies, and so the deficit grew, made up by borrowing from banks

---

[3] Agencies that made loans or direct investments, or refinanced or guaranteed old loans, include the Reconstruction Finance Corporation, the Federal Farm Mortgage Corporation, the Federal Land Banks, the Home Owner's Loan Cor- poration, the Rural Electrification Administration, and the Federal Housing Administration.

and from the public. It is curious to remember, in view of later expenditures from the federal Treasury, that the main charge of the Democratic campaign of 1932 against the Republican administration was extravagance. Budget deficits and the loans of the RFC were the particular targets of attack.

After the Roosevelt administration came into office in March, 1933 the deficits continued. But during the next several years there was hardly any evidence that influential administrators, research men, and legislators had any thought that recovery might be effected through a higher rate of government expenditures into the economy, than of taxation out of it. The deficits continued and grew because of apparent necessity, not because of policy: tax yields continued low, and relief and other emergency expenditures grew. Emphasis remained for a time on monetary policy. The aim of raising prices to their 1926 level was repeatedly stated, the two principal means being devaluation of the dollar (by making our money cheaper to foreigners we would encourage their buying in this country) and the NRA (whose codes of fair competition encouraged monopolistic price-fixing). The early public works program was a relief measure, not a means of recovery. In the meantime, state and local governments over the nation cut expenditures as their incomes collapsed. State and local public works declined steadily from nearly 3 billion dollars in 1929 to a little over 1 billion dollars in 1935.

In June 1934, there was a visit of J. M. Keynes to this country, during which he said that if the federal government spent in excess of revenue only 200 million dollars a month, we should decline to the bottom of the depression of 1932, that 300 million dollars would hold us where we were, and that spending 400 million dollars a month would bring us to complete recovery. Many influential government economists and administrators agreed in general with this prognosis—even if they were not impressed by its precision. But such was not the official administration view. The official view continued hopeful that a balanced budget might induce such confidence in businessmen and consumers as to cause them to expand their own expenditures sufficiently to bring about high employment and output. In England, Winston Churchill, when Chancellor of the Exchequer in 1929, had put this conviction firmly: "It is the orthodox Treasury dogma steadfastly held that, whatever might be the political and social advantages, very little employment and no permanent additional employment can . . . be created by State borrowing and State expenditure." [4]

The annual budget messages sent to Congress by the President repeatedly promised that the budget would soon be balanced.

There was considerably unofficial advocacy from 1933 to 1935 of "pump-priming." If a well pump on the farm does not work, one can generally get it working by pouring a little water into it. The priming wets and swells the leather valve, thereby causing better suction. So with the economy. It was argued that a bit of additional spending by the government would expand consumer buying, necessitate more investment expenditure, and thereby increase confidence in the future. Businessmen would be encouraged to invest more heavily, and we should soon find ourselves well on the road to a recovery in which government deficits would no longer be necessary, but would instead turn into surpluses. The government budget would, it was thought, be balanced in the long run, with deficits in depression just about equaling the surpluses that would accumulate in prosperity.

The official administration view did not seek to make use of the stimulating effects of an unbalanced budget until the sharp downswing of 1937–1938. The budget has temporarily come into balance, partly through the rise in federal revenues as business conditions were improving, and partly through the building up of a social-security reserve. A new spending program was put together hurriedly in the spring of 1938 and was

---

[4] Sir William Beveridge, "The Government's Employment Policy," *Economic Journal*, Vol. LIV (June–September, 1944) , pp. 161-162.

passed by Congress. The federal government's net contribution to income, which had fallen from 4.3 billion dollars in 1936 to 1.1 billion dollars in 1937, rose in 1938 to 2.4 billion dollars.[5]

After 1937 there was little heard of pump-priming. Obviously, the pump had not been primed: the deficits of government had not started a cumulative upward movement of private consumption and investment spending that would continue under its own momentum. It was best to let the matter drop in an embarrassed silence.

Instead, discussions grew as to whether we were not in for "secular stagnation"—a continuing, decades-long era of such inadequate investment and consumption as would lead to continuing heavy unemployment unless government expenditures should fill the gap. And if the government should, for this purpose, tax less than it spent, its debt would continue to rise—a prospect alarming to many people who were already worried by the growth of the debt from 14.8 billion dollars in 1930 to 31.4 billion dollars in 1937.[6]

Such discussion soon became academic, as defense and later war expenditures of the federal government boomed our national income and output to heights that no economist had seriously thought possible. All predictions turned out to be too low. Money income expanded from (in round billions) 40 in 1933, to 73 in 1939, to 184 in 1944. Even when we allow for the rise in prices, the comparison of real output still shows a very large rise: from 74 billion dollars in 1933, to 127 billion dollars in 1939, and 239 billions in 1944.[7] The over-all rise in real output, from pit of depression to peak of war boom, is about 222 per cent. Evidently, the extent of concealed unem-

---

5 Revised data of Laughlin Currie, in Mordecai Ezekiel, "Saving, Consumption, and Investment, I," *American Economic Review*, Vol. XXXII (March, 1942). p. 27.

6 These figures are for federal debt only, data of the end of the year. State and local debt would add another 14.7 billion dollars in 1930, and 15.8 billion dollars in 1937.

7 At average prices of 1950.

ployment, and the degree to which we could stretch ourselves to produce more when our hearts were in the job, were uniformly underestimated.

Meanwhile, the national debt was expanding vastly, passing 263 billion dollars by the end of World War II. But less was heard during the war about the menace of public debt. The booming prosperity of the United States and its immense productivity gave renewed confidence to that wing of business and economic thought which urged that a freely operating economy could be trusted to solve the problem of unemployment itself.[8]

---

8 A fuller statement of the policies of the 1930's is in John H. Williams, *Postwar Monetary Plans*, New York, Knopf, 1944; Chap. IV. See also Alvin H. Hansen, *Business Cycles and National Income*, Norton, 1951, Ch. 26.

CHAPTER TWELVE

Fluctuations in Production and Employment

A. The Earning and Spending of Income

IN CHART 15B TOTAL INCOME IS PLOTTED AGAINST THE SOURCES of that income. In Chart 15A total income is plotted against the disposition, or uses, of income. The 45-degree line OB at every point measures the aggregate of sources, or of disposition, in income; and so it measures total income. For example, in 1950 the gross national income was 279.8 billion dollars. We can think of this as measured by OL in both figures. The sources from which this income came must total 262.4 billion dollars, and when we add up the uses of that income, we must also have 262.4 billion dollars. LT in both figures, therefore, equals 262.4 billion dollars.

In 1950 (as we have seen in Table 10, p. 68) , the values of the main subdivisions of the sources of income and of the channels in which that income was disposed were as follows:[1]

Disposition of Income	*Sources of Income*
IN BILLIONS OF DOLLARS	

Disposition of Income		Sources of Income	
Savings	40.3	Gross investment	46.6
Taxes and transfers [2]	48.7	Government expenditures	42.5
Consumption expenditures	193.6	Consumption expenditures	193.6
Gross national income (or product)	282.6	Gross national income (or product)	282.6

[1] *Survey of Current Business, National Income Supplement,* 1951, pp. 150-151.
[2] Adjusted for statistical discrepancy.

187

The lines separating the elements that make up the sources and disposition of income are drawn to indicate roughly the ordinary pattern of changes as income rises. Savings, taxes, and consumption usually all become larger with higher income. But we have less assurance as to how private investment and government expenditures will behave. In an ordinary business boom the main expansion is in private investment, but during

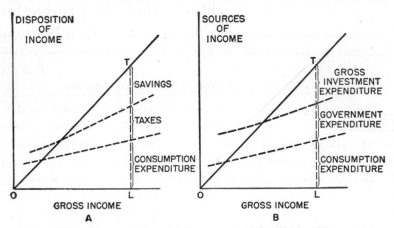

Chart 15. Income: Its Sources and Its Disposition.

wartime government expenditure rises hugely, and may do so at the expense of investment or even of consumption.

An increase in any one of the sources of income—consumption, government expenditure, or private investment—means that total income rises, ordinarily by a magnified amount. An increase in private investment swells income not only directly, but also by tending to expand consumption. A rise in government expenditure increases income directly, and usually also induces more consumption and more private investment.[3] An increase in consumption (which is the

---

[3] This assumes that there are no (wartime) controls imposed on the economy to restrict consumption and investment. It is also possible under peacetime conditions that certain increases in government expenditure might, on net balance, decrease private investment, so that the multiplier is less than one, or even negative. (A negative multiplier would mean that total income declines when the government increases its expenditure.)

same thing as saying that there is a decreased disposition to save out of current income) increases income directly, and also through encouraging private investment.

On the other hand, an increase in taxes will ordinarily absorb some funds that otherwise would have gone into consumption; and is likely also to discourage private investment, both because consumption expenditure is less and because businessmen anticipate higher taxes to be added to their costs or subtracted from their receipts.

Consumption is, of course, the same in both Chart 15A and 15B: just to the extent, at any level of income, that people spend on consumption, income is derived from consumption-spending. This means (as we have seen, pp. 67-69) that savings plus taxes always equal investment plus government expenditure. This equality can be rearranged into the form: Savings equals investment plus (government expenditure minus taxes). Since the expression within the parentheses is the government deficit, we can say, alternatively,

Savings *equals* Investment *plus* Government Deficit

An increased desire to save, if not offset, will lead to lower national income by means of a drop in consumption. But this decline in income will not occur if the increased savings is offset by an increase in private investment and/or the government deficit.

These quantitative relationships underlie much of what we say later, but they do not themselves offer much of a guide with respect to detailed issues of policy. Suppose that our problem is that of deficient total expenditure.

1. One range of issues, on which no light is shed above, is concerned with the possibilities of expanding consumption and private investment by policies not making use of the government budget. There are many activities of government that affect total income and employment other than its budgetary practices. Among them are such specific policies as those concerned with the checking of monopoly, job guarantees, security

issues, even the general tone of unrelated government policies. To be included also are the general powers of government over money and credit.

2. Qualitative matters of the budget are neglected above, but these may be crucial. The indirect effects of government spending on consumption and private investment can be more important than the direct stimulus to income; and the indirect effects depend, in large degree, on *where* the government does the spending and from what *kinds* of taxes and loans it secures its funds.

3. Expansion of government expenditures may change the dividing line between public and private enterprise. The choice of this dividing line need not, and should not, be the accidental by-product of policies directed toward increasing employment and production.

We will return to these matters below.

Determinants of the Level of Employment

Chart 15B illustrates the simplest possible device for estimating the national income. If we know the normal relation of consumption to income—not the amount of consumption, but only the relationship—and also can estimate the amount of investment plus government expenditure, we can calculate total amount of income.

We start out with

Income *equals* Consumption *plus* Investment *plus* Government Expenditure.

It is convenient to use gross measures of each of these. In the period 1929–1940, consumption had the following average relationship to gross income. The data are for real consumption and real income, at prices of 1950.

Consumption *equals* $19.47 billions *plus* .52 *times* Income.

Suppose we can trust this relationship to hold. Then:

Income *equals* ($19.47 billions *plus* .52 *times* Income) *plus* Investment *plus* Government Expenditure.

If investment plus government expenditure is running continuously at 80 billion dollars a year, a bit of arithmetic shows us that income will approach [4] 207 billions a year:

Income *equals* $19.47 billions *plus* .52 *times* Income *plus* $80 billions

or,

$$\text{Income} - .52 \cdot \text{Income} = \$ \ 99.47 \text{ billions}$$
$$.48 \cdot \text{Income} = \$ \ 99.47 \text{ billions}$$
$$\text{Income} = \frac{\$ \ 99.47 \text{ billions}}{.48}$$
$$\text{Income} = \$ \ 207.2 \text{ billions}$$

No trust should be put in these as being exact figures. Consumption does not have as consistent a relationship to net or gross income as we might like, nor does investment plus government expenditure stay at a constant level year after year so that its effect on income has a chance to work itself out.

1. The cumulative process

In this and the following two sections we are concerned with explaining, first, why any contraction or expansion tends to continue for a while, once started; and second, why any contraction or expansion tends ultimately to be checked and reversed.

A contraction is likely to be set off rather suddenly by a drop in investment below the volume of savings that people want to make at a high level of income and employment. A "collapse of the marginal efficiency of capital," which we associate with the mushroom growth of pessimistic expectations, may have found its origin in a speculative down-flurry in the stock market, in conspicuous business failures, in foreign events, or elsewhere. Or there might have been a fall in consumer

---

4 Income will rise at first rapidly, then more slowly, toward 197 billion dollars as a limit. This will become clearer later, when we consider the leverage principle (pp. 203-204) .

buying, or a drop in government purchases, or a collapse of important foreign markets (this last is hardly possible for the United States, but could be significant for a small country like Belgium, whose foreign trade is large relative to its domestic trade).

Once the contraction is underway, pessimism has reason to deepen. With a decline in investment, consumption also declines; and declining consumption justifies still further decline in investment. As demand falls, prices sag, losses are experienced, buying is postponed. The output of capital and durable goods drops more than that of consumer and perishable goods. Alarmed creditors hound debtors for payment, and debtors are compelled into forced sales to pay off debts, thus pushing prices lower still. Banks decide not to lend out again as old loans are paid off, and individuals want to hold cash rather than other kinds of assets. And so purchasing power drops further.

An expansion process is set off by a change in some underlying condition; perhaps new methods of production have been developed; perhaps there has been a change in consumer tastes. In a large proportion of upswings, we will have put our finger on the strategic cause when we have answered the question: Why are businessmen more willing to invest than before? Any increase of demand will set off favorable repercussions: an increase in investment increases incomes, and so stimulates consumption; and a rise in consumption, in turn, gives businessmen cause to invest more. If the banking system has become liquid at the end of a previous period of depression, then interest rates have tended to fall. To some extent this encourages investment, especially in relatively durable investment goods. Prices rise to some extent as demand grows, with favorable psychological effects toward still more investments and anticipatory buying generally. Output of investment goods and durable goods rises faster than that of consumer and perishable goods. The improved prospects make banks and other lenders more ready to give up cash (either newly created money or past savings) for lending in investment channels. And so the boom feeds on itself.

2. Fluctuations within a range of relatively high and relatively low employment: simplest explanation

A back-door way of looking on these matters helps to explain why national income tends to fluctuate within a range, neither rising indefinitely in a continued inflationary boom, nor falling indefinitely toward complete business paralysis. The reasoning of the last several pages says that income is the total of expenditures on consumption, investment, and government activities. We could look closely instead at the parallel relationship: Savings equals investment plus the government deficit.

We can simplify our reasoning by assuming what has often been true in past decades, that government taxes and expenditures are unimportantly small compared with private expenditures on consumption and investment, and so drop them out of the picture. Then savings always equals investment.[5]

Savings is the gap between income and consumption: it is a "leakage" out of the income stream. Since savings tend to be large at a high level of income, investment, an injection into the income stream, must be equally high in order for that high level of income to be realized at all. Hence in any boom, investment spending is heavy.

But investment spending may not be so large as this. Then income realized is smaller. Consumption is smaller and savings are smaller also. Income has shrunk to the level where the smaller sums that people save at that level are equaled by

---

[5] It is possible to portray, also not very happily, the determination of national income of a country at the level of income where *normal* savings equal *normal* investment. This indirect method requires one to differentiate between temporary equality of savings and investment, which always exists by definition; and the equality of normal savings and normal investment, which exists only when a stable income level is achieved.

the smaller sums that are being spent for investment. If the decline in investment and consumption is moderate, the economy will run along at some level of employment moderately below the level corresponding to full employment and maximum output—perhaps, in the United States, with 5 to 10 millions unemployed. The economy may be fairly stable at this level. The fall in investment may, however, be drastic down to levels where present plant and equipment are not being maintained. Income falls, also, to a level where people are so impoverished that they spend for consumption a sum that exceeds their incomes (they use up their savings or go into debt) by the amount of the negative investment. The economy is then in deep depression, with 20 to 25 per cent or more of the work force unemployed.

We may conclude, then, that the sums which people decide to save must be matched by investment spending, or else incomes, output, and employment fall until the community is so poverty-stricken as to save no more than is being invested. Since people and firms save less when their incomes are low, at some lower level of income the savings that they try to make are equaled by the investment expenditure that is going on. Income falls no further.

If less is being invested than people try to save, there is a drop in incomes downward toward stagnation, bankruptcies, and soup lines. If more is being invested than people try to save, there is a boom in incomes up toward high employment, or past this into inflationary price rises. Incomes rise or fall over the whole economy as people carry out their decisions to consume or not to consume, and the total saving accomplished remains equal to the total investment actually made.

In brief, an expansion of production and employment is brought to a close and reversed by investment falling below what people wish to save; and a contraction is brought to a close and reversed, by investment rising above what people wish to save. (We continue to assume that government taxes and expenditures are unimportantly small). We have, then, a picture of fluctuations within some range of levels of employment and production. This range need not, of course, be close to a full employment level. It might be considerably below.

No "normal" level of unemployment equilibrium is implied by this reasoning. It is only that employment and production may persist within a range *somewhere* below full employment.

3. Fluctuations within a range of relatively high and relatively low employment: a more realistic explanation

At any point of time, the level of income and employment in an economy is in balance between forces tending to raise it, and forces tending to lower it. In the same fashion, the level of a pool in a stream is in balance between the flow of water into it, tending to raise it, and the flow of water out, tending to lower it.

In the section above, we looked on investment as an inflow tending to raise income, and saving as a leakage tending to lower it. But we can be more accurate and go into more detail: these are not the only influences that tend to keep the income stream from rising above a certain point, or falling below a certain point.

Any fall in spending tends to lower the income stream: less consumer spending, less investment spending by businessmen, less government spending, or less export sales to foreigners. Why does not income and employment fall indefinitely, once it is started on the downgrade?

(1) It is true that savings tend to fall with lowered income. In fact the statistics indicate (*a*) that personal savings usually fall by a *greater* percentage than income, as individuals reduce their savings, draw on past savings, and go into debt in order to try to maintain their standard of living. In other words, consumer spending usually falls by a *smaller* percentage than income. (*b*) Another influence supporting consumer spending

is a fall in the amount of taxes taken out of the income stream. The take from excise and sales taxes will be smaller as national income falls. More important, corporate and personal income taxes fall rapidly. Lower incomes are taxed at lower rates, thus releasing funds for corporate and consumer use. (c) Corporations reduce their saving as their receipts fall. They try to maintain their dividends, and may even pay out dividends in excess of current earnings. This supports *disposable* income of individuals as national income falls. (d) A final influence toward maintaining consumer spending is the rising volume of payments of unemployment compensation.

(2) There are kinds of investment that will not be discouraged by currently falling incomes, since their justification rests on the long-run prospects of the economy. Among them are public utility investment, and certain kinds of public works.

(3) Government expenditures are not likely to fall as rapidly as income. Some are contracted for long in advance, some expenditures are increased by depression (relief, and support of weak businesses), some are not much affected by the state of boom or depression (military spending, foreign aid programs).

(4) As income falls, the value of imports will decline, since there will be less spending by individuals and by businesses *both* at home and abroad. (Imports are a leakage out of the income stream.) And there are likely to be falling prices in the economy to encourage buying by foreigners: exports tend to rise.

All these four influences work toward checking and eventually reversing any fall in income. Each of them can be approximately reversed to explain why a rise in income also tends to be checked.

It is plain that actual influences on total spending are so various and complex that it is misleading by geometry or algebra to define exactly where the income level will be, under assumed conditions. Any such definition has at best only a rough illustrative value. Actual predicting of the national income level, six months or a year or so hence, requires prayerful meditation on all the complex influences on total spending, and a sharp awareness that the most important single item, consumer spending, is significantly influenced by other factors than current income (Chapter 9).

But our analysis does indicate that there are strong pressures tending to keep income from falling indefinitely, or from rising indefinitely. There are "stabilizers" in the system, even though they work in a rough fashion.

The Equality of Savings and Investment

An awkward logical problem arises from the way our national income data are set up. The savings made in a country are always equal to investment plus the deficit of government.[6] And yet it is obviously possible that people might *want* to save more than the total of private investment plus (any) government deficit.

We can avoid the unnecessary complication of always talking about the government budget by assuming, as before, that government taxing and spending are unimportantly small compared to private spending; or that they are fixed amounts, and so can be neglected when we are talking about the causes of changes in the situation. We can then say without further qualification that savings always equals investment.

The difficulty remains that people might *want* to save more or less than is being invested.

Of course, some people save in order to invest personally—we may save in order to buy a house. In such cases, though investment spending may tend to lag behind savings, it will not, on the average, be higher or lower. But in general, different people save than invest, and for different reasons. We save for

6 This is true whether we are defining savings and investment on a net or on a gross basis, since the same correction (for depreciation and other reserves) is made to both.

a rainy day, because we want to buy some expensive article in the future, for prestige, or because we should like to receive the interest and dividends our savings might earn, and so on. On the other hand, individuals and business firms invest mainly because they hope to add to their incomes—that is, because the marginal efficiency of investment opportunities open to them is higher than the interest rate.

The question that we face is: How does it happen that, although people in a society may want to save more than others want to invest, it always turns out that the total savings made are identically equal to the total investment made?

1. If all, and no more than all, income were regularly and promptly spent, then the stream of income in the economy would continue at a given level, neither swelling to a flood nor dwindling off to a trickle.

Suppose that some person, A, decides to save $10 more than usual (that is, he withdraws $10 more than usual from the income stream). Then, if someone else happens to invest $10 more than before (that is, injects $10 additional into the income stream), all is still well. The income stream continues as before, neither shrunken nor swollen. Savings continue to equal investment.

2. But suppose instead that when A saves his additional $10, no one else invests additionally. Then incomes received in the economy immediately drop by $10. Some other person (or persons), B, does not receive the $10 that A has decided to save.

If B continues his consumption expenditure as usual, despite the fact that his income has dropped, then he has saved less by $10 compared with the preceding period. The net result of A's savings is that the national income has dropped, and that B has canceled A's savings by saving less. Saving over the whole economy has not changed, and investment has not changed. They remain equal, just as before.

On the other hand, if B reduces his consumption expenditure by $10 as his income drops, and C (whose income derives in part from B) finds his income cut and reduces his expenditure by $10, and so on, we have a series of falling incomes initiated by *A*'s original savings. (But at any point of time, some person or persons have suffered a cut in income of $10 while still spending as before, and therefore have temporarily saved less by $10 compared with the original situation.) Incomes of *B, C, D, E,* . . . successively drop.

There is reason to expect this series of decreases in incomes eventually to come to an end because, as we remember, lower incomes are correlated with lessened savings. Suppose that when the income of *F* drops, he permanently reduces his savings by $5. *G* then receives an income drop not of $10, but of $5. The series of decreases in income ends when total decreased (permanent) saving has canceled out *A*'s original saving. No additional investments being made, savings over the whole economy continue to equal investment at the old level. The only difference from the original situation is that incomes have been lowered.

3. There is a third possibility, parallel with the above. Suppose that *A* now upsets the applecart of the stable economy by deciding to *invest* $10 more than usual at a time when no one else happens to save $10 additional. Then some other person (or persons), *B*, finds his income raised by $10.

B might decide to consume as usual, despite the fact that his income has risen: then he has saved $10 additional compared with the preceding period. The net effect of *A*'s investment is that the national income has risen, and that investment and saving are both higher by $10; hence, investment still equals saving.

If *B* spends his additional $10 of income, and others down the line also, then we have a series of rising incomes initiated by *B*'s original investing: *C, D, E,* . . . receive successively $10 of extra income. (But at any moment of time some person or persons have the extra $10, which has not been spent and which is, therefore, temporarily savings.)

This series of increased incomes is not to be expected to continue indefinitely because, as we also remember, higher incomes are correlated with higher savings. Suppose that when F receives his income rise he permanently saves an additional $5. Then G receives an income increase not of $10, but of $5. The series of rises in incomes ends when total increased (permanent) saving has canceled out A's original investment. Over the whole economy incomes have risen, and investment and savings are both $10 higher and, therefore, are still equal.

The inequality of savings and investment

The main argument for using definitions of savings and investment that make them equal—or more fully, savings, and investment plus government deficit—is that one can find this equality directly in our national income data. The accounts are set up in that way (Chapter 2). In these measures of income, savings and investment measure real flows of goods and services in the economy. But a demonstration of how the equality works out through money payments among individuals, which we have just worked through, is not immediately obvious.

Professor D. H. Robertson has developed an alternative, attractively simple method for explaining the rise, constancy, or fall of national income. His method appeals to many students as a common-sense approach. He is explicitly concerned with money income (rather than with real income). By breaking up the life of the economy into separate time periods, and defining savings as being made out of the income of the previous time period, his system tells us that savings may be less than, equal to, or greater than investment—and national income in consequence rises, is constant, or falls.

One time period differs from another in that income earned in any time period 1 (Ye_1) can be disposed of only in time period 2 (Yd_2). It is disposed of either in consumer spending (C), or it is saved (S). On the other hand, income earned in any time period can arise only in consumer spending (C) or in investment spending (I) of that period:

(Illustrative Figures in Billions of Dollars)

Time Period 1	Time Period 2	Time Period 3
$C_1 + I_1 = Ye_1 = Yd_2 = C_2 + S_2$		
. . . . . $= 100 = 100 = 88 + 12$		
	$C_2 + I_2 = Ye_2 = Yd_3 = C_3 + S_3$	
	$88 + 20 = 108 = 108 = $	

Income earned is shown in the example as rising from 100 in time period 1 to 108 in time period 2. Any such change in income is always equal to the difference between savings and investment in the second time period. Here investment, an injection into income, exceeds saving, a leakage out of income: 20 *minus* 12 *equals* 8, the amount *of* rise of income. If income were falling, saving would exceed investment by the amount of the decline.

Hence in the Robertson system we can explain a rise in income in two ways: because investment was greater than saving of the period, or because the total of consumption and investment rose between that period and the former.[7] By the national accounting (or Keynesian) approach we follow generally in this book, we must say that income rises because the total of spending on consumption and investment rises, or because more was being invested than people want to save at the existing income level.[8]

A difficulty of the Robertson definitions (aside from the fact that they cannot be applied to the national income accounts) is that between any two periods of time—say, between the years 1952 and 1953—there is not necessarily one, but perhaps a fraction of one, or several, or many income periods.

[7] If we want to take account of government taxing and spending, we can say that investment plus government expenditures exceeded saving plus taxes of the period, or that the total of consumer spending, investment, and government spending rose between the two periods.

[8] Compare J. M. Keynes, *General Theory of Employment, Interest, and Money*, pp. 61–65, 74–85. New York: Harcourt Brace, 1936; and D. H. Robertson, "Saving and Hoarding," *Economic Journal*, Vol. XLIII, **pp.** 399 ff.; and pp. 699 ff.

The number depends on our uncertain estimates of the average time required for earned income to become disposable. And over the whole economy the income periods of individuals and businesses are overlapping and confused.

A third aproach has been developed by a group of Swedish writers, among them conspicuously Professor Ohlin. In accordance with the reasoning we have already given, they agree that, looking *backward* on the events of any time period, savings equal investment—that is, both are equal to income minus consumption. But looking *forward,* the two need not be equal: planned (or *ex ante,* or expected) savings need not be equal to planned (*ex ante,* expected) investment. If so, a process is set in motion that makes realized (or *ex post*) savings and investment equal.

Suppose, the explanation runs, planned savings are less than planned investment. In other words, individuals and businesses are saving less out of their incomes than businesses are investing. Then either incomes rise and people find, to their surprise, that they have more savings than they expected (and realized savings equal realized investment); or else inventories are depleted through the heavy investment, and unplanned, lessened investment in inventories cancels out the excess of planned investment over planned savings (and realized savings equals realized investment).

This is an approach that should be used very cautiously. For, as one of its main authors has granted[9] even if planned savings equal planned investment, income might still rise or fall. It would rise if people expect their incomes to rise, and so increase their consumption spending; it would fall if people expect their incomes to fall, and so cut their consumption spending. The approach holds water only if one cautiously adds to a statement about inequality or equality of planned

---

9 Bertil Ohlin, "Some Notes on the Stockholm Theory of Savings and Investment," in the *Economic Journal,* Vol. XLVII (March and June, 1937) ; reprinted in *Business Cycle Theory,* pp. 87–130. Philadelphia: Blakiston, 1944. In the latter printing, see p. 103.

savings and investment, that the planned savings assume maintenance of current incomes.

The simplest, and universally acceptable, explanation of a change in incomes is that the total of spending (consumption plus investment, or consumption plus investment plus government spending) changes.

B. The Leverage Effect of Changes in Spending

Any change in expenditure for output is apt to have a magnified effect on incomes and employment. This is true whether we have decided to classify the original expenditure as investment, or consumption, or government spending. There usually is a magnified effect on incomes and employment because the original outlay stimulates a series of changed respendings. These effects will continue over a considerable period of time. If *A* spends more than before, and hence *B* finds his income up, *B* is likely to increase his consumption spending, which, in turn, will cause *C*'s income and then his consumption spending to rise, and so forth. Meanwhile, business managers may decide that in view of the increased consumer buying, they had better carry larger stocks of goods, and perhaps add additional machines to their plants. If so, investment also increases.

We might find, in the end, when all these effects have worked themselves out, that an original increased expenditure of $100 has led to a total increased (consumption and investment) expenditure in the economy of $400. We will say in this case that the *leverage* of the original expenditure was 4. Leverage, in other words, is the number by which we multiply an original expenditure in order to obtain the total changed expenditures which it brings about.[10]

That a leverage greater than 1 is likely will be clearer if we look, first, to the effect of the original expenditure on con-

---

[10] This concept of leverage is only slightly different from Professor Hansen's *leverage coefficient*, to whose treatment the following section is much indebted. Alvin H. Hansen, *Fiscal Policy and Business Cycles*, pp. 264 ff. New York: W. W. Norton, 1941.

sumption outlays, and second, to the effect of the original expenditure on investment outlays.

The Multiplier Effect

The effect of a change in spending on consumption expenditure is called the *multiplier effect.* Suppose that *A* spends $100 more than usual, drawing down his savings for the purpose or perhaps borrowing the money from his bank. Suppose also that people in the economy, as an average, spend on consumption 2/3 of any increase in their net incomes, saving or paying off debts with the remainder. In other words, the marginal propensity to consume is 2/3. This is, in fact, the rough estimate for the United States given by J. M. Clark and Lord Keynes.[11]

When *A* spends the $100, the person (or persons) to whom he pays the money, *B,* finds that his income is up by $100. *B* spends on consumption $66.67, which becomes income to a person (or persons) *C. C,* in turn, spends on consumption 2/3 of $66.67, or $44.45; and so forth. The series runs as follows:

ADDITIONAL INCOMES TO

B	*C*	*D*	*E*	*F*	*G*	*H*	*I*	*J*
$100	$66.67	$44.45	$29.63	$19.75	$13.17	$8.78	$5.85	$3.90

The effect of the original spending evidently goes on and on, but since some remains in the hands of each person in the series as a "leakage," the amount passed on steadily becomes smaller. At the point when *J* receives his $3.90, the total of all the additional incomes received is $292.20. If we followed this series of income increases further, we should find that the total of all additional incomes received approaches closer and closer to $300. This is the limit of the increases of income that were started by *A*'s original spending of $100, if people spend on consumption 2/3 of their marginal incomes.

---

11 "Income" is here taken as net income created, not as disposable income.

The multiplier, which relates the original change in spending to the total increase in incomes *eventually* resulting from the induced consumption, is in this case 3. The larger the marginal propensity to consume, the larger is the multiplier.

The value for the multiplier is best calculated as follows: Of each original dollar spent in our example, 2/3 was respent on consumption by the first income receiver, 2/3 of this 2/3 by the next, and so on. In other words, the total rise in incomes is $1 + 2/3 + (2/3)^2 + (2/3)^3 \ldots$ The fraction 2/3 is the marginal propensity to consume, which we have before defined as

$$\frac{\text{change in consumption}}{\text{change in income}}$$

or in symbols $\triangle C/\triangle Y$.

This means that we can express the value of the multiplier, k, by the following equation:

(1) $\qquad k = 1 + \Delta C/\Delta Y + (\Delta C/\Delta Y)^2 + \ldots\ldots (\Delta C/\Delta Y)^n,$

where n is the last income period we take account of.

Multiply equation (1) by $\triangle C/\triangle Y$, and we have:

(2) $\qquad k(\Delta C/\Delta Y) = \Delta C/\Delta Y + (\Delta C/\Delta Y)^2 + (\Delta C/\Delta Y)^3 + \ldots$
$$(\Delta C/\Delta Y)^{n+1}$$

Subtracting equation (2) from equation (1):

(3) $\qquad k - k(\Delta C/\Delta Y) = 1 - (\Delta C/\Delta Y)^{n+1}$

Or:

(4) $\qquad k(1 - \Delta C/\Delta Y) = 1 - (\Delta C/\Delta Y)^{n+1}$

Which means that:

(5) $\qquad k = \dfrac{1 - (\Delta C/\Delta Y)^{n+1}}{1 - \Delta C/\Delta Y}$

This is a general formula for the multiplier, for any kind of injection and for any number of time periods.

But what is the value of $(\triangle C/\triangle Y)^{n+1}$, when n, the number of income periods, is very large? The fraction $(\triangle C/\triangle Y)$, which we usually think of as being greater than zero and less than 1, is being multiplied by itself a large number of times—for example, $2/3 \times 2/3 \times 2/3 \times \ldots$ —and so comes to be of smaller and smaller value. Hence if n is very large, we can neglect $(\triangle C/\triangle Y)^{n+1}$ as being unimportantly small, and say approximately:

$$k = \frac{1}{1 - \triangle C/\triangle Y}$$

which is the ordinary, simplest formula for the multiplier.

The time required for multiplier effects

Of course, it takes time for the spending of the original $100 to affect successively these incomes. How long on the average is required for additional income of one person to become income for another? Estimates of this *marginal income period* for the United States run between 3 and 3½ months. Suppose we assume that the former estimate is about right. Then, after B in our example above receives his $100, 3 months go by on the average before C receives $66.67; 6 months go by before D receives $44.45; and so on. An infinitely long period of time (an infinite number of income periods) is, strictly speaking, required before the full effect of the original expenditure is worked out, and additional incomes resulting from it actually total $300. On the other hand, at the end of a year, 87 per cent ($260.50) of the full rise in income has been received; and at the end of two years, when J has received his increase of income, 97 per cent. The bulk of the stimulating effect on income and employment of changed expenditures occurs rather soon.

The total of leakages

When at the end of an infinite number of time periods the effect of the original new expenditure has completely worn off, the total of "leakages" all along the line—of savings or debt payments—equals the original expenditure. As much has been withdrawn from expenditure as was originally expended, and when this is true, the original stimulus is canceled out. For example, *B* withdrew from further spending $33.33, *C* withdrew $22.22, and so forth. When *J* received his income increase, $96.10 had leaked out from the income series. If we followed the series further, we should find leakages approaching $100, and as this occurs, the original injection of $100 is canceled out, and the total of additional incomes approaches $300.

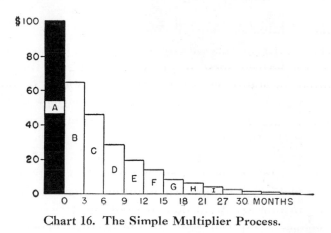

Chart 16. The Simple Multiplier Process.

We can graph the expansion of this multiplier process as shown in Chart 16. The shaded area is the original expenditure. The areas numbered 1, 2, 3 . . . are the secondary expenditures on consumption which are realized at the end of 3, 6, 9 months, and so forth. All of these represent *changes* above some basic level of income.

The multiplier effect of a continued injection of new expenditure

We have traced out over the course of months the effect of a *single* additional expenditure. Suppose that, instead, *repeated* additional expenditures are made. Then, each one of them will have its series of secondary expenditures. In Chart 17, we

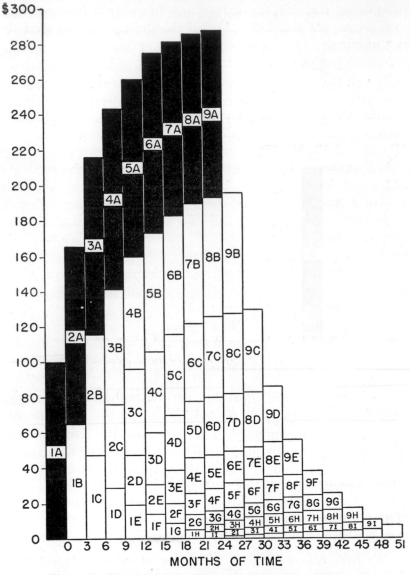

Chart 17. The Multiplier Process Following Repeated
Injections of New Expenditures.

show the cumulative effect of such repeated additional expenditures, assuming as above that the marginal propensity to consume remains 2/3, and that the average income period is 3 months.

Nine injections of new expenditure into the economy are represented, one at the beginning of each income period. In each case the original expenditure is shown by the dark rectangles 1A, 2A . . . and the series of consumption expenditures derivative from it by the light rectangles labeled 1B, 1C, 1D . . . and 2B, 2C, 2D . . . and so on.

As these successive new expenditures are made, the total of additional incomes received in any period mounts rapidly toward a limit of $300, or three times the new expenditure made every period. At the end of a year, 87 per cent of this maximum rise has been achieved. So long as the injection of $100 every period continues, incomes will approach closer and closer to the limit of $300 above the original level, assuming that the consumption and investment behavior of the economy remains otherwise unchanged.

But if the injection of $100 every period is stopped, then incomes rapidly fall back toward their old level. Chart 17 shows the effect of stopping the injection of new expenditure at the end of 24 months. One year afterward, incomes have fallen 80 per cent of the way back to their original level. There is, in brief, a multiple effect from a fall in expenditure, just as there is from a rise in expenditure.

The stability of the multiplier

Our example is based on rough estimates for the United States. It would appear, then, that it shows us approximately what we could expect out of the stimulus to consumption from a single new expenditure or repeated new expenditures. These expenditures might be made by the government, by foreign buyers, by businessmen who are investing, or by consumers who are splurging on a new consumption good. We might just as well think of the expenditure as 100 million dollars every three months, rather than $100 only, and thereby magnify all our figures by a million.

It is on the basis of reasoning similar to this that Lord Keynes, when he visited this country in 1934, predicted that if the United States government spent only 200 million dollars more every month than it took in through taxes, we should slump back to deepest depression; and that the spending of 400 million dollars would bring us full recovery.

But there are a number of considerations that make it hazardous to predict closely just how large the multiplier effect will be. (1) We have assumed that previous consumption and investment expenditures continue unchanged, but there might be outside causes of a change in consumption. And the derivative consumption expenditures illustrated above are rather likely to have an influence toward increasing investment. (This we discuss below.) On the other hand, it is possible that certain kinds of new expenditure—perhaps the government is increasing its debt or is thought to be spending ineffectively—will diminish business confidence, and so diminish also private investment. (2) The value of the multiplier is not a stable and unchanging figure. If people who receive the flows of new income have been unemployed before and have run up debts, they are apt to use a part of their new income to pay off these debts rather than spend on consumption. The multiplier is lower than it will be later on; the new funds are being soaked up in liquidating debts rather than having their full effect toward increasing consumption. There is also reason to think that changing distribution of income as incomes rise, the varying responses of consumer spending to income changes, and varying expectations of future income changes will affect the marginal propensity to consume, and so affect the value of the multiplier.

For these reasons, we cannot predict closely the amount of the stimulating effect on consumption from any given expenditure.

The Acceleration Effect

Changes in the demand for goods relatively close to consumption may give rise to much larger changes in the demand for (and output of) the capital goods used in their production. This relationship is known as *the acceleration effect.*

Suppose that 80 metal-forging machines are used in the production of lathes, and that 8 of these machines need to be replaced every year—that is, these machines last on the average 10 years.

1. If demand for lathes remains unchanged, the capital goods industry producing the machines will produce 8 per year.

2. But if demand for lathes should in some year rise by 10 per cent, then 88 forging machines would be required (assuming no change in techniques takes place allowing greater output from the existing machines). The capital goods industry must, therefore, produce 16 machines in that year: 8 for replacement and 8 for additions. A 10 per cent increase in demand for lathes has given rise to a 100 per cent rise in demand for the forging machines that makes lathes.

3. Suppose that through the next year demand stops rising, remaining constant at 10 per cent above its original level. Then a total of 88 forging machines are needed, of which 8 wear out in the course of the year and must be replaced.[12] The output of the forging-machine industry has fallen from 16 to 8, a decline of 50 per cent, merely because consumption is no longer rising.

4. Suppose, finally, that in the following year demand for lathes itself falls to the original level. Then, 80 machines are required. Since there were 88 at the beginning of the year and 8 wear out during the year, none need be produced. A decline of 9 per cent ($^8/_{88}$) in demand for the product nearer to consumption (lathes) has led to a complete shutdown in production of the product further from consumption (forging machines).

---

[12] In this year $1/_{10}$ of the original 80 will wear out. The 8 new machines produced the year before will not wear out.

The above example shows that a small change in demand for goods relatively close to consumption can transmit itself with accelerated force to capital goods industries.[13] Here is the basic element in explaining why the main capital goods industries, such as steel, are "prince or pauper" industries. While consumer spending is falling moderately, capital goods output collapses. (Over the years 1929–1932, consumption goods output fell 23 per cent; capital goods output fell 78 per cent.) And when consumption output is rising moderately, the capital goods industries are booming. (Over the years 1932–1938 when consumption goods output was rising 29 per cent, capital goods output was rising 240 per cent.)

Types of acceleration effects

The acceleration effect can be seen operative in three cases.

1. If the demand for the services of durable consumer goods (automobiles, washing machines, radios, refrigerators) varies, then demand for the capital instruments which make them is apt to vary in an accelerated fashion. If refrigerators last 14 years on the average,[14] then if demand for them drops by about one-seventh, none need be manufactured. But if demand rises a bit, then not only must those that wear out be replaced, but also an additional number must be produced in accord with the increased demand.

2. If demand for capital instruments changes, then demand for the capital equipment that makes these capital instruments can vary in an accelerated degree (that is, the acceleration effect moves in a direction away from the final consumption goods ultimately to be produced). This was our example above of the forging machines, which were used in making lathes.

---

13 It is only a *change* in consumption which influences the volume of net investment (which we define as a change in the total quantity of capital goods). The *level* of consumption (that is, any continued level of consumption) has no influence on net investment; it determines only the normal level of *replacement* investment.

14 —And their age distribution is random.

3. Finally, if the demand changes for any good which is carried in stock, there may be an acceleration effect. Suppose that demand for a good is running at the rate of 1000 units a week and that dealers are, on the average, accustomed to keeping an equal quantity in their inventories. Then their orders run also at the rate of 1000 a week. Suppose demand rises to 1100 a week; then the dealers, if they want to retain the old proportion between inventories and demand, must buy not only 1100 to equal their sales, but also 100 more for the increase in inventories, or 1200 in all. A 10 per cent rise in sales by the dealers has led to a 20 per cent rise in purchases by dealers. A similar acceleration effect follows from a downswing in sales.

The stability of the acceleration effect

As with the multiplier, we have reason to believe that acceleration also is not a reliable staff to lean on. Usually, we shall be uncertain how much acceleration to expect.

1. We have assumed above a fixed ratio between capital instruments or inventories and output. But if there is excess capacity of capital equipment or excessive inventories, as often there will be during depression, an increase of consumer demand will not have any acceleration effect, but merely cause some of the excess capacity or inventories to be absorbed. Or, if the capital equipment is improving in quality, so that productive efficiency is rising, then an increase in demand for its products need not stimulate any increase in its quantity.

2. We have assumed fixed durability of capital instruments—that they are worn out a given number of years after they were constructed. But the date when a capital instrument is worn out is, in fact, very uncertain, depending as it does on the care it receives, availability and cost of repair parts, the technical change going on, the cost of a new instrument, the interest rate, and so forth.

3. Finally, we have assumed that investment depends closely on current consumption. But much investment depends only on long-run prospects of returns. In the United States, canals,

railroads, and electric railways have persistently been constructed far ahead of effective demand, almost independent of
existing need.

In all that we have said about the acceleration principle, we
were relating *changes* in demand for goods relatively close to
consumption to the magnified (new) investment to which they
may lead. The new investment might be thought to lead
(through the multiplier effect) to further enlarged consumption changes, and so on indefinitely. But it turns out, in fact,
that in ordinary stable situations, the acceleration effect does
not alter the ultimate result that the multiplier effect alone
leads to. It only causes fluctuations around the path to that
result. In the longer run, therefore, we are justified in minimizing acceleration and in emphasizing the multiplier.

The acceleration principle is probably most useful in helping
us to understand how the expansion (or slowing up of contraction) and contraction (or slowing up of expansion) of a major
industry can have a magnified effect on supplying industries.
As examples, we might take the expansion of railroads in the
middle of the nineteenth century and the slackening of expansion toward the close of that century in their effects on steel
production and fabrication; or we might take the rise of the
automobile industry in the 1920's and its slackening in the
1930's in their effects on steel, rubber, plate glass, and other
contributing industries.

Conclusion on Leverage Effects

The *leverage* of any new expenditure is, we have seen, the
total increase in investment and consumption outlay resulting
per dollar of that new expenditure. Leverage is the total of the
multiplier and acceleration effects that work themselves out
over a period of time, though in ordinary cases, acceleration
only modifies the path taken to the same final level of income
as would have been achieved by the multiplier acting alone.

Leverage tends to magnify significantly the ultimate total
effect of any dollar of new expenditure. But the relevant in-

fluences are too complex and uncertain for us to have confidence that we can predict the exact magnitude of that total effect.

C. Business Cycle Experience

In primitive economies lowered production has been the simple consequence of physical events like war, pestilence, blight, fire, drought, and flood. And in the more developed economies of western Europe, as far back as the eighteenth century and before, there have been occasional flurries of speculation, with the prices of land, buildings, and securities rising to extravagant levels when people bought because other people were willing to buy rather than because of any reasonable long-run earning power of the assets.

But, in western Europe, the United States, and some other developed economies, there have been, since about the beginning of the nineteenth century, recurring periods of good times and bad times of a different sort. These fluctuations have penetrated generally through the economy and even through the world, as better communications have strengthened ties of all kinds, as trade and resulting interdependence have grown, and as complex money and banking systems have developed. The characteristic of "business cycles" since about 1800 is that, in their depression phases, there has been unemployment of available resources at times when people *need* goods and services as much as ever. This is a new phenomenon.

In the United States the acute crisis of 1837 followed heavy land speculation in new western territory, fed by expansion of bank lending. When banks could lend no more and were inclined to demand repayment of some of their existing loans, the boom ended. A fall in the price of cotton in London, crop failures, and the collapse of the large United States Bank and of other smaller banks intensified the collapse. Southern areas suffered most. Several of the southern states repudiated their debts—some attic trunks in the south still contain these bonds. Banks in the Tennessee region were forced to make the sad entry GTT—"Gone to Texas"—as the final item in many of their loan records. The crash was severe—but unemployment was not the important problem in depressions that it became later. A larger proportion of the work force then consisted of farmers and other independent businessmen. They could be distressed, but not unemployed.

Later business depressions repeat the persisting theme of banking trouble. 1857 saw the peak of another expansion, and a drastic crash. Cotton, slaves, and land had been rising in price; railroads were expanding. To finance the boom, capital was flowing in from Europe, and banks were extending credit freely. In 1857 an outflow of specie to Europe cut financial reserves and put pressure on banks, and some railroads failed when they could not borrow further to meet interest due on their bonds. The collapse of a major insurance and trust company spread general alarm: each bank and business tried to get outstanding debts paid off in specie. When people are demanding more specie than exists, some are sure to be disappointed. A number of banks failed, and general depression followed. Prices remained low until after the outbreak of the Civil War.

In 1873 again, a period of expansion—especially in railroads —and of extension of bank credit was followed by contraction of bank lending and depression. Outflow of specie to Europe in payment for rising imports was a major cause of financial contraction and bank failures. Depression lasted some four years. Recovery came in part because good grain crops in this country then found a booming market in Europe due to crop failure there.

The crisis of 1893 occurred when railroad bankrupties forced a number of banks also to fail. Uncertainty about the future of the gold standard discouraged business sentiment. Recovery came in 1896: there was a presidential election that guaranteed the gold standard, an inflow of specie from abroad into bank reserves, and other favorable developments in farming and industry.

In 1907 a brief but sharp financial crisis had repercussions

in stagnant trade and business failures. The financial tightness
was quickly relieved, in part by government credit; and by late
1908 recovery was under way. There was mild recession in 1910
and 1911, with revival before World War I.[15]

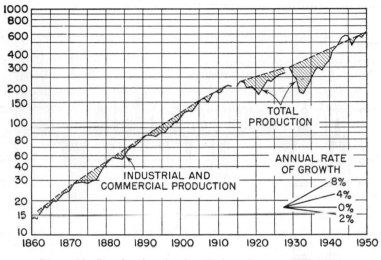

Chart 18. Production in the United States, 1860-1950.

Source: Data for 1860-1914, Industrial and Commercial Production from
E. R. Frickey, *Economic Fluctuations in the United States.* Cambridge:
Harvard University Press, 1942, p. 180. Data for 1915-1950 is taken from
Chart 1, p. 81 of this text. The barred areas are rough estimates of the loss
from underemployment of resources.

The charts attempt to portray the general level of business
activity since 1860. Chart 18 shows estimates of actual production on a ratio scale, so that any given slope represents a given
percentage rate of growth. The barred areas are rough measures of loss of production from underemployment of resources.
Chart 19, with data from different sources, shows business activity as deviations from a calculated "normal." But the decision as to what is normal business activity is a difficult and

---

15 A more complete summary of U. S. business cycle experience is given by
H. M. Somers in H. F. Williamson (editor), *The Growth of the American
Economy*, 2nd Ed. Chaps. 5, 17, 38. New York: Prentice-Hall, 1951.

partly arbitrary one, especially for recent years. What will seem a normal level of business activity for 1940 when we look back, not from 1950, but from 1980? A fringe of uncertainty is introduced into the chart from the operations performed on the original data.

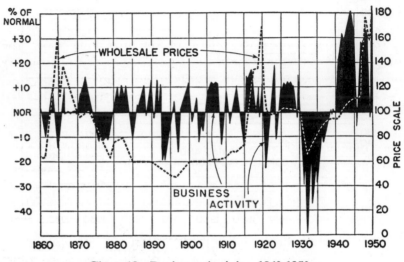

Chart 19. Business Activity, 1860-1950.

Source: Cleveland Trust Company. Business activity is shown here as deviations from a calculated "normal" level of activity. The basic data are for the most part measures of production.

"Long waves" in prices—the Kondratieff Cycle

There is convincing evidence that over the past 150 years, in the United States and in certain countries of western Europe, there have been *long waves* in the level of average prices, including interest rates—long periods of rising prices, followed by long periods of falling prices, followed in turn by rising prices, and so forth. There is also some evidence (the inadequacy of data bars a firmer statement) that there may have been parallel waves in rates of industrial growth and geographic expansion. During these upswings of prices, business contractions tend to be relatively short; during downswings, business contractions are longer and perhaps more severe.[16]

Approximate dates for these periods or long waves in the United States appear to be:

Long Wave	Rising Prices	Falling Prices
1	1790–1814	1814–1844
2	1844–1873	1873–1896
3	1896–1929	1929– ?

During the rising-prices phase of the first long wave, the major influences appear to be (a) repercussions in this country of the heavy expenditures of European government during the Napoleonic wars and (b) the industrial opportunities afforded by expansion in the use of Watt's steam engine, by improvements in textile machinery and by other innovations of what has come to be known as the Industrial Revolution. After 1815 government expenditures dwindled off, and the increased flow of products from the new machinery and processes depressed prices. In consequence production had to be adapted to worsened cost-price conditions, and resources shifted from unprogressive to progressive industries.

The good times following the middle 1840's are dominated in the United States by heavy investment in railroads and by

---

[16] The basic study on this matter available in English is that of the Soviet economist Nikolai D. Kondratieff, "The Long Waves in Economic Life," *Review of Economic Statistics*, Vol. XVII (November, 1935), pp. 105–115.

Violent attacks were made by other Soviet economists on Kondratieff's work. The main reason lay in the implication that capitalism would revive from its epochs of "bad times," since the Kondratieff cycles were temporary deviations from the continuous course of capitalist evolution. The leaders of Soviet Russia anticipated the period following 1914–1920 to be one of wars and revolutions preceding the final collapse of "capitalism." But if the period were only the downswing of a Kondratieff long wave, there would be an upward turning point and better times ahead. The official Russian Encyclopedia published in 1929 referred to Kondratieff's views in one sentence: "This theory is wrong and reactionary."

In the fall of 1930 Kondratieff was arrested and deported to Siberia without trial. The outside world has not heard of him since.

An excellent detailed survey of the controversy (the source of the above note) and a criticism of Kondratieff's findings is given in George Garvy, "Kondratieff's Theory of Long Cycles," *Review of Economic Statistics*, Vol. XXV (November, 1943), pp. 203–220.

government expenditures incident to the Civil War. The discovery of gold in California in 1849 worked toward expanding the money supply; hence toward higher prices, hence toward heavier business investment.

After the 1870's railroad investment slackened toward a steady level, and declined in the 1890's. A fall in the rate of addition to the monetary gold supply from the early 1870's to the 1890's furnished a depressing influence on demand and prices, and so also on the marginal efficiency of investment.

The price upswing and general prosperity of 1900—1929 seems in large part identified with the rise of four major industries. (*a*) The automobile industry is the most important of the four. A negligible infant in 1900, with a production of 4000 cars, it had expanded to an annual output of 5.6 million cars by 1929, carrying along in its wake the auxiliary industries of road construction (a government-directed industry), petroleum, steel, glass, and rubber—until, it is argued, there is no business in the United States that does not contribute goods or services, directly or indirectly, toward the making of cars. (*b*) Electric power, in which investment was likewise negligible in 1900, expanded rapidly thereafter to a maximum investment expenditure of over 8 billion dollars in the 1920's. (*c*) Street railways were growing most rapidly in the decade of 1900—1909. It was the most important of these four industries in that decade, and also in the previous decade. (*d*) Investment in the telephone industry rose sharply after 1900, reaching its maximum also in the 1920's. Aside from these four industries, we should include in our list of stimulating factors the very important effects of heavy government expenditures during World War I and, in the 1920's, the housing boom.

Throughout this century and a half, some injustice is done by concentrating attention on the few "major" industries, because sometimes the total investment in "minor" industries was increasing at just as fast a pace. The major industries are the most conspicuous, but not the only ones of importance.

The onset of the great depression of the 1930's

Why was there a collapse of output and employment after 1929? This is the 64-dollar question repeatedly asked and answered as often with varying degrees of profoundness and positiveness. And there is valid ground for difference of opinion, since there is no sure criterion for degree of emphasis that ought to be put on each element, and since one can speak in terms of immediate, or of distant and abstract causes.

Our answer is brief, and in terms of immediate causes. The depression of the 1930's came upon us when and because private expenditure on investment dropped. There was an accumulation of causes for lowered private expenditure.

1. A conspicuous cause lies in the speculative fevers of 1927–1929 afflicting real estate and the stock market. Such speculation was bound to lead to reaction, even to collapse, once the people gambling in these markets—innocent of serious knowledge of long-run values, and hence of stable convictions—came to doubt whether prices would move upward forever.

Once the decline began, the vulnerable mortgage situation of farmers and of urban holders of real estate piled despair upon distress. Collapsing real estate values, as foreclosed properties were unloaded on the market, directly forced a further contraction of construction expenditures and undermined the position of banks holding mortgage loans. More important, and with continuing repercussions, was the crushing psychological effect of the loss of farms and homes.

2. Faults of structure and of policy in the banking system had their share in converting recession into catastrophe. In the early years of depression our monetary authorities permitted to take place, despite some countermeasures, an unexampled contraction of the money supply. In three years, 1929 to 1933, the quantity of money dropped by one-quarter.[17]

---

17 Money is taken as demand deposits adjusted plus currency outside of banks, on June 30 of these years. The actual figures are, respectively, 26.2 and 20.2 billion dollars.

This was in large measure a result of lessening desire by businessmen to borrow from banks for investment purposes. But it was also a *cause* of their lessened investment, in that banks generally, hard hit by shrinking reserves and falling value of assets (in part results of monetary contraction), were less able to lend even to those businessmen who still wanted to borrow.

As the depression deepened, three waves of bank failures spread economic paralysis, and intensified the growing sentiment that all was lost. These failures would have been, in the main, avoidable had salvaging operations been undertaken in time. But the banking system of the United States is peculiarly subject to distress: it is characterized by the existence of multitudes of small banks—in contrast with the systems of Canada, England, and other industrial countries. This has its advantage in dispersing financial power. It also has its disadvantage in the weakness of the small bank, due to its substantial dependence on the fortunes of a particular community and to its often low level of management ability.

3. The speculative and banking factors we have mentioned would have had their effects postponed and diminished had there been strong incentives for investment inherent in the situations of a number of major industries. But it appears likely that the automobile industry, and perhaps several others, had exhausted, at least temporarily, their possibilities of expansion. (The construction industry, following its own peculiar pattern of behavior, had been declining since 1927.)

When technical advance, population growth, and the like stimulate the development of a new industry, that development takes place over the course of some years or decades. The rate of expansion is limited by the often gradual increase of demand and by the competition of other industries for raw materials, labor, and managers. But as the industry grows beyond a certain point, it comes upon an increasing obstacle: that the wants of consumers for its product are becoming more and more nearly satisfied. An increased output per capita can be sold only at a lower real price. For some kinds of products, price will drop drastically with only a moderate increase of output.

If, for example, two-thirds of American families have a new or used car, automobile manufacturers may well find that they can increase appreciably the number of cars in the hands of the public only by reducing prices considerably. And costs may be high enough so that they are unwilling or unable to cut prices much.[18] If this is their situation, automobile manufacturers will not want to expand plant and equipment by further investing.

If a number of dominant industries have shrunk their investment outlays, one or several industries that are in a better position will be unable to stem the general tide of contraction. The latter industries must expect now, not the demand of normal times, but the dwindled demand of depression, and they will view this lessened demand through the gray-green spectacles of loss of confidence.

4. As fourth among the influences causing the 1929 collapse one may list a number of foreign policies and events having both real and psychological repercussions in this country. After 1925 many of the developed countries of western Europe raised their tariffs skyward, blocking imports from agricultural countries and forcing the latter off the gold standard in 1928, 1929, and after. The gathering collapse of the gold standard had its effect on confidence abroad and in the United States, and, with other causes, led to a sharp decline in our foreign lending after the middle of 1928, and induced a change in type of lending, from long term to short term. This in turn, coupled with other causes, led eventually toward a decline in our exports and also toward the later collapse of the banking system of central Europe, set off by the failure of the Credit-Anstalt bank of Vienna in 1931.

---

18 Costs may not fall greatly even though raw materials are in abundant supply and a good deal of labor is unemployed, because of rigid (monopolistic) pricing—that is, monopolistic policies on the part of raw material suppliers and union stipulations on the part of labor.

We could give further details of the causes of the 1929 debacle, and of the decline into deep depression that followed. No two students of the subject would, in a detailed list, include quite the same items or emphasize them in the same way. But we can bring strategic causes together under the heading, "What caused investment spending to decline." [19]

Secular Stagnation?

At the end of the 1930's when, after much thought and government effort, we still had not attained high employment, much discussion developed over the question of secular stagnation—whether or not the United States and the western world generally would experience chronically insufficient demand during the rest of the century and beyond so far as one could see.

The argument that the United States economy is faced with secular stagnation can be briefly formulated. We have never in peacetime years experienced satisfactory levels of employment and output except when investment was heavy. Now investment is called forth by a rise in the marginal efficiency of capital. This rise is in turn induced mainly by factors associated with (1) population growth and geographic expansion, and (2) inventions. Population growth is argued to be favorable to investment because it leads to demand for increased housing,[20] government and business buildings, railroads and roads, water and sewage systems, and so forth, and for equipment for the larger number of workmen. Inventions give profitable opportunity to individual businessmen to increase output from a given force.

As output has increased in the past half-century, the quantity of capital equipment has increased by about the same proportion as output. This is a rather surprising conclusion, but

---

[19] For policies used against the 1930's depression, see pp. 179-185.

[20] More accurately, an increased number of *families* is closely correlated with a demand for more housing, and this is not the same thing as an increase in population. *Cf.* p. 227.

the statistics leave no doubt of its approximate truth: over recent decades in the United States we have retained about the same amount of capital equipment for each unit of output.[21]

The argument continues to the effect that the end of the first kind of stimulus to investment is close upon us. Population in the United States is still increasing, but at a declining rate. The *rate* of population increase began to decline after the middle of the nineteenth century, and has continued to decline until recently. In the decade of the 1920's, our population rose by 17 millions; in the decade of the 1930's the increase was about 9 millions. War and prosperity in the 1940's brought a remarkable rise of 19 million.

Most population specialists, though they confess there is more short-run variability in birth rates than anyone thought possible a few years ago, still think that the long-run trend of population has probably not changed. They still expect that the United States population will be rising only very slowly, or be stable, by the year 2000. If they are right and there are no new surprises in the offing, we face, from an economic point of view, a basically optimistic prospect. We are *not* faced, as Malthus feared, with a multiplication of mouths until our average standard of living falls to a minimum of subsistence. But there may be disadvantage from the viewpoint of the effect on employment.

Furthermore, ever since the passing of the western frontier a half century ago, opportunities for the kinds of investment occasioned by people living over a wider geographical area—new roads and railroads, buildings, and utilities—have been narrowing.

Professor Hansen estimates that population increase and geographical expansion taken together were responsible for

21 The figures of Paul Douglas are that the quantity of real capital in the United States (1890–1922) rose at the rate of 4 per cent a year. The rise in output appears to have been slightly less than this. *Theory of Wages*, pp. 464–465. New York: Macmillan, 1934.

something like half of the real investment of the nineteenth century.[22]

The question therefore confronts us as to whether, in the future, investment stimulated by inventions will expand additionally enough to make up for the ending of population growth and geographical expansion. One can think of inventions that will lead to much investment, among them electronics, plastics, atomic energy, and synthetic textiles. But, of course, we have had in the past also hugely expanding industries, such as railroads, canals, and the electrical and automobile industries. If one is pessimistic about the chance that innovatory investment can fill the gap, then he expects "secular stagnation," and anticipates that our primary problem is not going to be that of controlling the ups and downs of the business cycle, but of lifting ourselves above a persisting level of heavy unemployment and inadequate output.

There is reason to question the secular-stagnation thesis. We mention four sources of doubt.

1. If our population ceases to grow, it will be composed to a greater extent of older people, to a smaller extent of younger people. In 1870 there were about 29 people over 65 years of age for each 1000 people in the population; by 1940 there were about 68. Now, older people are to a considerable extent dissavers rather than savers: many of them are using up the savings of their youth, either directly or by using up annuities they have bought. Few of them are trying to accumulate savings as people do when they are younger. In brief, an older society is likely to want to save less,[23] and to this extent our problem of finding investment outlets for savings is lessened.

2. To some extent, savings are made for specific purposes—

---

[22] *Fiscal Policy and Business Cycles*, pp. 358–360. New York: W. W. Norton, 1941.

[23] On the other hand, individuals in a growing society may be *able* to save little, because of the expense of rearing children.

to buy a house or a car or to obtain college education for children. Some of these purposes will be less important when the population is no longer growing, and to that extent, savings will be diminished also.

3. The extent of demand for housing is a special problem —and a very important one. Residence construction made up from one-tenth to three-tenths of total (gross) investment between 1919-1935. The demand for housing units depends not so much on total population as on numbers of families. The family is ordinarily the buying unit. How much a family is willing to spend for housing accommodation depends mainly on two factors: its income and the size of the family. The size of the family has been shrinking in the United States in recent decades, and the interesting question arises as to what effect this will have on demand for housing. Smaller families "need" less housing; on the other hand, at any given income level they are able to afford more. Data from the census of 1940 gives evidence that the latter dominates: within any given income level, the smaller the size of the family, the greater the expenditure on housing. This conclusion is comforting: increased expenditure per family for housing will tend to offset other depressing influences on investment from the predicted slowly rising or stationary population.

4. Finally, there is the appeal to experience. Certain European countries have been far along the road to population decline. England and Wales, Sweden, and Austria, for example, had before the war net reproduction rates so low that their populations were tending to fall by 50 per cent within 60 years. And yet such countries were not in peacetime necessarily depressed. Some of them got along very well, and where there was low investment, it seemed more obviously explained by other causes than population decline. Economies seem to be able to adapt themselves to declining numbers.

It appears, therefore, that although the argument that our economy confronts secular stagnation is impressive, it is much less than conclusive.[24] And of course, tendencies within the private economy can be completely swamped by government taxing and spending policies. In the spring of 1951 it seemed likely that heavy government expenditures would continue for a long time, mainly because of continuing international tension.

---

[24] For an impressive argument against the stagnation thesis, see George Terborgh; *The Bogey of Economic Maturity*. Chicago: Machinery and Allied Products Institute, 1945.

CHAPTER THIRTEEN

Some Doubtful Analyses and Proposals

NOT ALL ANALYSES OF EMPLOYMENT RUN IN TERMS OF THE consumption - savings - investment reasoning we have given. Today the difference among trained economists is usually one of emphasis and wording, and so is not substantial. Sometimes, especially as we go back to the past, the difference is real. It is helpful in understanding the problem of employment to look at several questionable analyses, to see where they are partial or wrong.

Special Views on the Cause of Unemployment

Say's Law

Many of the economists of the nineteenth century denied that it is possible for general unemployment ever to appear, on the grounds that so long as human wants are not completely filled—and when have they ever been?—a demand for labor exists. This reasoning was in the background of the extreme doctrine of the early French economist, J. B. Say. He was willing to grant that a glut of goods would appear, and hence unemployment, "if we lived on bread and water and did not employ our savings,"[1] but that men should refuse to buy as much of commodities as their means allowed seemed as unlikely to him as that the moon should fall upon the earth. More exactly, he wrote:

---

[1] *Letters to Malthus.* London, 1821. Reprinted 1936, George Harding's Bookshop, Ltd., p. 37.

A product is no sooner created than it, from that instant, affords a market for other products to the full extent of its own value. When the producer has put the finishing hand to his product, he is most anxious to sell it immediately, lest its value should vanish in his hands. Nor is he less anxious to dispose of the money he may get for it; for the value of money is also perishable. But the only way of getting rid of money is in the purchase of some product or other. Thus the mere circumstance of the creation of one product immediately opens a vent for other products.[2]

One can agree with Say that few of us are misers and want money for its own sake. We want money in order to spend. But it is also evident that we may decide to postpone the spending of part of our incomes (that is, save), and such postponement does not necessarily imply that other people and organizations in the economy are spending an equal amount in excess of their incomes, which is necessary if total expenditure remains unchanged.[3] In other words, money may be kept idle (hoarded), or it may be destroyed by contraction of the banking system—and so purchasing power falls.

Our statistics suggest what our reasoning predicts: that one kind of private expenditure — consumption expenditure — usually depends fairly stably on income created, but that the other kind—investment expenditure—has a strong dynamics of its own. Government expenditure does not necessarily vary in an appropriately offsetting way. Hence the total of these three kinds of expenditure cannot be trusted to remain at a stable and adequately high level.

But Say's kind of thinking was not unrealistic in view of the kind of world he lived in.

1. To accuse Say of neglecting the peculiarities of money is a less serious charge than if we made it against a present-day economist. Money was less important in 1820: the western

---

[2] *A Treatise on Political Economy*, Fourth edition, pp. 78–79; translated from the French by C. R. Prinsep. Philadelphia: John Grigg, 1830.

[3] Say appears to assume that prices are rising: "the value of money is also perishable." If people expect prices to rise, their buying now will be stimulated. But, by the same token, if they expect prices to fall, their buying now is curtailed.

world was closer to a barter economy. In the United States of 1840 quantity of money was 10 per cent of the value of the national income; by 1900, 55 per cent; by 1940, 85 per cent. There has been a growing possibility of "investing in cash," and so of withdrawing money from purchasing.

2. In Say's time a much larger proportion of total output was made up of consumption goods and non-durable goods. Consumption goods tend to be bought in relatively sustained volume, and nondurables, once produced, must be promptly sold.

3. The greater proportion of simple, direct processes of production in Say's time blocked the operation of the acceleration principle, with its influence toward magnifying changes in consumer demand.

4. The rise in real income in the last century is a source of instability. As the most urgent wants have been more fully satisfied, wants have become increasingly peripheral and postponable, and so saving competes more strongly against current wants.

5. In the small shops and on the farms of Say's time variable costs (costs whose total changes when output changes) were a smaller proportion of total costs. In consequence, there was a general tendency, in times of slackened demand, toward sustaining output at lower prices rather than toward cutting output and maintaining prices. Consider the small farmer, as a type of the producer of Say's period. His running costs consist mainly of his labor and that of his family (that is, they are negligible in terms of money). His chief money costs of production are likely to be taxes and the payment on the mortgage —fixed costs, which do not change with changing output. Hence, in times of low prices he may well work all the harder and produce all the more to meet his fixed payments. In contrast, producers with high variable costs tend in times of low demand to cut output and maintain price, rather than the reverse. (Compare pp. 111 ff.)

6. Finally, in Say's time government expenditure was

usually a very small part of total expenditure. This is no longer true. As government expenditure grows in relative size, it must be taken into account, either as a source of instability, or as a possible offset to the instability of private expenditure.

Say's analysis fitted his world fairly well. But despite the fact that the world was changing in the nineteenth century, many classical economists repeated his reasoning without change.

The argument that general unemployment is caused by rigid wages

The long line of classical economists who accepted Say's doctrine in one formulation or another agreed that the problem of unemployment is not important. The economy constantly tends, they reasoned, toward full employment. If we do not have it, it is because of temporary, frictional causes, which the natural working of the economy tends steadily to eliminate.[4] In one evolved form, the reasoning runs that general unemployment in the society can only be explained by excessively high wages.

It is important to notice that the effect of lowered wages in some one firm, industry, or occupation is not in question. Agreement is unanimous that the effect of such a local wage drop is to increase employment in that firm, industry, or occupation. There is a favorable substitution effect, and a favorable expansion effect: (1) More labor will be used because it is now relatively cheaper than the machinery and materials used in production, and hence will be substituted where possible for these other resources. (2) More labor will be used also because the lowered costs in the area where wages have dropped tend toward lowered prices, and hence expanded output, which, in turn, requires more of all resources, including labor. If wage

---

[4] Say likewise admitted that there might be a temporary overproduction of a particular kind of commodity or service, above what would be bought at the usual price. In other words, he granted that there might be temporary unemployment (of a sort we have called *frictional*) because the right man is not in the right place at the right time.

rates drop 20 per cent in the rubber products industry, there is no doubt that the effect will be to increase the quantity of labor hired there.

But this is not the issue. The issue is what would happen if wages dropped 10, 20, or 30 per cent for *all* employees in the nation. Would employment increase?

It is easy to find businessmen arguing that employment would increase, that the way out of depression is through reduction of wage rates. Professor Taussig presented the businessman's reasoning (and the view of many classical economists) in this way. He assumed, to begin with, that total demand can be relied on to continue undiminished:

> [It is an erroneous notion] that lavish expenditure creates a demand for labor, and is good for laborers. On this ground luxury and extravagance of all sorts have been commended. . . . The fallacy that underlies it has often been pointed out. That which is saved is spent quite as much as that which is not saved. . . . The money which is put by is turned over to someone else, usually to a person engaged in operations of production. It is simply spent in a different way.[5]

If our savings (what we do not spend on consumption out of our net incomes) promptly flow through a bank or other intermediary into the hands of someone who does spend them, then of course (as we have reasoned above), there is no chance for total spending in a society to fall below its current level, and hence no chance for unemployment to grow.[6] But, awkwardly enough, heavy unemployment often exists. How can Professor Taussig and the classical economists explain it?

The essential answer is that it is explained just as any other surplus of unsold goods is explained: the price of labor is too high. If you lower the wage rate enough, employers will buy more labor, and unemployment will shrink. If it were not for

5 F. W. Taussig, *Principles of Economics*, Second edition revised, Vol. II, pp. 192–193. New York, 1915. Copyright 1939 by The Macmillan Company and used with their permission.

6 Assuming that there is no depressing influence from the government budget.

the "frictions" of time and place that we have mentioned—seasonal fluctuations, changes in consumers tastes, technological changes, the slowness of labor and industry to move, and the like—unemployment would altogether disappear.

Taussig's reasoning is plausible enough. If we accepted it we should feel, like others of the older economists, that there exists no problem of deep unemployment unless unions and government regulations prevent wages from falling, as is their healthy tendency when there is a large amount of unemployment.

But if we are tempted to follow this doctrine, let us reflect that although classical economists and businessmen often recommend a drop in wage rates as a cure for depression, they *never* urge in time of inflation—of booming prices and high employment—that a rise in wage rates is the cure. On the contrary, they seem confident that this would be adding fuel to the flame. We may wonder suddenly whether a selfish interest is not, consciously or unconsciously, involved—that since wages are a cost to businessmen, they are normally disposed to regard lower wages as a blessing, and seize upon the catastrophe of depression as a convenient excuse for emphasizing what is their chronic preference. This would not explain the view of Taussig, who was a conscientious scientist, but it certainly is in the background of many similar analyses.

Our distrust of the above reasoning is apt to grow when we remember that employees and union leaders argue frequently and emphatically that the way out of depression and unemployment is to *raise* wage rates. For, they reason, wages are purchasing power, and unless consumption-spending is maintained at a high level, depression must follow. The Steel Workers' Union during the 1946 strike for higher wage rates broadcast over the radio a tune whose plausible refrain was: "Money in the pocket is money to spend."

But what if employers hire decidedly fewer workmen when the cost of labor is raised? Then total labor incomes and spending by labor would be less.[7]

It looks as if these two arguments cancel each other, or, more accurately, as if neither one is satisfactory.

We return, then, to the reasoning we have developed earlier. The effect of lowered wage rates must be found in their influence on consumption and investment spending. (Of course, lower wages and prices would lead to higher employment *if* total money demand remains unchanged, but the precise question is *whether* total demand remains unchanged.)

What will be the effects of lowered wage rates on consumption and investment spending?

1. The most important consequence is probably to be found in people's expectations of future prices. Lower wages mean lower costs and (if administered price policy does not prevent) lower prices. Will people expect wages and prices to keep on falling? If so, they have reason to postpone their consumption and investment to a later date. (Why should we buy today a gadget for $10 that later on we can get for $8?) This means that the wage cut has tended toward more unemployment. But, on the other hand, if people think that wages and prices have now reached bottom and later on will rise, their consumption and investment buying will be encouraged. Our wage cut will then have had its intended effect toward stimulating employment.

2. If, when we lower wages, prices fall, the worth in terms of goods of such quantities of money as people have at their disposal[8] is increased. If their cash balances are worth more in

---

[7] The *wage rate* (pay per hour, week, and so forth) is distinctly different from *total wages*, which equals the wage rate times the hours (weeks, and so forth) of labor employed. It is, therefore, possible for the wage rate to be increasing while total wages are decreasing, and *vice versa*. Suppose that when the wage rate is $6 a day, 1000 workers are employed in a given plant. Total wages are $6000. If, when the wage rate falls to $5, the management decides to hire 1500 workers, total wages rise to $7500.

It is total wages, not the wage rate, which is to be closely identified with purchasing power.

[8] This includes not only pocket money but also deposits in the bank and claims on cash, such as insurance policies and loans outstanding.

real terms, they may be encouraged to spend more on consumption out of current incomes—that is, their consumption will be increased. Also, people may be encouraged to lend out more readily if the real value of their cash balances is increased. This will tend to lower the interest rate, and to some extent to encourage investment—though, as we have seen, the interest rate is probably not a very important influence on investment.

3. The fall in wage rates and prices will affect the distribution of real income. This may to some extent affect the total of expenditure (pp. 149-150).

4. We should notice finally that, if when costs fall, prices also fall, a given consumption and investment expenditure will bring about a larger volume of production and employment than if prices had been maintained. Also, there will be stimulus from an increased volume of net exports out of the country. This will be important only if foreign trade is large compared to domestic trade.

In view of these consequences of lowered wage rates (and the ramifications may be very complex) we are forced to conclude that the *net effect is uncertain.* There are certain favorable consequences, but it is possible that these would be completely overcome by others, especially adverse expectations of further price changes. This is not a trustworthy road out of depression and unemployment.

Do savings inevitably cause unemployment?

We have surveyed briefly two parallel views on unemployment: first, that it could not exist unless caused by temporary frictions, and second, that one kind of friction might be permanent—wages might be kept "too high" and so lead to chronic unemployment. We have found reason to reject both doctrines. A third doctrine is worth looking at—namely, that savings inevitably cause unemployment. With this doctrine, one may associate such names as those of Marx, Foster and Catchings, and Major Douglas, though these gentlemen would be surprised to find themselves in the same company, and though grouping them together does violence to the details of their thoughts. Marx holds that inevitably consumers cannot buy as much as the capitalist machine can produce.[9] Foster and Catchings find that the existence of savings inevitably causes purchasing power to be less than the total value of goods coming on the market for sale.[10] Douglas thinks that part of the value of goods coming on the market goes into certain B payments made to other businesses rather than to individuals, and hence the total purchasing power of individuals is always less than the total value of goods coming on the market.[11] (These B payments we might term the *savings of business.*)

Our analysis has already undermined these doctrines. Of course, it is true that consumers do not receive enough income to buy all the output of the economy. But the output of the economy does not consist only of consumer goods: it consists also of investment (or capital) goods and the goods and services purchased by government. The real question is whether the buying of consumption goods plus the buying of investment goods and the purchases of government bodies are all together sufficient to absorb the output of the economy at full employment. The fact that savings exist or that they tend to be large does not necessarily lead to unemployment—not if the sum of investment spending and the government deficit is equally large. Neither the investment spending of businesses nor government spending is limited by the current level of consumption. Investment spending is determined mainly by expectations of returns in the future, and perhaps the distant future. Government spending is determined in large part by non-economic—that is, political and social—considerations.

---

9 See for example *Das Kapital*, Vol. III, Part I, p. 231; or the account of Marx's theory in M. Dobb, *Political Economy and Capitalism*, Chap. IV. New York: International Publishers, 1937.

10 W. T. Foster and W. Catchings, *Money*. Boston: Houghton Mifflin, 1923; and *Profits*. Boston: Houghton Mifflin, 1925.

11 C. H. Douglas, *The Control and Distribution of Production*, pp. 19–20. London: Palmer, 1922.

In conclusion: Savings, or large savings, are perfectly compatible with full employment. When found together with full employment, they simply mean that the economy is accumulating capital plant and equipment and/or that the government is running a deficit. The former may go on indefinitely, as it has already gone on for centuries; and the latter, we shall see, has no close limit.

Proposed Remedies for Unemployment

Stamped money

One of the simplest proposals for increasing total spending, and hence employment, is that of introducing *stamped money*. During a time of falling prices and deepening depression, people are disposed to postpone expenditure until prices are lower and to save up against the rainy day which is visibly approaching. Suppose, then, that we replace the ordinary paper money in existence with money that deteriorates in value as time goes on[12]. Each dollar bill might, for example, be worth 99 cents a week after original issue, 98 cents in two weeks, and so forth. There might be provision that the dollar bill could be kept up to its full value by the weekly purchase of a one-cent stamp to be pasted on the back of the bill in its proper square. Every individual, therefore, has cogent reason for spending his dollar bills promptly. The velocity of circulation of money, it is argued, will rise, and purchasing power will expand; and this is what we want.

This plan for expanding total expenditure was originated by Silvio Gesell, a German businessman who migrated to Argentina in 1887, and whose experience in that country with prolonged depression led him to think seriously about measures for economic reform. The plan has been tried in the

---

12 The Aztecs of Mexico had developed such a currency before Cortez landed. Cacao beans were the usual money. A slave could be bought for 100 cacao beans; taxes and debts were payable in them. Large bars of crude cacao were the "monetary reserve" of the government. The cacao deteriorated in time, hence it could not be hoarded for long periods. The money had to be spent or eaten while it was fresh.

towns of Schwanerkirchen in Bavaria, and Wörgl in Austria, and in at least 19 towns of the United States. The most extensive trial was made in the province of Alberta, Canada, under Premier Aberhart. In August, 1936 the issue of stamped money was commenced by the Province, through payments to the unemployed and to government employees. The provisions were as we have indicated: On the back of each of 262,000 dollar bills issued was space for 104 one-cent stamps. One stamp was to be attached every week. At the end of two years, when 104 stamps would have been pasted on the back, the bills were to be redeemed at face value. The provincial treasury would have a 4-cent margin, most of which would be clear profit.

In order to keep the bills circulating at full value, the provincial treasury pledged itself to accept them in payment for taxes and other obligations, whether the two years were up or not.

In consequence, the bills did not circulate rapidly from hand to hand among the general public as was hoped, but instead flowed rather promptly in the channel of least resistance back to the treasury. The treasury was the only willing receiver of the money: all other individuals and firms preferred to receive and hold assets that did not cost them 1 cent per dollar per week. Within seven weeks of the first issue, almost half of the money issued had been returned to the treasury; within fourteen weeks 86 per cent. Within eight months, 95 per cent had returned, and the scheme was abandoned[13].

Could a stamped-money scheme serve as an effective remedy against depression? We may perhaps neglect the nuisance and loss of time involved in buying stamps every week and sticking them on. More important is the consideration that people would in various ways avoid the use of stamped money, and hence the need for buying the stamps. They would barter goods so far as that was convenient or simply put down credits

---

[13] Margaret Myers, *Monetary Proposals for Social Reform*, pp. 157–163. New York: Columbia University Press, 1940.

or debits on account books, and so avoid the use of the money. And, most important, they would flee to the use of any un-stamped kinds of money or money substitutes, such as checks and money orders. (One element in the failure of the Alberta experiment was that Dominion currency, which required no stamps, circulated side by side with the provincial stamped money.) People would to some extent also put their assets into the form of inventories of real goods (flour, metal products, cloth). This might be thought to some extent desirable be-cause it encourages the production of the goods. But it is a real cost since the excessive inventories are not needed for con-sumption purposes and since they are subject to deterioration over time.

Suppose, therefore, we tax all money and money substitutes: all banking accounts will be subject to a weekly or monthly tax; all common money, paper money as well as coins, will be subject to stamping or taxing. To be complete, all barter and bookkeeping arrangements would also have to come under the tax rules. The mechanics of the matter will be difficult, especially the taxing of fractional currency—but suppose we manage it. We then meet a further objection, that this stimulus to the rate of spending (velocity of circulation) of money is an inflexible stimulus. Inflation (that is, a drastic rise in prices) is hardly less menacing an evil in the economy than depression and unemployment. Can we be sure our measures will not push us into a violent inflation, and that our last state is not worse than our first? We might perhaps, to meet this danger, try to arrange for flexible taxes or stamp values—raising them when we fear depression, lowering them when we fear infla-tion—though these measures would add further to our admin-istrative problems, and might anyway be inadequate to offset an inflation or collapse that is well under way.

It is clear that the difficulties of this method are so consider-able that we should do well to investigate further, and see whether some better depression remedy is not available.

A social dividend

Major Douglas, pursuant to his contention that purchasing power is always less than the value of output,[14] suggests that a fixed payment (a social credit, or national dividend) should be paid every week to each individual. Similarly, the Townsend Plan has advocated fixed pensions to aged persons. The "Thirty-Dollars-Every-Thursday" or "Ham-and-Eggs" plan was a California version of the Townsend Plan. It was expertly promoted, and came up for vote twice, in 1938 and 1939, only to be rejected both times. The scheme provided that a $30 weekly payment be made to aged persons in bills that should be receivable in trade and for state taxes. These bills were to be stamped money: a 2-cent stamp was to be attached every week, so that by the end of one year the state would acquire a retirement fund of $1.04, with 4 cents extra for its trouble.

1. Most social dividend plans are subject to the criticism of rigidity. It might, from the viewpoint of increasing purchasing power, be acceptable to give everyone or certain favored persons $30 a week in time of deep depression, but it would be foolish to do so at a time when the country is already at full employment or threatened with inflation. And if, as might be read into some of Major Douglas' statements, one should plan to vary the dividend in accordance with business conditions, there is still room for doubt as to whether the recipients would be good humored about the changes, or would vary their expenditures promptly and by the same amounts.

2. If we are going to increase the incomes of people in the society, ought we to give the same weekly bonus to everyone (the Douglas Plan) or to all oldsters (the Townsend Plan)? All countries, including the Soviet Union, try to encourage people to train themselves for skilled tasks and to work zealously by offering them the hope of higher money returns.

---

14 The Major has shown much uncertainty as to the proportion that purchasing power, as he conceives it, bears to value of output. The proportion of the former to the latter has been variously given by him as 40, 20, 25, 75, and 35 to 45 per cent.

(There are of course qualifications to this: we try also to set a floor beneath living standards, and we make it difficult for people to increase their incomes into the very high levels.) Is it necessary to desert this principle of incentive payments in order to expand purchasing power in time of depression? We shall see later that it is not necessary.

3. The taxation proposal of the California Ham-and-Eggs plan was fantastic. If all the older people eligible claimed their pensions, it would have been necessary to collect through sale of stamps a sum equal to nearly half the total incomes of all Californians in 1937. And since the stamp taxes would have been absorbed out of the ordinary flow of consumer incomes, the expansionary effect of the weekly dividend would have been approximately canceled. It was, therefore, rather a scheme to give pensions to old people than to expand employment and output.

Hundred per cent reserves

The 100-per-cent-reserve plan has attained considerable academic respectability in the United States. Its best known advocates probably have been Professors Fisher of Yale,[15] Graham of Princeton, Angell of Columbia, and Simons and Douglas of Chicago. According to Fisher, the chief screw loose in our monetary system is fractional reserves: the ability of our commercial banks to expand loans (and deposits) $4 or more for every $1 of reserves; and their possible need to contract loans (and deposits) by $4 or more for every $1 withdrawn from reserves.[16] The fractional-reserve system is said to make uncontrollable the upward and downward swings of price and employment. The proposed remedy, in the form urged by Professor Fisher, is to require all banks to keep as reserves against their demand deposits 100 per cent in cash plus gov-

---

15 Cf. *100 per Cent Money.* New York: Adelphi, 1935.

16 On November 1, 1951, banks of the Federal Reserve System were required to keep 14 to 24 per cent, depending on the size of the cities where they are situated, in legal cash reserves against demand deposits (checking accounts). That is, for each dollar of reserves, there might be roughly $4 to $8 of demand deposits.

ernment bonds. To enable banks to fulfill the new requirement, the government would lend to any banks so desiring
enough newly printed paper money to bring their reserves up
to the required 100 per cent. No bank would be permitted
thereafter to increase its reserve in bonds, but the government
would always stand ready to purchase from any bank its reserve
bonds at par.

If in the future, prices should fall, the Federal Reserve (or
perhaps the Treasury) would print and issue new money,
buying with it government bonds in the hands of the public.
And, if prices should rise, the Federal Reserve would sell government bonds, and so withdraw money from the economy.

There is an interesting contrast between this proposal and
the stamped-money proposal. The quantity of money in the
economy, M, times the number of times in a year that an
average dollar becomes income to someone (or the income
velocity of money), V_0, equals total expenditure or income.
We can, therefore, use MV_0 as a symbol for total expenditure
or income. The stamped-money proposal tries to increase total
expenditure by increasing V_0. The 100-per-cent-reserve plan
tries to increase or decrease the level of expenditure by controlling M.

This point suggests a vital weakness of the 100-per-cent-
reserve plan: 1. It has no means of controlling V_0, the rate at
which money is used. If the profit prospects are so glum that
businesses do not want to borrow and invest nor holders of
cash to lend, much of the new money pumped into the economy by the Federal Reserve would simply flow into idle balances, and not raise employment or prices at all. The income
velocity of money fell 39 per cent from 1929 to 1932,[17] and
still further during World War II. There seems no convincing

---

[17] The extreme change in the 20 years preceding 1929 was 23 per cent. (James
W. Angell, *The Behavior of Money*, pp. 175, 190. New York: McGraw-Hill, 1936.
Professor Fisher in a letter to me stated his conviction that the income velocity
of money would be nearly constant if his 100-per-cent plan were in operation,
but the uncomfortable recollection of its behavior during depression remains.

reason to believe that this change in V_0 would have been affected by the 100-per-cent-reserve proposals.

2. The plan as formulated by Fisher looks to the level of prices as the criterion of policy. But this is misleading. Some economists argue that it is healthy for average prices to fall gradually as productivity increases, as in fact they did during the prosperous late 1920's. (Professor Fisher himself preferred this.) Other economists argue that it is healthy for prices to rise gradually. The valid aim is high production and employment, rather than any particular level or rate of change of the price level. Even an ideal stability or ideal trend of the price level might fail to counteract a tendency toward *prolonged* low production and employment.

On the positive side, we can readily admit that stability of prices (or no more than a moderate rate of change) would tend to diminish *fluctuations* in production and employment and that insofar as the 100-per-cent plan helps toward price stability, it is also a help toward the latter and more important goal. Its principal contribution in this respect lies in its avoiding the forced deflation of the money supply during business downswings characteristic of our present system. Under present rules, when $1 is withdrawn from commercial banks or when $1 of debt owed to commercial banks is paid off, those banks must (*if* they were lent up to the maximum that their reserves permit) contract their deposits by $4 to $7. The Fisher Plan would permit only a dollar-for-dollar contraction, not this multiple effect. But the plan's effect is one-way only: it has no means of forcing banks to lend or businessmen to borrow when business prospects are dismal (even if bank reserves should be very high, say, 120 per cent of deposits), nor, as we saw above, has it any means of forcing individuals to spend on output the money that is put into their hands by open-market operations. Our experience of 1930-1945 gives clear evidence of the large extent to which banks may heap up excess reserves, and individuals invest in cash.

The advantage of the Fisher Plan in avoiding a forced contraction of the money supply suggests that it might be well for us to move gradually toward the higher-reserve requirements it advocates. Another advantage of the plan is a provision for eliminating the national debt over the course of years by monetizing it. But its weaknesses are very considerable, above all its neglect of the question whether total expenditure on output *normally* will be sufficiently large.

There is virtue even in the poorest crank plans: they dramatize the fact that something is wrong, and they propose to do something exciting about it. They continue preaching, for example, that total demand can be insufficient, until economists at long last think out analyses and policies that are in closer accord with current problems, and cease paraphrasing a Say's law that may have been relatively valid a century and a half ago but does not fit the facts today.

The usual fault of the maverick plans is that they present one-track cures, ignoring the complexities of the economy and the possibility of using alternative and complementary remedies. It is hard to make a serious proposal that does not have some merit in it. The important question to ask is: Can we obtain this good in greater measure and with less disadvantage in some other way?

The policies proposed in the next four chapters are not uncontroversial. They do not exclude other measures which may well be used, but which seem to us relatively minor and which, therefore, we do not detail. Different economists would emphasize individual aspects differently. But the program as a whole commands a general and a growing agreement among students of the problem.

CHAPTER FOURTEEN

Basic Problems of Employment

A Summary

OUR REASONING HAS CARRIED US TO THE CONCLUSION THAT whether we have low or high employment depends strategically on whether total expenditure for goods and services is small or large; and that the private consumption and investment expenditures plus the expenditures of government, which all together make up total expenditure, fluctuate for reasons that no one business or individual can forestall.

Consumers may or may not have accumulated deferred demand for durable consumption goods—though in ordinary times we can feel sure that their total consumption will remain in fairly stable relation to their incomes. Businessmen may or may not have exploited the possibilities of existing industries, may or may not have a swarm of innovations to develop, and may be inclined toward optimism or pessimism with respect to the general situation. The volume of government expenditures depends in large measure on political and social factors external to the economy.

Any increase or decrease in total expenditure has leverage and psychological effects tending toward a cumulative expansion or contraction. The magnitude of these cumulative reactions tends to become greater as we grow more productive and raise the standard of living (wants are more unstable), and as we increase the proportion of output that consists of investment goods and durable consumer goods (whose purchase can be postponed). The cumulative reactions are further exaggerated by expansion and contraction in the banking system.

In brief, a tendency to boom and bust is inherent in our economy.

To set the responsibility for attaining and maintaining full employment on the shoulders of individual consumers or individual businessmen is absurd. Each is caught in the upward spiral of inflation or the downward spiral of deflation. Although each adjusts himself as best he can, he buys and sells too little to affect the sweep of events over the whole economy.

Fluctuations in total spending are inevitable. Nor are these fluctuations in themselves all undesirable. When new inventions or other opportunities for increasing the productivity of the economy present themselves, it is desirable for the general good that they should promptly be taken advantage of. And this means a surge upward in investment. Under any kind of economic system—socialist or our own mixed variety—the complete ending of economic fluctuations can be achieved only at the cost of slowing down the rate of economic progress.

Our aim therefore is not to end fluctuations, but to moderate them—not uninterrupted full employment, but a softening of the violent cyclical swings of the past is the goal. We should normally have full employment with only occasional and mild dips below, plus a strengthening if possible of our already remarkable upward trend of productivity. We want to get from *A* to *B* in Chart 20.[1]

We have seldom during ordinary peacetime years of the past experienced the overemployment and booming prices that are the evidence of excessive expenditures. Our more frequent problem has been that of insufficient expenditure. At intervals over the past we have fallen into periods of acutely low output and employment—with the deterioration of human morale and skills and of capital assets that these involve. We have also over long periods carried on in a state of lower employment and lower output than was easily possible to us. This implies

---

1 Adapted from a chart of the Committee for Economic Development.

the prolonged existence of what we have called *concealed un-employment,* which escapes statistics because it is hidden in movements out of preferred kinds of work to the household and school, to makeshift jobs, to part-time work, to subsistence farming.

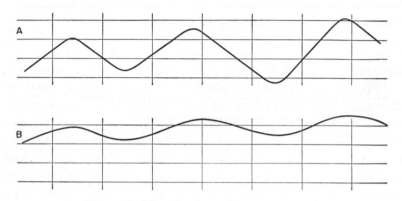

Chart 20. Two Business Cycle Patterns.

The evidence is emphatic that the problem of fluctuating output and employment will be with us in the future just as it has been in the past. But our weapons against depression have also been growing sharper. We know more than we did in the 1930's about the problem of productive employment. Full employment can be maintained in a free society and a free enterprise economy. But only through a run of good luck that we have no reason to expect can it be maintained without effort and action.

Democratic Freedoms and Full Employment

The future of democracy depends in large measure on its success in solving the problem of unemployment. It is far from sure that all the major democratic nations of the world could survive even one more depression as deep and prolonged as that of the 1930's. Many of the weaker democracies certainly could not. The personal freedoms of thought and action that a democracy offers to its citizens are superior to any that can be hoped for from a despotic regime. But if the democracies of the world again permit widespread and continued unemployment, the desperate among their citizens are likely to accept desperate remedies, and trade in the liberties that mean little in the midst of poverty and idleness to the demagogues who promise them a mission and work.

It is in the next depression that the new prophets will preach hatred and multiply their followers, that the Huey Longs will promise "Every man a King." Then the Communist Party expects to gather in a bonanza harvest of new comrades from among the frustrate. The Politburo in Moscow also anticipate the next depression hopefully. It is a basic article in Marxist dogma that capitalism can never escape its fated spiral of increasingly violent depressions and booms.[2] Future depressions will weaken the economic and political systems of the West, and so afford Soviet Russia maximum opportunities for expanding its power. The Kremlin will modify the official dogma only when it is proved by fact to have gone wrong somewhere—when the United States and other nations of the free world have shown that they can stabilize their free economics.

The next United States depression is also a chief fear of the British[3] and other democratic nations, as tending to broadcast the seeds of depression and disorder elsewhere in the world.

It will be obvious below that the relatively minor central policies required to obtain acceptably full employment are compatible with democracy. Democracy is menaced by the decay and hate that will corrupt society if general unemployment is allowed to persist, not by measures to avert depression.

---

[2] See the interesting collection of quotations from the Soviet press in the *Christian Science Monitor*, January 25, 1947, p. 11. Also nearly any issue of the New York *Daily Worker*.

[3] See for example in *British Speeches of the Day*, January, 1946, Lord Keynes, p. 798; Sir John Anderson, p. 769; Sir Stafford Cripps, pp. 773, 776. In the issue of July, 1946, Mr. Herbert Morrison, p. 439; and in the issue of December, 1946, Mr. R. H. S. Crossman, p. 709.

The use of the powers of government in this kind of service for the general good is of the nature of democracy.

Freedoms and Free Enterprise

The word *capitalism* has become increasingly useless. All modern economies, without exception, consist of mixtures of government and private enterprise. The only question is where the dividing line had best be put, and too much heat steams out of discussions as to whether that line ought to be moved a trifle one way or the other. In the United States the carrying of mail and the school system were once private enterprises. Many of our highways were once privately owned. In Western Europe, in recent decades, the telephone and telegraph, electric power, and railroads have generally been state enterprises. Furthermore, there are all varieties and all degrees of government control of privately owned enterprises. A large number of these deviations are gathered under the blanket label of capitalism or free enterprise or private enterprise, and so evoke our habitual personal responses of approval or disapproval. It is at some indefinite and subjectively determined point that the proportion of public enterprise becomes so large that we are inclined to call the resulting mixture a socialist system. (If the British Government should eventually complete the socialization program undertaken in the late 1940's, some 80 per cent of national production will still be in private hands, only 20 per cent in the hands of government.)

It is conceivable for political democracy to exist with either a free enterprise or socialist economy, and likewise free enterprise may coexist either with democracy or dictatorship. It is easy to think of examples of all of these. Nevertheless in the United States and a number of other technically advanced countries, democracy and free enterprise do exist together. That is, the freedom to set up and run one's own business is one of the freedoms that we enjoy.

The word *freedom* is a conditioned word, and often ought to be looked at with suspicious scrutiny. It carries a different context of meaning in every historical period: we are always implying freedom *from* some particular menace or *toward* some particular goal. The continuing aim is to maximize the area of freedoms, to accept no curtailment that is not overbalanced by expansion elsewhere.

Employment policy and the division between free enterprise and public enterprise

There is no necessary relation between the employment policies carried on by government and the proportion of a country's economic life administered by government. (This is true even though advocates of government action to increase employment have often carelessly recommended policies that carry with them as a by-product the shrinking of the private or free-market sector of the economy. Thereby they have brought down upon themselves the justified wrath of conservatives.) The choice by the people of an economy of a dividing line between private and public enterprise — a choice continuously being made through decisions on individual issues—need not depend and, therefore, should not depend, on the level of employment toward which the economy is naturally tending.

Suppose that a higher total of demand for goods and services is needed. (We anticipate some of the discussion of later chapters.) This might be obtained through methods that expand the private sector of the economy. A wide range of indirect measures can be used to encourage private consumption and investment spending. Tax rates might be lowered or the tax structure altered so as to bear less heavily on private spending. Social-security payments might be increased (which means that private individuals spend for goods and services, not the government).

The higher demand for goods and services might also be attained through measures that expand the relative size of the government sector in the economy. Special controls might be used to constrict private consumption and investment spending (as in wartime). The government might increase its expenditures for goods and services, meanwhile levying heavier taxes or requiring heavier social-security contributions or altering the tax structure to bear more heavily on private spending. In its spending for goods and services, the government always has the choice of hiring its own employees, or engaging private contractors.

All government expenditures tend to encourage consumption expenditures (through increasing incomes received); but the effect of government expenditure on private investment varies according to its type. The development and conservation of natural resources, road construction, and the like tend to stimulate private investment. Low-cost housing projects, health measures, and education grants might not appreciably stimulate or contract private investment. But should the government buy out and operate the coal industry, insurance companies, and public utilities, the area available for private investment is narrowed.[4]

Certain monetary problems of public debt and liquidity in the economy may or may not follow on the heels of a government employment policy. But such problems are on the whole, as we shall see, of moderate importance.

The social values of free enterprise

We ought to face explicitly, even though very briefly, the question of whether it is worth while, as we have been assuming, to retain a wide area of free enterprise. We cannot solve this major problem by laying *pro* arguments against *con* arguments to come out with a plain conclusion. There are estimates of probable causes and probable effects that no one can be

---

4 This logical separation between employment policy, and policy on the spheres of private and public enterprise, is illustrated in the views of English political parties. The Labour Party advocates nationalization of certain basic industries. But all parties—Labour, Liberal, and Conservative—agree, whatever their views on nationalization, that the state is responsible for maintaining steady employment.

sure about; and there are value judgments involved that no one can solve for his neighbor. The brief comments that follow are no solution. They do set up a working presumption about policy.

In the short run—say, for the next decade—the policies and problems implied by the need for continued high employment and production remain essentially the same no matter where we should like the eventual boundary between the free sector and the government sector.

1. Even if we want to avoid any use of the powers of government toward higher production and employment, the issue of government policy will nevertheless arise. Federal government expenditures in the postwar years, by reason of the costs of the armed forces, of veterans benefits, and ordinary department expense, are going to continue to be at least five times higher than any previous peacetime level. If federal expenditures are 40 billion dollars or more annually, the effect on the economy of the government budget forces itself on our attention.

2. If we, instead, set our face against private enterprise, we still need to confront the fact that any realizable alternative to our present setup must for a long time to come contain a strong admixture of this same private enterprise, merely because it takes so long to organize anything. One can be a socialist in principle, have no doubt that the United States will be completely socialized eventually, and still feel that the great problem of the 1950's is making private enterprise work.

But the longer run should also be considered. Probably majority opinion agrees with our own national policy that the right of a man to engage in business for himself is not a basic freedom, like freedom from fear, from want, of speech, and of worship. It is a right that only about one in five of our working force finds himself able, or finds it worth while, to accept.

If free enterprise is not a basic freedom, then it must be justified as a central principle of organizing production or fail to be justified, primarily on the grounds of whether it has "delivered the goods." Has it proved an efficient mechanism for producing the goods and services we want?

1. The evidence is strong that private enterprise *has* delivered the goods. Over the course of the last two centuries it has been correlated with a rise in, and, it seems valid to conclude, has lifted the general standard of life of the Western world to an extent never before achieved. We have surveyed some data on this for the United States.[5]

This does not deny the existence of evils of inequality and unemployment. With respect to the subject of inequality, it is no part of the logic of private enterprise that family dynasties should exist and continue over the generation to draw tribute parasitically from the flow of production. The logic of private enterprise is that high money returns should be available to individuals, but only as inducement and reward for performing services of high social value. Constant vigilance is demanded to plug up loopholes where returns are obtained without services being performed.

Nor does such a conclusion deny that the selfish principle in human action can be pushed too far. But the drive in human beings for power and prestige can, as we have seen in dictatorship societies, take far more malignant forms than pursuit of the dollar. And rising real income offers increasing facilities for softening the competitive struggle.

Casual reasoning in this field often suffers from the illusion that redistribution of income from the rich to the poor would appreciably raise the living standards of the poor. This is not true. There are too few of the rich and too many people of moderate and low incomes for the device to work. Suppose that, in 1945, we decided to skim off *all* incomes above the $10,000 level and divide the proceeds among the members of the working population who received less than $2000 a year. Each of them would have gotten a bonus of only $380.[6] The logic of this reasoning is even plainer when we remember that

---

[5] Chapter 4.

[6] This assumes that production would have remained unchanged.

it is not money but goods and services that low-income groups need—houses, cars, washing machines, refrigerators, and the like. These are not in the attics of the Rockefellers, Astors, or Mellons. They must be produced if the poor, or anybody, is to have them.

It is increased production alone that can significantly raise the living standards of the poor, and middle-income groups as well. And capitalist, or dominantly free enterprise, economies have succeeded very well in the Western world in raising tremendously the volume of production. There are nearly 10 million businesses in the United States, in each of which the entrepreneur is free to experiment and test new ideas. Where numerous independent businesses exist, there is wide opportunity for personal initiative: the self-interest of individuals is harnessed in the service of increased production—that is, in the service of the general welfare. We too easily forget how far and fast our real incomes have risen in the course of the past two centuries and more—and with them the wide range of personal freedoms directly involved in higher real income.

2. Private enterprise economies have achieved rising real income without resort to secret police, concentration camps and slave labor or mass purges and executions. And so a second point is that free enterprise seems to many students a central cause of the growth of political liberties and the rise of social conscience of recent centuries. The argument here is that liberty is correlated with decentralization of authority just as tyranny is implied in the unchecked power of the state, and to a lesser degree, of the huge-scale business. In the economic sphere, decentralization exists when economic decisions are made by thousands of small firms. Alternative opportunities are abundant in such an economy. These alternatives spell economic liberty and independence to the individual, and the practices and traditions of freedom grow on this basis.

3. Finally, there is the matter of the public will. Obviously, the American public do not want a nationalized economy or a totalitarian unity. We want to give up no segment of our area

of freedoms unless there is clear justification. To many of us, there is a profound psychological loss involved in giving up working for ourselves to be an employee of someone else—to give up running our own garage, operating our own contracting business, having our own medical practice, administering our own typing agency, writing our own book. We may be glad to work 14 hours a day for ourselves, with a confident sense of fulfilling the promise of our talent and energy, whereas we would be miserable working 8 hours a day under someone else's direction, subject to his judgment and caprice.

Although only about one-fifth of our working force are in business for themselves, many of the remainder—an additional one-fifth or more—prize the status and independence and "chance to get ahead" that their particular jobs in private business give to them. Nearly all the rest of us evidently, as we look to the voting records, like to live in the environment of a free enterprise economy.

Giant business, monopoly, and free enterprise

The American public want a dominantly free enterprise economy. But, after all, is the United States economy a free enterprise economy, even outside the area of government ownership and substantial government controls? There is a wide range of situations where the freedom of an individual to carry on his own enterprise is hindered or blocked by the policies and conspiracies of existing businesses.

The monopolistic power of the latter concerns comes from two sources: they dominate either because of the relatively large volume of output that they produce of their particular product, or because their product seems "different" and superior to buyers (because it is really superior or because of advertising or other sources of consumer goodwill). Some firms that have a high degree of monopolistic insulation from competition are of huge scale. Others are small, and secure their monopolistic power because of their size dominance in a particular village, city, or other small area, or because of differen-

tiation of product. All giant firms have a considerable amount
of monopoly power; but not all monopolies are large.

Mammoth-scale businesses—say, the 200 largest nonfinancial
corporations and perhaps an additional two score of financial
corporations—are suspect for a number of reasons in a political
democracy and in a free enterprise economy. But the price
rigidity that giant businesses and other monopolistic firms
show may not be a disadvantage when depression is tending
to spread in the economy. It offsets the tendency toward
expecting continued price declines and offers competitive
opportunity to other firms whose prices *have* dropped. Price
rigidity can be an advantage in recovery, because increasing
expenditure then tends to go more into output increases
than price rises.

Also, many monopolistic firms, some of them very large, have
given an exemplary level of performance in private hands,
through improvement of product and lowering of price in the
long run, since this is compatible with rigid prices in the
shorter run (p. 112). A good case can be made for du Pont,
Firestone, Ford, and many others on these grounds. Some people who praise "pure" competition seemingly would prefer the
old icebox to a Frigidaire, and a cheap horse and buggy to a
modern car as improved and priced by "monopolistic" enterprise. "Monopolistic competition" is plainly compatible with
rapid technical progress. There is reason to believe that in
some fields and up to a certain point, a monopolistic insulation against the "strong wind of competition" has proved the
condition for investment and entrepreneurship that will *eventually* bring forth better products at lower prices.

It is worth recalling again that even the well thought-of
village store and local bakery have their share of monopoly
power. In such cases, the society has neither the wish nor the
power to eliminate "monopoly."

We have, therefore, two problems, partly distinct and partly
overlapping: that of huge-scale enterprise and that of monopoly. Huge private enterprises are obviously on trial. They

have lost their case in the current general opinion of Europe and of England. The decades to come will show whether in the United States the managers of large business can convince the public that the privileges they enjoy are justified by the service they render to the public good. Monopolistic business, which is a more inclusive classification, also presents a more complex problem. Some "monopolies" are effective servants of the general good, others are clearly not.

Our aim of maximizing the area of freedom implies the general rule that increasing public control or public ownership, or both, are needed as we go up the scale from small to large enterprises, and from pure competitors to those whose monopoly power or whose particular monopolistic practices are more and more hostile to the public interest. The aim is that on net balance freedom in the economy shall be as great as possible.

The objectives of high productivity and employment, attained in part through specific measures of government policy, are not in conflict with this rule. (In fact, the prospects for small enterprises are rocky and uncertain *unless* we maintain acceptably full employment. It is mainly small enterprises that go bankrupt in depression.) The policies required for maintaining high production and employment are those that affect the environment in which business decisions are made. They need not, unless we want them to, involve direct controls over individual businesses.

The Formation of Policy

The problem of effective government decision and administration is a major one in any matter of employment and production policy. All too often in recent years, bills of general concern have become stalemated in the midst of conflict between the President and Congress. It is crucial, therefore, that employment policy be lifted as far as possible above partisan politics, and be made as efficient as possible.

A major landmark in United States government policy toward employment is represented in the Employment Act of 1946. The Act is an explicit acceptance by the federal government of responsibility to aid "in creating and maintaining, in a manner calculated to foster and promote free competition and free enterprise and the general welfare, conditions under which there will be afforded useful employment opportunities, including self-employment, for those able, willing, and seeking work; and to promote maximum employment, production, and purchasing power."

An Economic Council of three economic advisers is established under the Act, with the task of considering all federal activities that have a bearing on employment and production matters. The Council makes recommendations to Congress, and issues annual reports. The first came out early in 1947. By 1949 the circulation was near 50,000 copies, and rising. The reports have earned a central place in the endless public argument over inflation and unemployment, and prices, wages, government expenditures, and taxes. The Council is appointed by the President. It maintains close liaison with Congress, through a Congressional Joint Committee, before which the representatives of business, labor, the farm, and economists and others give their views on national economic policy.

The Council has no means of ensuring the prompt action that may occasionally be desirable to offset the gathering momentum of a downswing or of a speculative boom. But the mere existence of the Council is a long step forward: we now have a body whose function is to oversee government policy as a whole, and consider how it meshes with the particular state of the private economy. Some such distinguished coordinating and recommending agency is needed to lift employment policy above partial views and above special political and economic interest—an agency intelligently and obviously devoted to the public good. The economic reports of the Council repeatedly direct the attention of Congress and the public generally to the state of economic health of the nation and to the issues involved in maintaining stable prices, and productive and high employment.

Special policy considerations

At intervals in the future, and perhaps even chronically, the problem faced will be that of deficient demand. Although high employment is an aim in itself because of the psychological and loss-of-skills cost of employment, in the main it should be looked upon as a by-product. The chief objective of the economy is the highest output reasonably possible of those goods and services that we want most. Nevertheless, even from the point of view of output, it is better to employ men in digging holes and filling them up than not to employ them at all; it is better to employ men to make products that we dump in the middle of the ocean[7] than to leave them idle. For these men will spend their pay on food, shelter, and clothing, which in turn gives useful employment to others, and so the leverage effect cumulates.

Pyramid-building, earthquakes, even wars may serve to increase wealth, if the education of our statesmen on the principles of the classical economics stands in the way of anything better. . . .

If the Treasury were to fill old bottles with banknotes, bury them at suitable depths in disused coal mines, which are then filled up to the surface with town rubbish, and leave it to private enterprise on well-tried principles of laissez faire to dig the notes up again (the right to do so being obtained, of course, by tendering for leases of the note-bearing territory), there need be no more unemployment and, with the help of the repercussions, the real income of the community, and its capital wealth also, would probably become a good deal greater than it actually is. It would, indeed, be more sensible to build houses and the like; but if there are political and practical difficulties in the way of this, the above would be better than nothing.

The analogy between this expedient and the gold mines of the real world is complete. . . . Just as wars have been the only form

---

[7] If critically scarce natural resources are not used up on the process.

of large-scale loan expenditure that statesmen have thought justifiable, so gold mining is the only pretext for digging holes in the
ground that has recommended itself to bankers as sound finance;
and each of these activities has played its part in progress—failing
something better. . . .[8]

What is mainly wrong with useless "make-work" projects is
not that they cannot make us richer than we should have been
without them. It is that there are other, and useful, projects on
which the unemployed can and should be used.

In addition, the morale value of employment is in large
part lost if men realize they are being employed on worthless projects. People want to feel significant and needed. The
man who is doing useless work has little cause to feel content
with himself or to respect the society that so employs him.

We return to a statement of the basic goal of the economy—
the fulfilling of our needs for food, clothing, shelter, education, health conservation, recreation, and so forth, to the full
extent that we have resources available. We will push our
utilization of labor and other resources further in those areas
where the needs are larger. We obviously want to use all our
resources, but the full utilization of them should be looked
upon primarily as the *means* toward satisfying our present
and future wants.

In such a context of thinking, one has gotten away from the
demoralizing make-work notion and sees the unemployment
problem for what it is—a problem implied by the success
of the economy, not proof of failure. That is, unemployment
is evidence of unutilized productive power. It is the abundance
of our productive power—which means high savings, which, in
a specialized economy, need not lead to high real investment—
that is, in a basic sense, at the root of the trouble. But there is
no need to let the nation's productivity be the cause of its
poverty.

---

8 J. M. Keynes, *General Theory of Employment, Interest and Money*, pp.
129–131. New York: Harcourt Brace, 1936.

In the suggestions made below, guiding principles (in addition to the major aims of high living standards and full employment) are to move in the direction of lessening inequalities of wealth and income and to maximize the area of freedom of the individual. These are not necessary concomitants of a full employment policy: it would be possible to attain full employment with greater inequality of wealth and, still more readily, with less freedom. But there is no need to affect neutrality with respect to every social issue save higher output and employment.

With respect to the second principle, maximizing the area of individual freedom, it is our general assumption that government should not do anything that individuals or voluntary associations can more efficiently do for themselves. (On the other hand, it should do whatever cannot be done by private individuals, or what can be done by them only with clearly lower effectiveness.) In connection with the unemployment problem proper, it is our postulate that government extend even its indirect controls no further than is necessary to secure efficient full employment. That extension is moderate—on net balance, a retraction from the level of government action that would be necessitated by an economic collapse.

Any economic policy implies elements of social judgment. There will be little disagreement with the major outlines of the kinds of policy suggested below. But there may be much difference of opinion on the advisability of particular measures, on the emphasis that should be placed on them, and on the possibilities of other measures. Time and experience will serve to correct our earlier judgments, and any program embarked upon by Congress will be subject to the continuous modifications that all living things undergo.

The following three chapters consider what can be done toward maintaining adequate total expenditure in the economy (assuming that without such effort, expenditure would be inadequately low). This is the most important single element in securing high employment and output. The outline of the solution is simple. Government and strategic private groups must do what they can to encourage private consumption expenditure and effective private investment expenditure (Chapters 15 and 16). If total expenditure is still insufficient, government must, through use of its budget, make up the difference (Chapter 17).

CHAPTER FIFTEEN

The Encouragement of Consumption

THE PROBLEM OF THE VOLUME OF PRIVATE EXPENDITURE ON goods and services is twofold—the encouragement of a higher average level (if there is a continuing deficiency of expenditure), and the discouragement of fluctuations (to the extent that we are troubled with cyclical upswings and downswings).

Many economists see the problem of increasing consumption as the central problem of high postwar employment, since ordinarily about two-thirds of gross expenditure is consumption expenditure. It is certainly a major problem. The bulk of consumption, we remember, is done by lower-income groups. (In 1949, four-fifths of total money income went to families receiving under $7500 a year.) It is also in the lower-income groups that consumption needs press most urgently on the heels of income. In order to conserve our human resources and for humanitarian and democratic considerations, we should concentrate any program directed toward expansion of total consumption on raising the consumption of the poor rather than that of the rich.

We might try to obtain higher consumption through diverting income by taxation from high to low-income groups. But our data indicate that there is not sufficient difference between the marginal propensities to consume of high and low-income groups for this device to increase consumer spending *much*. There is further reason to doubt that such a transfer would have any significant stimulating effect on total expenditure when we consider that there would probably be a general shift in consumer habits in the direction of less consumption, and that investment would be discouraged by heavy taxes on high incomes (p. 149). This reasoning does not deny that greater equality in the sharing of a given income will probably increase economic welfare,[1] and can bring non-economic advantages in greater social and political democracy.

1. Taxation is a major instrument of government for influencing the amount of disposable income of individuals, and the channels in which individuals spend their incomes. The merit of particular taxes can be judged by the basic criteria of (a) their effect on income and employment, (b) their effect in causing greater or less inequality of wealth and income and the extent to which they otherwise seem fair or unfair, (c) the extent to which they interfere with the most effective allocation of resources and products (by causing price changes), and (d) their political and administrative feasibility. The problem of developing an optimum system of taxes is not only that of getting in the right amount of revenue from the right sources, from the point of view of a government program directed toward the maintenance of over-all high production and employment. The problem is, in addition, that of getting together a group of taxes that complement and balance each other so as to have the best possible combined effect on the functioning of segments of the economy—on particular industries, firms, and consumers.[2]

All taxes are depressing. No one likes to pay them, and they siphon off money that would otherwise be used, at least in part, for consumption or investment spending. From the point of view of increasing income and employment, our problem is to obtain government tax revenues from those sources where the taxes are *least* depressing on private spending. Both personal

---

[1] A. P. Lerner, *The Economics of Control*, pp. 29–32. New York: Macmillan, 1947.

[2] See H. M. Groves, *Postwar Taxation and Economic Progress*. New York: McGraw-Hill, 1946. This is a research study of the Committee for Economic Development. Also A. H. Hansen and H. S. Perloff, *State and Local Finance in the National Economy*, pp. 243–284. New York: Norton, 1944.

income, and excise and sales tax (on tobacco, gasoline, alcoholic beverages, leather products, automobiles, watches, radios, and so forth) are, by the criterion of their effect on consumer spending, undesirable. They extract funds that would otherwise be mainly spent for consumption. Corporation income taxes in general discourage investment by incorporated businesses.

Excise and sales taxes have especially heavy counts against them because most of them absorb a greater proportion of the incomes of the poor than of the rich—and so seem to most of us unfair; and because they alter market prices of goods and so distort consumer spending from the channels it would follow if prices were everywhere proportional to costs of resources. Certain taxes on consumption, it is true, may be justified because of equity considerations (the gasoline tax, which goes for highway upkeep), or because of the desire to discourage consumption of supposedly harmful commodities (taxes on liquor and tobacco).

The balance of considerations points toward the personal income tax as the major single source of federal government revenues. The Committee for Economic Development has recommended that about 60 per cent of federal revenues come from that source.[3] The income tax is "fair," being the only tax that can be closely adjusted to ability to pay; and unlike taxes on individual commodities, it distorts little the consumer's choice as to how he would like to allocate his expenditure.

The consumption expenditures that take place under given social conditions reflect habits slow to change. It may be possible to encourage private consumption expenditure somewhat by publicly emphasizing the higher level of consumption now

---

[3] The income tax levied on corporations accounts for only 11 per cent, and excise taxes on tobacco, liquor, and gasoline for only 16 per cent. These two are the most important other federal taxes in the CED recommendation.

The federal government actually received in 1950 about 46 per cent of its tax revenue from the personal income tax, 23 per cent from taxes on corporations, and 20 per cent from excise taxes.

possible and desirable. But on the whole, such publicity is doubtless a weak device.

Appreciable reliance can be placed on various kinds of social consumption expenditures, which either provide services for general public use, or put products or purchasing power directly into the hands of consumers. Some types of these are described below.

2. Such social consumption expenditures should be directed toward the establishment of a new and higher minimum standard of living. That standard expresses in concrete terms the level of consumption of food, shelter, education, medical care, and recreation opportunity (including leisure) below which it is the national aim that no one shall fall. There exists a vague notion in the United States today of such a minimum: no one is supposed to starve, freeze, or go without shelter. But the minimum can be much higher. The formulation and steady raising of such a minimum standard of life is a measure of the economic progress of a people.

3. People may lose their incomes and so their ability to consume through sickness, accident, and old age, as well as through unemployment. Under existing unemployment compensation laws, only 32 million were covered, in mid-1947, out of a work force of 63 million.[4] Under federal old-age insurance, 42.5 million were covered at the beginning of 1948. The old-age insurance provisions gave, in mid-1948, $40 a month to the average retired man and his wife; the average single man received $24. Under the unemployment insurance program, an average payment of $18.19 weekly was made to each recipient in 1947—1948. The average maximum time for which benefits were payable was 20 weeks. There is no general federal law for workman's compensation for industrial accidents, and existing laws vary widely in their provisions.

Evidently, we have made only a good start toward the obvious target of protecting everyone against all the hazards that

---

4 Unemployment compensation laws would not be necessary if proposal (4) (*below*) were adopted.

might leave him without minimum necessities and comforts. Our social conscience is coming over the course of the years to demand such a program; a full employment policy automatically includes it.

The social-security program, with the cooperation of state and local governments, should, therefore, be made universal in coverage, and its benefits increased to the end of assuring a new and higher minimum standard of living.

4. A simple and direct measure for increasing private consumption is a guarantee by the federal government, in cooperation with the states, to employ anyone who cannot get a job elsewhere. The work so offered should be adapted to the types of skills available and to local needs, with pay rate and other conditions less attractive than the other employment usually available. The proposal puts a floor beneath wage rates, but there is no reason why it should diminish incentive to find better jobs and earn higher income. Guaranteed employment is a last resort, and little application would be made for it if the other proposals we list are effective. Such a policy keeps incomes from falling below a moderate level so long as people are able to work, and so it provides funds for consumption. But the psychological effect may well be its most important aspect, encouraging as it does consumption out of people's ordinary incomes by assuring that they will always be able to find work, and encouraging investments by business through assurance of greater stability of consumption.[5]

5. Consumer expenditure, especially on durable consumer goods, can be increased also by Federal Reserve measures to encourage installment buying—to reduce the "down payment" and increase the number of months over which the rest of the bill can be spread.

6. Another proposal having the tendency to maintain consumption is worth mention. This is *separation wages*, a lump payment made to anyone who is discharged. The amount of

[5] E. A. Goldenweiser makes this suggestion in his "Jobs," *Postwar Economic Studies No. 1.* Board of Governors, Federal Reserve System, August, 1945.

the payment is proportioned to the number of months or years the worker has been employed by the given firm. Such separation wages are justified not only from their effect on consumption expenditure, but also because they require the firm to enter into its calculations a sum representing in some degree the social cost of discharges—the psychological cost of losing a job, the effort and money cost of searching for a new one, the possible expense of moving. Thus, it helps to improve the utilization of the nation's work force.

Secular and Cyclical Policy

It is possible, but not likely in the visible future, that the United States is faced with a long-run, or secular, problem of deficient production and employment. All of the above six measures for encouraging consumption are useful against this contingency. But suppose, instead, we normally make full use of our resources, and only occasionally come into the downswing of the business *cycle*. To meet this kind of need, we want, if we can find them, measures which through their structure automatically stimulate consumption when private expenditure is falling off—that is, which have a built-in counter-cyclical effect. All the above suggestions fall also under this heading. For example: The siphoning off of income by income taxes automatically falls sharply when incomes are declining; unemployment insurance benefits then rise in volume; consumer credit will be applied for more freely; and separation wages will be paid in greater quantity.

But all of these measures for stimulating consumption put together may be of only very moderate effectiveness. It is likely that we shall need to do much more.

CHAPTER SIXTEEN

The Encouragement of Investment

The Social Atmosphere

IT IS A PERVADING AND SUBTLE FACT THAT THE SOCIAL atmosphere of our society has become, in some real degree, hostile to the capitalist, or free enterprise, machine; and consequent laws and the spirit in which the laws are conceived and administered have become in some measure antipathetic to its functioning. It is not so much that existing measures—increased personal and business surtaxes on income, heavier estate and gift taxes, government-supported unionism which restricts the freedom of action of management, antitrust action, public utility legislation, special requirements with respect to security issues, and the like—are in themselves flatly discouraging to business enterprise. Many or most of these measures are favored by business sentiment; all would be acceptable, taken by themselves.

It is rather that these measures, coupled with the tone and slogans with which they are advocated, the spirit with which the laws are administered—more important than the laws themselves—and the general trend of public opinion toward business, seem to the businessmen to prophesy menacingly with respect to the future. "If," he reasons, "these trends continue and grow, I should be foolish to make heavy investments that can be realized only over a number of years."

The desire for profit is only a special case of the general urge we all have to improve the lot of ourselves and our families.

The urge for self-advancement exists in every kind of social system and we have generally thought it a useful social drive. If profit-seeking, the essential drive in the private enterprise machine, meets increasingly with political obloquy and moral disapproval; if the businessman, from whom the society wants effective and abundant investment expenditures, is increasingly hampered by heavier taxes and more legal restrictions, then it is clear that the free enterprise machine will gradually run down. Its worsening performance will increasingly justify its bad repute, and the latter will in turn lead to still more hostile measures.[1]

But, as we have seen, there are conclusive short-run and strong long-run reasons for preserving a dominantly wide area of free enterprise. Is it possible for such a downward spiral of continuing collapse, feared by Professor Schumpeter and other students, to be broken?

It is probable that over future decades, the area of government will continue to expand somewhat in the economy, as it did in the nineteenth century and the first third of the twentieth century. Formerly, postal service, roads, and general education were private enterprises, run for profit. There came a time when it seemed better, in the common interest, to have them administered by government. But whether or not this trend continues into the future, it is not wise for us to carry through measures hostile to private enterprise, that prevent it from functioning, while we continue to reject any general socialist system of production. We must not paralyze one system of production at a time when we are unwilling to accept any other.

A clue to the solution of the problem may lie in the recognition of when and why anti-private-enterprise sentiments have appeared. They were not important in times like the 1920's,

---

[1] Arguments of this tenor have been developed most impressively by Joseph A. Schumpeter, *Business Cycles*, Vol. II, pp. 1038–1050. New York: McGraw-Hill, 1939; and *Capitalism, Socialism and Democracy*, pp. 131–163. New York: Harper, 1942.

when the capitalist machine was working well. The Greenback, Populist, and Free Silver movements of the late nineteenth century were mainly a reflection of three decades of falling prices and hence of pressure on debtor groups. The Interstate Commerce Act of 1887 and the Sherman Antitrust Act of 1890 came only after abuses were flagrant. Trust-busting of 1901–1911 coincided with muckraking and revelation of abuses. Similarly, the reforms and anti-free-enterprise sentiments of the 1930's followed the major economic collapse of which we have statistical record.

The reasonable suggestion emerges from this that private enterprise will retain our allegiance and respect if it deserves it; that we are overquick to imagine a long-term growth of disaffection suddenly come to flower. Specific evils have evoked attack and measures of reform. And to reform is to preserve, though the medicine may not be pleasant to take.

With respect to the major disaster of depression, private enterprise will not be blamed for depression if depression does not occur, and its avoidance is the purpose of all our suggested policies in this section. With respect to the evil of concentration of wealth and power, the taxation and other policies to diminish it should be carried through gradually and in such ways as interfere least with incentives to expand businesses and to produce, and so earn income. With respect to a social attitude of hostility toward profit and profit-makers, an effort should be made to direct that hostility toward *unearned* income (income from monopolies of the antisocial sort, and from large inheritances). Respect should be inculcated for the earning of high incomes through the efficient directing of businesses serving the public good.

The conflict between our desire for incentives to encourage efficiency and larger output, and our desire for no-more-than-moderate inequality of income and wealth, is a conflict that exists in all societies, that of the Soviet Union included; and its solution lies in compromise.

It is the threat of future, unpredictable anti-private-enterprise policies that is a vital deterrent to investment. To minimize it, the policies which government will follow with respect to business should be clear and adjusted only gradually—"a government of laws and not of men." Antimonopoly measures should be firm, plain, and as predictable as possible: once again there is a call for sophisticated measures. The policy of non-interference, unless the public interest clearly requires it, should be an obviously established one. If there is an extension of public ownership—and it may often be more economic to own "monopolies" than to carry on a running warfare of regulation and suits—present owners should be generously recompensed. In general and emphatically, the spirit of democratic cooperatives should prevail; men in business are presumed to be serving the common good unless, in specific cases, they are clearly proved to be acting otherwise.

A spirit of general goodwill is likely to exist if, as a result of measures like those we are suggesting, the society maintains its achievement of recent years—reasonably full employment, high and increasing productivity, and diminishing inequality of income and wealth.

Taxes

Our second proposal is more specific—namely, *tax changes* to encourage investment are of primary importance. Our present tax laws give a premium to investment of funds in safe channels where they are not effective in creating jobs and increasing productivity—away from risk investment and into idle balances and bonded indebtedness.

1. It is dangerous for corporations to finance themselves by issuing bonds, since bondholders have a fixed claim against the business. This is especially true of risky projects, some of which offer the greatest promise of increased jobs and productivity. But the alternative, that of issuing stocks, is at present discouraged because income belonging to stockholders is taxed twice, once when the corporation pays a tax on its earnings, and once when the stockholder pays an income tax on the dividends he receives. In addition, the poor stockholder is at present discriminated against, since his share of the total earnings

of the corporation is subject to a corporate income tax at just the same rate as that paid by the rich stockholder.

In partial defense of the corporate tax, we should mention that it is in the main flat-rate [2] rather than progressive, and loss carryover provisions permit considerable offsetting of losses in one year against profits in another.[3] The depressing effect on investment is mitigated, but it is not cured.

One proposal, made repeatedly in recent years, to correct these and other faults of the present corporate- and income-tax relationships, is that the United States should follow its own former, and the current British, practice. Each corporation would pay a tax on all its earnings at the lowest-bracket personal-income-tax rate (in 1950 this was 20 per cent). For any part of the earnings distributed in dividends, this acts as a withholding tax: the stockholder owes nothing in personal income tax unless his total income is high enough to subject him to the surtax rates. Stockholders with low incomes or many dependents get rebates. For the rest of the earnings of the corporation, which it retains, credit for the tax paid will be realized by stockholders only when dividends are actually distributed.[4]

Proposals to diminish the burden of corporate income taxes (and emphasize personal income taxes more) have the greater significance because a larger proportion of funds for investment comes from retained earnings of corporations than from outside investors.

2. It is possible to diminish greatly the burden of taxes on small and growing businesses without substantially reducing federal government revenues. It appears desirable that, no matter in what way or to what degree corporations are taxed in

---

2 But flat rates do not give the preferential treatment to small corporations which is desirable. See p. 275.

3 According to the Revenue Act of 1950, net operating losses can be carried back one year, and forward over a period of five years, thus averaging losses over a seven-year period.

4 Harold M. Groves, *Production, Jobs, and Taxes*, pp. 35–51. New York: McGraw-Hill, 1944.

the future, small corporations should have a tax advantage—
the purpose being, for economic and for social reasons, to
diminish concentration of production and of economic power.

Given rates of income and excess-profits taxes tend to discourage investment by small corporations more than by large
ones. Large enterprises can offset the loss, when an investment
goes sour, against profits made in the remainder of the business,
and so reduce their total tax bill. Small enterprises have less
chance to do this.

It has been calculated that if corporate income of over $100,-
000 were taxed at 40 per cent, and that under $100,000 at only
20 per cent, federal revenue would fall less than one-sixth under
that from a general 40-per-cent rate.[5]

However, the attainment of continuing general prosperity
probably would do more toward encouraging small enterprises
than any specific tax measures we could suggest, since small
firms are at special disadvantage in time of depression, especially in connection with getting capital.

3. With respect to personal income taxes, it is discouraging
and unjust to risky enterprises that individuals who have fluctuating incomes should not have credit for years of loss or low
income to set against years of high income. Returns from risky
investment are usually fluctuating: a period of loss usually must
be faced before positive returns can be hoped for. Our personal income taxes do not permit such early loss to be set
against the later possible gain. We have urgent reason to favor
persons with fluctuating incomes, instead of penalizing them,
as is the case at present. Tax burdens on these people should
be equalized by a liberal loss carryover, or averaging provision.

Realized capital gains and losses—that is, a rise or fall in the
value of property realized through sale, or transfer at death, or
by gift—should be treated like any other personal income.
They should, similarly, be subject to a generous carryover

---

[5] J. K. Butters, and J. Lintner, *Effect of Federal Taxes on Growing Enterprises*,
p. 133. Cambridge: Harvard University Press, 1945.

privilege, and losses should be fully deductible (now they are only partly deductible).[6]

4. A basic principle of fairness in taxing is that individuals with high incomes should pay high percentage taxes on those incomes. But the principle can be pushed too far. The risk, work, and responsibility which investment in new business requires will not be undertaken unless there is hope of a considerable return. This leads us to the conclusion that tax rates should rise only moderately through the range of moderately high incomes (say $20,000 to $60,000 a year) from which come a strategic portion of funds for risk investment. Above this range, since the total quantity of investment funds forthcoming will in any case be small (because so few people receive incomes above $60,000), the rate can again rise steeply for equalitarian reasons. The marginal tax rate of 56 per cent on $20,000 incomes in 1950, and the 78 per cent on $60,000 incomes were probably too high, though we can justify the 89 per cent on incomes over $100,000. The Committee for Economic Development has proposed taxes of 39 to 46 per cent on incomes within the $20,000 to $60,000 bracket. This seems more reasonable as a compromise between the basic aims of discouraging investment as little as possible, on the one hand, and less inequality of wealth, on the other hand.

In the past, the income tax has been criticized on the ground that it is an unreliable source of revenue: returns shrink far more in depression and swell far more in prosperity than, say, the returns from consumption taxes. This variability is, in fact, as we have seen, a principal virtue of the income tax, and helps to justify our choosing the personal income tax as the chief single source of government revenue. We want a tax system with *built-in* flexibility, a system that automatically absorbs much more funds away from private investment and consumption in time of high boom, much less in time of de-

---

[6] At present, a major loophole exists in the taxation of capital gains. See p. 278.

pression, and so lessens the violence of fluctuations of total expenditure.[7]

5. Finally, we may note that one cause of the recent housing problem, and a source of declining property values and local blight, is heavy and inequitable real estate taxation by local governments. The great bulk of the revenues of cities, towns, and counties comes from this source. But the local property tax has been abused. Part of the trouble comes from the excessive reliance placed on it. One major improvement would, therefore, be for the burden of the real estate tax to be lightened through greater support by state and federal governments of continuously growing municipal responsibilities. In addition, reform is needed in administration, especially to the end that assessments may be more equitable and frequently reviewed.

A note on equality

What we have suggested above with respect to lowering personal-income-tax rates in the moderately high brackets, and to eliminating double taxation of corporate income suggests that in pursuit of the goal of increased incentive perhaps we are losing sight of the goal that a healthy democratic society must keep in view—avoidance of great inequality of wealth and income. In our desire to encourage investment, we have been encouraging accumulation.

We should try to make the best both of *incentive* and *equality*. Men do not live forever, and the huge fortunes that can be accumulated from scratch within the lifetime of a single individual are, even with future surtaxes considerably lower, not going to be numerous or dangerous. As for inheritances, the prescription is plain.

Estate taxes (on the entire property of the deceased) and inheritance taxes (on the amount bequeathed to individual heirs)

---

[7] Some economists have gone so far as to suggest that taxes should become *negative* in time of depression—that is, turn into subsidies in order to shore up consumption and investment expenditure.

should be consciously aimed at the goal of ending transmissions of hereditary fortunes. Beyond the modest aims of securing to the widow and dependents unable to work a sum adequate to maintain them, and of completing the full education of all children, the justification for bequests tapers off rapidly. It is not allowable in a democracy to set up the goal of establishing a family dynasty.

At present, an exemption of $60,000 is permitted by federal law to all estates. Above this, the rates begin at 3 per cent and rise to 77 per cent on the portion in excess of 10 million dollars. The exemption of $60,000 should be lowered, and rates of taxation on larger estates should be raised further. But the main defects of death taxes lie in the existence of notorious loopholes through which part or all of the tax can be avoided.

1. The most important of the loopholes results from the possibilities of disposing the estate before death through gifts. For example, the owner of a $100,000 estate can obtain a 90-per-cent tax saving by giving it away to his beneficiary before death.[8]

2. Capital gains can remain untaxed from generation to generation so long as the gains are unrealized. Furthermore, each successive heir gets a new base price from which to figure.

3. It is possible to escape some of the death taxes through changing residence from one state to another.

These loopholes should be plugged. There is no reason why we cannot achieve at least the level of success of the British in increasing the productivity of death taxes.

An additional suggestion to end family dynasties is to tax at increasingly higher rates fortunes that are passed on to successive heirs—for example, the first inheritor might be taxed at the rate of 50 per cent; at his death the tax might be at the rate of 80 per cent on the portion he had inherited; the next

---

[8] H. M. Groves, *Production, Jobs and Taxes*, p. 90. New York: McGraw-Hill, 1944. The gift must be made "in the fullness of life"—that is, *not* in contemplation of death. Trusts set up to manage the property being given away, when the gift is irrevocable and income from it goes immediately to the beneficiary, secure exemption both from the federal death tax and most state death taxes.

death tax on the remainder of the original estate might be 100 per cent.

Estate taxes are relatively easily borne by the heirs, to whom the bequests are a windfall. They are not easily evaded, since estates of any size are probated in courts. They are a much milder discouragement to enterprise than taxes paid during the lifetime of the income receiver. They are unimportant as revenue producers, having as justification only our desire for less inequality of income and wealth. Toward this aim they can be, over the course of time, very effective. In 1935, 14 per cent of incomes below $5000 came from property sources. The percentage rose steadily with higher incomes until, for incomes over 1 million dollars, 98.5 per cent came from property sources.[9] In brief, high incomes arise mainly from property, much of which is inherited. With heavy taxes on inheritance, a chief cause of inequality of incomes disappears.

Monetary Policy

Under this heading we include all matters of policy relating to the money supply of the country. Monetary policy is, therefore, concerned with encouraging a high and stable level of income through varying the supply of money. But we face the immediate difficulty that the quantity of money does not bear a close relationship to (either the net or gross) national income. Money and national income usually vary in the same direction, but one cannot be closely predicted from the other.

In Chart 21, money is plotted against gross national income (or product) for the years 1909—1950. Money is here defined as the total of money outside banks plus checking accounts. In the 1930's and 1940's the volume of money was much larger relative to income than it had been in the previous two decades.

1. If money were used only for the purchase of newly produced goods and services, then we should expect money and income to vary in close proportions to each other. The amount

---

[9] *Concentration and Composition of Individual Incomes, 1918–1937.* TNEC Monograph No. 4 (Washington, 1941), p. 48.

of money needed to transact a given volume of production is probably quite stable: it depends on the average interval between the receipt of income and its payment out again as income, and this, in turn, depends on such slowly changing matters in the economy as the average frequency with which businesses and consumers make payments, the organization of industry, transportation facilities, and the like.

2. But not all money is used for the purchase of newly produced goods and services. Some money is held instead for use in financial transactions, for buying bonds, stocks, real estate, or other previously produced goods.

3. More important still, people may decide to "invest in cash,"—that is, to hold part of their wealth in the form of currency and checking deposits, and not to buy anything at all.

This last use of money furnishes the chief explanation of why money expanded relative to income in the 1930's and during World War II. An increased volume of money was available in the economy—in the 1930's owing to inflows of gold from abroad, to open-market operations, and other banking policies; and during World War II, to creation of money through government borrowing from the banking system. But the money flowed into the hands of people who decided to hold a large part of it idle, to use it *neither* for investment or consumption. During the 1930's investment possibilities were not attractive, and during the war private investment and consumption were constricted by special government controls.

This looseness of relationship between money and income does not mean that monetary policy is to be neglected. Perhaps economists are at the present time unduly pessimistic about what can be done in the monetary field.

Wartime financing brought major changes to our monetary and banking system. A principal legacy is that the quantity of money got out of hand. By the end of 1950 about 197 billion dollars of United States government securities had come into the hands of the public and of banks. The holders of these could, if they wanted, exchange them for money at the prices for these securities guaranteed by Federal Reserve policy; and the volume of money at the disposal of the public can expand far beyond this, since bank reserves would be increased, making possible a further multiple rise in deposits. The ultimate increase in the money supply that *might* take place was therefore several times 197 billion dollars. (The existing money supply at the end of 1950 was only 117 billion dollars.)

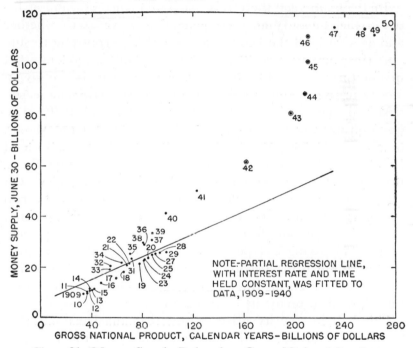

Chart 21. Money Supply Related to Gross National Product.
Source: Survey of Current Business, Vol. XXVI (May, 1946), p. 10; *The Economic Report of the President* (January, 1950), pp. 149, 174; (January, 1951), pp. 171, 198.

The continuance of the Federal Reserve and Treasury policy of low and stable interest rates on government securities—that is, the continuance of the policy of standing ready to buy federal securities at fixed rates—was incompatible with effective use of the main traditional powers over the money supply (open-market operations, changes in discount rates, and changes in reserve requirements). The most important determinant by far of the volume of money was the form in which the public wanted to hold their liquid assets. If they were content to continue to hold federal securities, the money supply would not increase; but if they unloaded them, then the Federal Reserve would support the market by buying them up, and so place additional money in the hands of the public.

In 1949 and 1950 there was sharp difference of opinion between the Treasury and the Federal Reserve as to whether and at what level the Federal Reserve should continue to support the prices of government securities. Only a moderate fall in the prices of government securities (that is to say, a moderate rise in the interest rate paid on government securities) had been permitted between mid-1947 and 1949. The question was whether a decided rise in the interest rate should be allowed by lowering the price level at which the Federal Reserve stood ready to buy government securities. The Treasury opposed, the Federal Reserve favored, such a policy. On March 3, 1951 an "Accord" was announced between the two agencies, in accord with which there were successive lowerings of the price support levels, and the issuance of a new long-term bond paying 2¾ per cent, higher by ¼ per cent than that of any existing negotiable long-term bond.[10] Up to the end of April a fall of three cents on the dollar occurred, and was allowed to occur, in bond prices.

This fall in security prices meant that any bank or other holder of governments who was tempted to sell the securities before their redemption date in order to lend to private borrowers had to face the sharp discouragement of a capital loss. To this extent, lending to businesses and consumers would be lessened, and inflationary pressures checked.

But no wide change in the interest rate is to be expected in the visible future. "Easy money" will continue. The level of

10 The Series E savings bonds, which are not negotiable, pay 2.9 per cent if held for their full 10-year term.

interest rates, following the huge rise in government debt during the war, too closely affects the credit of the government (because the price of government bonds fluctuates inversely to the interest rate), the interest burden faced by the Treasury, the solvency of banks, and the incomes of endowed institutions and private individuals, for it to be raised or lowered *much* in the hope of discouraging or encouraging private investment expenditure.

As we have reasoned before, the level of interest rates, even in past years when the public debt was small, has not been of first importance among anti-depression measures. Profit prospect faced by businessmen (the marginal efficiency of capital) fluctuates far more than does interest rates. In addition, the rates on certain kinds of loans are inflexible, or inversely flexible, or else are not subject to control by the monetary authorities. But it would always have been possible, by raising interest rates *enough*, to discourage investment, even though we are not sure that lowering them (to any point above zero) would encourage investment much.

There are, however, special measures that might be undertaken to reduce interest rates and make funds more abundant in strategic areas. Through the Reconstruction Finance Corporation, the National Housing Agency, and other federal agencies, including the Federal Reserve, funds can be made available (or guaranteed) at especially low rates in loans for residence construction and to industry.

Housing is an especially favorable area for such activity. Before World War II, 70 per cent of privately financed homebuilding was supported under programs of the Federal Housing and Home Loan Bank Administrations. It might be possible to lower interest rates and down-payment requirements in order to stimulate construction during times when building activity and general business activity are declining. With respect to loans to industry, the RFC and other agencies could make loans at favorable rates during time of recession, especially to small businesses, which are handicapped compared to large businesses by their inability to borrow at low interest rates.

Special Measures

There are a number of special measures that can be a help toward increasing investment, and some of them, toward increasing productivity.

1. The federal and state governments have for many years carried on research work in experiment stations and universities for the benefit of agriculture. The individual farm is typically too small to carry on effective research for itself. There appears to be every reason for expanding government-supported research into the fields of industrial problems of production and quality of product, as well as into basic fields of physical, chemical, medical, and other research, which will have their inevitable by-products at the practical level. The extraordinary success of government-inspired research during World War II has encouraged in the postwar years a remarkable volume of support of both basic and applied research in the physical sciences by the Department of Defense and its subdivisions. Other divisions of the government have smaller programs of research support. Dr. Bush's original recommendations [11] for continuing into peacetime the research that developed radar and unlocked the secrets of atomic fission would cost every year, at its full development, less than the cost of half a day of war.

The results of any research program supported by government and useful in commercial channels should be available to all industry. It would therefore help to redress an advantage that larger enterprises have had in the past, since they alone can support large-scale research. And it would lead toward a more rapid growth in technical efficiency and hence in volume of national output.

2. Any method of reducing the cost of housing would in-

---

11 Vannevar Bush, *Science, the Endless Frontier.* Report of the Office of Scientific Research and Development (Washington, July, 1945).

crease output in this vast field where our need will inevitably be, for years, in excess of our ability to produce—and to pay for—unless effective measures are taken. One needed reform is the modernization of building codes and building methods, which in city after city are far behind the times, enforcing obsolete and wasteful construction practices. A study in some 100 cities showed all of them specifying masonry walls 8 to 17 inches thick, although it is now possible to construct sturdy 4-inch masonry walls, and there are many new wall materials available that do not depend on thickness for strength. Chicago has distinguished itself by its blockade against modern practices: provisions in the code have, in effect, banned the use of anything but plaster in interior walls, a requirement that bars experimentation in prefabricated, dry wall construction. Steel buildings have been prohibited. The hod-carriers' union has prohibited the use of centrally mixed concrete.

The Department of Justice has charged that plumbing manufacturers with four-fifths of total output sell only to approved distributors, who in turn sell only to approved master plumbers, with prices fixed all along the line. A manufacturer who wishes to cut prices may find it impossible to get his fixtures installed.

Obviously, the expansion of low-cost home construction can be encouraged by efficient factory assembly of kitchens, bathrooms, and other structural units, by standardization of parts, and modification of some of the habitual construction methods. The need is urgent. Part of the resistance to change originates in the habitual efforts of building-supply producers to defend their share of a formerly compressed and shrinking market, and in the effort of unions to defend their members against unemployment. The resistance of city councils to better codes, and back of them, the resistance of material suppliers and unions to more effective materials and practices, may be lessened if, from policies like those we are suggesting, the economy continues with a high and stable level of output and employment.

International Monetary and Financial Cooperation

The United States is the only major industrial nation whose productive ability was expanded rather than disrupted by World War II. Many of the countries engaged in the war have been in need of consumer goods to tide them over postwar years of hunger and want of clothing and shelter, and also in need of industrial raw materials and equipment to replace what the war has destroyed, and to get them started in peacetime production. Other parts of the world—India and South America among them—want to industrialize their agrarian economies. The United States in its good fortune has an obligation to help its neighbors; it has also a vital interest in continued peace, and hence in stable economic prosperity.

The adherence of the United States to the Bretton Woods plan for the establishment of an International Fund and, probably more important, an International Bank for Reconstruction and Development, will help to stabilize the relations of world currencies, and to facilitate and guarantee the flow of funds for rebuilding and raising productivity elsewhere in the world. Under the U. S. program of aid to unproductive areas of the world, there were 520 million dollars of grants and credits in 1949–1950, and 690 million dollars in 1950–1951. The International Bank, to which the U. S. is the major single contributor, advanced 134, and 119, million dollars in these two years.[12] Our cooperation will promote international responsibility and goodwill and the establishment of stable trading relationships, to the common benefit of the countries of the world.

If a country exports more than it imports, the level of domestic production and employment is, of course, raised (assuming the existence of a margin of available unemployment resources). Nevertheless, the attainment of a large net export

---

[12] Fiscal years of the U. S. Government running from July 1 through June 30, *Economic Report of the President*, January 1952, p. 127.

balance by the United States is not an important route to higher employment. There are two reasons. First, our foreign trade is small compared to our internal trade (see page 176). Second, any efforts to export without importing will bring deflationary influence on foreign countries and pressure on their reserves of gold and dollars. They will attempt to defend themselves by tariffs, quotas, embargoes, exchange controls, and bilateral agreements, which will vitiate our efforts and, in addition, disrupt international division of labor and so worsen the economic condition of the whole world.

Our foreign trade balance is best looked on as a consequence, rather than a cause, of any given level of employment. Any country that expands its production and employment—in consequence either of an ordinary business boom or of government fiscal policy measures—tends to experience an adverse balance in its international payments. That is, its imports rise, and its exports lag behind. This is the result of an income effect and a price effect: as incomes rise, demand rises both for home-produced and for foreign-produced goods; and if prices rise, as it is likely they will to some extent, imports will be further encouraged and exports discouraged.

An adverse balance of payments can be met for a limited time by a gold outflow, by drawing down balances of foreign currencies, or by loans from abroad. If the adverse balance continues, more decisive adjustments must be undertaken—the reversing of a domestic inflation of prices and money incomes, cooperative international action to expand production and employment abroad, depreciation of the currency, or specific measures to expand exports or contract imports (such as export subsidies, and tariffs and other blocks to imports).

International trade matters are not of primary significance for determining the level of income and employment of the United States, though the political implications are far-reaching and though the economic stability of many other countries depends considerably on our internal employment and our trade policies.[13]

Measures to Combat Monopolistic Restriction of Output

We have reasoned before that the general problem of "monopoly" is a complicated one, with both good and bad aspects. This is still true when we look to the restricted question of the effect of monopoly on employment. We have seen that greater short-run price flexibility would not necessarily increase employment and that the longer-run shifts of relative prices, which are desirable, are not incompatible with monopoly.

The effect of monopoly on total expenditure is twofold: Up to a point, monopoly induces investment by giving innovators a better prospect of gaining from their improvements. It is, in part, for such a purpose that our patent law gives a monopoly to inventors for a term of 17 years. But beyond a certain point, monopolistic policies discourage investment (and so diminish output and employment) by hindering or blocking the entry of management, capital equipment, and labor into the monopolized area. It is such monopolistic restriction of output and of investment that we do not want.

If price-cutting competitors in the insurance business are boycotted (South-Eastern Underwriters' Association), if patents are misused in the glass-container industry to divide the market and restrict output (Hartford Empire), if national loan-shark syndicates can block competition and exact extravagant interest rates on small loans, if the Railway Express agrees to pick up and deliver packages for airline shipment only on condition the airlines keep their rates high—if such policies exist, evidently competitive investment is choked off in the par-

---

13 Calvin B. Hoover, *International Trade and Domestic Employment.* New York: McGraw-Hill, 1945; Gottfried Haberler, *Prosperity and Depression,* third edition, Chap. 12. Geneva: League of Nations, 1941; and *Economic Stability in the Postwar World,* Chaps. 6, 13, 17, 20. Geneva: League of Nations, 1945.

ticular fields, and unless there are offsets elsewhere, total employment and output are diminished.

There are a large number of policies that have the effect of combating the power of monopoly to restrict output and employment. Some of the policies we have already mentioned would have that effect; and the success of a full employment program would diminish some of the defense incentives for monopolistic policy. Measures specially directed toward the problem include some or all of the following.

1. Strengthening of the antitrust agencies of government. The mere knowledge—following Thurman Arnold's suggestion—that one or two representatives of the Antitrust Division of the Department of Justice are in every state to receive complaints and to give publicity to antisocial business practices can have an effective influence toward toning up business morals. For the men who violate the antitrust laws are respectable, prominent in the community, and therefore sensitive to public opinion.

2. A federal incorporation law to replace the "competition in laxity" of state laws might also be desirable to this end.

3. Government ownership and operation is desirable for those monopolies that are, for one reason or another, difficult to regulate and cannot be broken up into efficient competing units. The aim again is to replace restriction with expansion. Present owners should be liberally compensated to avoid what would otherwise be a discouraging effect on private investment in those and bordering fields.

4. Undesirable legal support now given to monopolistic sellers should be withdrawn. Lowering of tariffs would introduce more effective foreign competition.[14] Reform of our patent laws is long overdue. Though they retain their original purpose of stimulating innovation, it is also true that patent mo-

---

[14] This has a short-run depressing effect on investment in the home industries that compete with foreign products. In the longer run, this negative effect will be offset by expansion of relatively efficient industries.

nopolies have been, since 1890, a chief strategem of big business trying legally to control its market. Perhaps compulsory licensing of patents at reasonable rates to all applicants is necessary. The administrative difficulty of this suggests that other measures of reform should be tried first or in addition—the judicial eviction of monopolistic practices from patent protection (as in Hartford Empire); the beginning of the term of the patent at the time of application (so that applications cannot be deliberately kept "pending," and so protected, for many years); and perhaps the development of a second class of "petty patents" to run for a brief time, five or seven years. In addition, the expansion of cooperatives would limit the power of monopolistic sellers to exact high prices. Finally, there has grown up in recent years an ominous tangle of barriers to trade between the states. The motive behind these is generally the protection of local producers. Public policy should be directed toward their removal.

Secular and cyclical policy

All the above measures for encouraging private investment are useful for the purpose of encouraging a continued, secular increase in investment expenditure. If our problem is that *occasionally* private investment expenditure is inadequately low, the tax measures recommended above are especially useful. A progressive tax system with averaging or loss carry-over provisions diminishes its burden sharply when business activity and incomes fall—in other words, the taxes are not only levied on lower incomes, but also at lower *rates*. In addition, policies affecting monetary matters (especially direct lending in strategic areas) can be of some use in the cycle, though measures affecting the cash position or liquidity of lenders are of greater effectiveness toward choking off a speculative boom,[15] and toward maintaining demand at the onset, rather than toward stimulating demand at the bottom, of a depression.

---

15 P. 168.

These measures for stimulating investment, like the previous ones for encouraging consumption, are relevant to other social values than those of high production and employment. We have tried to choose measures with the best possible over-all effect.

CHAPTER SEVENTEEN

Fiscal Policy

WE HAVE SURVEYED A LIST OF MEASURES DIRECTED TOWARD encouraging private consumption expenditure and private investment expenditure. Though there is obviously room for difference of opinion as to what measures should be included and what measures emphasized, some such items as those we have listed must find a place in any policy directed toward full employment.

There is no certainty that even an ideal group of measures for encouraging consumption and investment will suffice to maintain a full employment level of expenditure. The profit prospect may still be too dismal, for many diverse reasons, to allow businessmen to invest heavily—even with all the measures of encouragement in effect that central policy can devise. What further action can be taken? Specifically, what use can be made of fiscal policy; that is, of the government's revenues and expenditures?

In past decades the tasks of government have been seen as essentially those of maintaining internal order and external defense. Hence, in ordinary peacetime years federal government expenditures were only a small proportion of the gross national product: 2.0 per cent in 1909, 1.8 per cent in 1913, 3.2 per cent in 1926. Under such conditions there could be little influence on the volume of national production and employment from the side of the government budget. Government revenues and expenditures were not in a range of size where they could significantly affect costs or incomes over the whole economy.

Nor was any stimulus to expenditure in the economy felt to be needed. It was argued, in accord with Say's law, that the private economy naturally tends toward full employment levels of production. The plausible conclusion followed that the government budget should be as neutral as possible in its effect on the allocation of resources as determined by private expenditure. A useful rule of thumb on the totals of government revenue and expenditure was developed: The budget should be balanced annually. The rule was often violated—in the 156 years from 1792 through 1947 we had 90 years of appreciable surplus and 58 years of appreciable deficit in the federal budget. But it remained as a convenient check on the propensity of legislators to vote new expenditures (generally politically popular) without voting new taxes (politically unpopular.

In recent years the percentage that federal government expenditures bear to the gross national product has been rising from an unimportant less than 5 per cent to a significant 10 per cent or more. In 1932 it was 7.2 per cent; in 1939, 10.0 per cent; in 1950, about 18 per cent.[1] The reasons for this rise are several: outlays on defense have grown (about 5.8 per cent of the gross national product in 1950); the national debt has expanded during depression and above all during World War II (interest charges were about 1.7 per cent of the 1950 gross national product); and finally, outlays for agriculture, social welfare, international affairs, veterans, national resources and the like, are larger than before (about 10.3 percent of the 1950 gross national product).[2] There is no likelihood that in the visible future government expenditures—or taxes—will shrink back to the pre-1930's level. Hence, whether we like it or not,

---

[1] The percentage always rises during wartime years: in 1918 it was about 20 per cent; in 1944 and 1945 about 50 per cent.

[2] 1932 and 1939 data are for the fiscal year, ending June 30 of the given year; 1950 data are for the calendar year.

the relationship of the government budget to production and employment in the economy forces itself upon our attention.

The new relationship implies the need for a higher level of administrative responsibility to replace the old rule of thumb. We can hope that the reports and procedures of the Employment Act of 1946 will work toward this end. Equally important, the new relationship requires public understanding of the purposes and means of fiscal policy, since this is the condition of the necessary public cooperation.

The fundamental rule of government finance, to which only minor qualifications exist, is that nothing shall be decided on financial grounds.[3] The basic realities of the economy are resources (labor, management, raw materials, plant, and equipment), and the wants of the people of the economy (for a high standard of living and for useful employment, gained with freedom of choice and equal opportunity). Money is simply a tool for the effective utilization of these resources toward fulfilling wants. Like other tools, money can get out of order, and can be used skilfully or badly. Government can, through its monetary authority and through its revenue and expenditure policy, exert a considerable influence on the flow of money in the economy, and so upon the allocation of resources to one use or another and upon how much of the resources are to be used and how much left unemployed.

Basic Reasoning on Government Finance, and Employment

1. First, we look to the flow of purchasing power in the economy as related to the government budget. Suppose unemployment exists. Then any government expenditure increases production and employment (unless there are indirect effects, to be considered below, toward contracting private consumption or investment expenditure). This stimulating effect exists whether the expenditure is directly for output or whether it is only a transfer payment that increases the money incomes

---

3 The rule is attributed to the London *Economist.*

of people who will subsequently spend on output. On the other hand, taxation withdraws money from the economy and, by contracting private expenditure, diminishes production and employment. Therefore, if budgetary policy goes too far in the direction of heavy taxing and light spending (that is, in the direction of avoiding deficits or generating surpluses),[4] total expenditure, production, and employment will be inadequate.

Production and employment can be stimulated, therefore, either through increased government expenditure or through decreased taxation. Also, and rather surprisingly, it is possible, as we shall see below, to secure a net stimulating effect through increasing equally both expenditure and taxes.

2. But reasoning on this monetary level is less significant than reasoning about the utilization of real resources in the economy. If any government expenditure is justified, the gain to the economy must exceed the loss that results, directly or indirectly, from the process of getting the funds.

The real gain is the increased production resulting from the expenditure. Sometimes it is easy to measure this real gain in value terms. When a toll bridge is built with government funds, we can find out how much people are willing to pay for the privilege of using the bridge. But often it is very difficult to measure the gain: new roads, new school buildings, public health work do not come on the market for sale, and we shall have to give our own subjective estimate of their social value. Some such projects have a very high social value and cannot be effectively performed by any agency other than the government. (The mere fact that the government does not charge us for facilities and services does not, as some journalists claim, indicate that they may not be completely justified by increased social productivity and social welfare.) Other projects are of slight value or can be performed better by private in-

---

[4] The surpluses will ordinarily be devoted to reducing government debt. But if an investment boom is in progress, then the best Treasury policy may be not to place more money in the possession of private investors, but instead to accumulate idle balances in the Federal Reserve.

dividuals. Logically, we should set up a scale of social priority for possible projects and direct government expenditure into projects of highest social value.

The real cost to offset against the above real gain is the loss of possibility of private use of the resources in question, plus the "burden of public debt" that results if the expenditure is financed by a loan. We shall see later that this "burden" is mild.

It is, therefore, true that if the resources made use of through government policy would otherwise have been left idle and if those resources are either abundant (like air, water, and perhaps coal) or perishable (labor time), there is no *real* cost to the expansion, though there will be a *money* cost. The increased production and employment are pure gain. The newly employed workers will certainly not think themselves worse off because they now have jobs. The whole economy is better off now through the higher production and will not be worse off in the future.

3. Suppose that we are facing the problem of setting up a budget policy for the government. We start out by assuming for the moment that the problem of adequate production and employment is solved. Then, the relevant question is: How far and into what channels should government expenditures be pushed, assuming that the resources which the government uses would otherwise go into private consumption or investment or into desired leisure? We must ask ourselves such a question about every specific project for government expenditure that is proposed and assent to the expenditure only when its gain (by our estimate of social values) overbalances the loss it involves. We assume, first, that the budget is balanced. The tax structure is set up without reference to employment effects, being based on such criteria as equity, nondisturbance of private allocation of resources, and administrative feasibility.

But suppose that this happy condition is upset by the appearance of unemployment. We must now ask ourselves additional questions: How far is it justifiable because of the unemployment (a) to increase government expenditures, (b) to reduce average rates to taxation, and/or (c) to mold the structure of taxation and expenditure into one as stimulating as possible to private consumption and investment? The effects of each such policy need to be evaluated in turn, including effect on social priorities and influence on the division betwen the spheres of government and the private economy. It is likely that we shall decide to follow all three of these possibilities up to a certain point.

Allocation of Resources and Government Expenditures

There is always room for doubt as to whether demand, expressed in offers of money on the market for the purchase of goods and services, rightly measures the social usefulness of the goods and services that are bought. The rich man's purchase of a yacht means that labor and other resources are used up that could otherwise have gone into the building of perhaps 10 houses, and we may feel sure that the houses would contribute more to human welfare—even though they are entered in the national product at the same figure as the yacht.

Our doubts on this matter are less pressing if there is heavy unemployment. If the resources used in a doubtful channel would otherwise have been idle, the society is still ordinarily better off as a consequence of the expenditure. But there is reason for special qualms when we look to the effect of government expenditures at a time of nearly full employment.

1. A problem of nearly full employment

Suppose the economy is approaching full employment of its resources as a result, in part, of the expansion of government expenditures. There is increasing danger that the government expenditures will bid resources away from private uses where they contribute more effectively to the fulfillment of human wants. Few resources are then idle, and of those that are idle many are relatively immobile, being attached to their old location or occupation. Hence, the government's expenditures will bid some resources away from private uses where, conceivably, their social value is higher. The government might build a dam, in part through the use of labor and materials that would otherwise have gone into house construction, and houses may be needed much more than the dam.

Government expenditures must always be made in some local area, and local interests compete strenuously for grants. Their representatives, moreover, want to be re-elected. And so the national interest must endure the sharp competition of many local interests; and national and local interests are often, to some extent, in conflict. Point is given to this fear of worsened allocation of resources by the recollection that in the fall of 1946 some 2 billion dollars of federal funds were allocated to public-works projects at a time when employment was at higher than "full employment" level and inflationary pressures on prices were the chief economic problem.

When we are considering the concrete possibilities of expanding employment and production through government expenditures, we must take into account this political danger. The higher the existing level of employment, the greater the risk that increased government expenditures will lead to worsened allocation of resources.

2. Structural changes

Over the course of the years major changes in the structure of the economy are gradually taking place. Among such structural changes are the following.

(*a*) Agriculture in a progressive economy absorbs, over the decades, a shrinking proportion of the working force, and urban occupations a rising proportion. It is the pressure of relatively low incomes in agriculture that furnishes a main incentive for farmers, and especially for farm children, to seek jobs in town. In the shorter run there have been acute dislocations in agriculture: in each of the world wars, farm output in the United States has expanded greatly; after World War I our agriculture suffered acutely as European areas again came into cultivation, as European countries after 1926 raised tariffs, and as productivity rose both in this country and abroad. This kind of distress to United States agriculture may appear once again. Also, technological advance has its specialized effects— wool and cotton are increasingly subject to the competition of synthetic fibers. There are, in addition, shifts in consumer preferences. Especially important are long-run shifts in demand resulting from rising average incomes; as people grow better off over the course of generations, they consume less cereals and more meat, vegetables, and fruit. This means relative distress in cereal-producing areas.

(b) Other industries than agriculture experience pressures to expand or contract from technological change and from changing conditions of supply and demand. Magnesium, aluminum, and specialized steels tend to supplant ordinary steel, cast iron, and other metals. The plastics and glass products industries are expanding, in part at the expense of other producers.

Our recent declining rate of population growth tended toward less investment in public utilities and perhaps in housing. There is a general tendency for the undeveloped parts of the country to show more rapid industrial growth than the older parts: the South and West are expanding more than the Northeast. Over the course of the decades increasing average real income means, as basic wants are more adequately filled, that consumer demand tends to become unstable and fickle, more subject to the whims of fashion.

The structural changes resulting from these causes are, in the main, inevitable and desirable in a healthy economy. They suggest a political danger, however, for a program of government expenditures directed toward higher employment: the relatively poor showing and distress that are the means by which resources are allocated from less to more useful purposes may be seized upon by the politician as justification for largess from the public purse.

Relief of special distress is, of course, in order, but it should be directed toward emergency needs and toward facilitating adjustments—not toward shoring up lost causes. Public grants can merely delay and frustrate the healthy shifting of resources from areas and occupations where they serve the wants of consumers badly to where they serve them well.

The two points we have mentioned—the danger that public expenditures may lead to worsened allocation of resources when full employment is being approached and periods when significant structural changes are taking place—suggest that perhaps there is a general advantage in having the stimulus from the government budget arise from lower taxes rather than from higher expenditure. But there are counterarguments.

1. Government expenditures can be directed toward specific areas and occupations where there is unemployment (and where the structural-change argument we have just given is not relevant), whereas the effects of reduced taxes are much less subject to control.

2. There are deep social needs for social-security measures, health services, educational support, low-cost housing, and other public works—for meeting what Sir William Beveridge calls "the giant social evils of Want, Disease, Ignorance, and Squalor." A wide area of social needs cannot be adequately met by private expenditure.

It is better not to come to any over-all conclusion but to return to our earlier pattern of argument: we should weigh individually the social advantages and disadvantages of specific types and volumes of increased expenditures and decreased taxes.

A. Quantitative Aspects of the Budget

We have said that, if the budgetary policy of government goes too far in the direction of avoiding deficits or generating surpluses, total expenditure in the economy, and hence production and employment, will be too low. Suppose that a group of favorable policies to encourage private consumption and investment of the sort we recommend in Chapters 15 and 16 have, in fact, been carried through, and that, with the federal budget balanced, there is still a considerable deficiency of expenditure below the value of gross output at full employment. It is possible to illustrate approximately but rather simply how government taxes and expenditures can be used to bring about full employment.

The example below is subject to three simplifying assumptions. It is assumed that: (1) Private investment is not affected by government policies. (We will consider this assumption later). (2) The marginal propensities to consume of the people who pay taxes and who receive government payments are taken as the same. (These may differ and affect the results. Hence the *kinds* of expenditures and taxes of government—also considered below—are critically important.) (3) Finally, we neglect the budgetary possibilities of state and local governments, despite the fact that their total expenditures, 1920-1940, have on the average been larger than that of the federal government. (In the middle 1930's and afterward, federal expenditure grew much larger.) Our reasons for this omission are two: (a) Their taxing and borrowing capacity is strictly limited by local revenue resources, whereas the federal government has not only country-wide tax resources but also control of the banking and currency system of the nation. Only the federal government has the resources to maintain its expenditure nearly irrespective of revenues, or to vary its budget countercyclically. (b) It is not likely that state and local governments could be induced to integrate their policies fully with the fiscal program of the federal government. In fact, through many of the interwar years, the expenditure practices of state and local governments were directly contrary to those of the federal government. It is to be hoped that, in the future, effective forms of cooperation will be devised between them and the federal government—for example, federal expenditures may be channeled through state and local units.

There are three routes to full employment through use of

the federal budget, illustrated in Table 15. The figures are illustrative only, but are in accord with the general magnitudes to be expected. We assume as our original situation that the government budget is balanced at 30 billion dollars of tax revenues and expenditures, and that after all acceptable nonbudgetary policies to encourage private consumption and investment have been carried into effect, gross national production is running about 24 billion dollars short of that necessary to buy the full employment output of the economy.

TABLE 15

FEDERAL BUDGETS

(*in billions of dollars*)

	Taxes	Expenditures for Output	Deficit
Original situation	30	30	0
Route *I* to full employment: Expenditure is increased sufficiently, with the *rates* of taxes unchanged	38	46	8
Route *II* to full employment: Expenditure is increased, taxes are increased equally	54	54	0
Route *III* to full employment: Expenditures are kept unchanged, with taxes reduced sufficiently	6	30	24

Route I shows the kind of result that would follow a maintained increase in government spending for goods and services,[5] with the original tax schedule unchanged. The govern-

---

5 The calculations assume that any change in government expenditure is in the government's purchases of current output, not in transfer payments. If a rise in expenditure consists of increased transfer payments, the stimulating effect is weaker. The original recipients are likely to save some part of their receipts; that is, to increase their spending for goods and services by only a portion of their increased disposable incomes. But if the government spends directly for goods and services, *all* its spending swells demand for current output.

ment spending raises national expenditure both directly, through the immediate market it provides for idle resources and men, and indirectly, through the effects of initially higher incomes on the chain of re-spendings. This latter is the multiplier effect. The multiplier effect will be larger to the extent that people spend more of their increased incomes for consumption. But the multiplier effect is checked in Route I by the circumstance that people have to pay heavier taxes out of their larger incomes (even with unchanged *rates* of taxation).[6]

Route II leads to full employment through an equal increase in both taxes and expenditure. The stimulating effect of this

---

[6] Route I leads to full production and employment in the following way: the increased government spending for current production is 16 billion dollars a year, or 4 billion dollars a quarter year. We assume that the "income period" is also 3 months, or a quarter year (p. 206); and that the marginal propensity to consume, when income is defined as gross national income, can be estimated, as a rough average, at $\frac{1}{2}$. The increased government spending of 4 billion dollars every quarter will have added to it $\frac{1}{2}$ of 4 billions when the first recipients, A, increase their consumer spending by the normal proportion to a second group of recipients, B. The B group spend additionally $\frac{1}{2}$ of $\frac{1}{2}$ of 4 billions to a third group, C; and so on. The complete series of income changes runs, in billions:

$$4 + \frac{1}{2} \times 4 + (\frac{1}{2})^2 \times 4 + (\frac{1}{2})^3 \times 4 + \ldots ;$$

which eventually approaches the value of *plus* 8 billions a quarter (p. 206) or *plus* 32 billions a year.

Partly offsetting this stimulus is the increased volume of taxes taken out of the economy. We have assumed that the pattern of taxes is such that 2 billion more a quarter, or 8 billions more a year, is taxed away as income rises to its final level. What is the effect of this 2 billions a quarter toward checking the rise in income? The first group of people, R, who are taxed, suffer no loss in income created and received; they simply are forced to turn over to the government 2 billions out of their incomes. But when they have time to react to their lower *disposable* incomes, they cut their spending to people from whom they buy consumer goods and services, S; as we assume again, for simplicity, by $\frac{1}{2}$ of 2 billions. As the incomes of group S drop, they cut their spending to group T by $\frac{1}{2}$ of $\frac{1}{2}$ of 2 billions; and so on. The complete series of income change runs:

$$0 - \frac{1}{2} \times 2 - (\frac{1}{2})^2 \times 2 - (\frac{1}{2})^3 \times 2 \ldots ;$$

which eventually approaches the value of *minus* 2 billions a quarter, or *minus* 8 billions a year.

The effect of the changes both in expenditure and taxation is, per year, plus 32 billions minus 8 billions, or plus 24 billions.

The data are designed to show the ultimate effects of given policies, when the multiplier has worked itself out to its ultimate level, rather than the lesser intermediate effects.

comes from the fact that an added dollar of taxes does not initially reduce incomes created and received at all—it immediately reduces only disposable income; whereas an added dollar of expenditure for output initially raises income created and received by a full dollar. Hence, if taxes are collected from, and government expenditures paid out to, people with the same marginal propensities to consume, a rise in government taxing and spending by one dollar causes a rise in national income of exactly one dollar.[7]

Route III leads to full employment by way of reduction of taxes only, expenditure remaining the same. The reduction of taxes is stimulating to the extent that it frees funds that will then be spent on consumption.[8]

Which Route is best?

What choice (we still continue our assumption that private investment is unchanged) should be made among these Routes? Those who most fear government expenditures—on the grounds that they are made inefficiently on make-work projects

---

[7] The increased government expenditure, and taxes, are both 24 billions a year, or 6 billions a quarter. The multiplier series from the increased government expenditure is:

$$6 + \tfrac{1}{2} \times 6 + (\tfrac{1}{2})^2 \times 6 + (\tfrac{1}{2})^3 \times 6 + \ldots$$

The multiplier series from increasing taxes starts with 0, since the people who pay the taxes do not suffer a cut in incomes created and received. But as their disposable incomes drop, they reduce their spending to others. (We assume, obtaining a simple formula, that reduced taxes of t amount cause people to raise their consumer spending by $\tfrac{1}{2}t$.) The series runs:

$$0 - \tfrac{1}{2} \times 6 - (\tfrac{1}{2})^2 \times 6 - (\tfrac{1}{2})^3 \times 6 - \ldots$$

These two multiplier series are identical save for the plus 6 in the first series. National income, in other words, is up by 6 billion dollars a quarter, or 24 billion dollars a year.

[8] When the 24 billions a year in taxes is remitted, or 6 billions a quarter, the people previously taxed experience no immediate rise in incomes created and received. But they increase their consumer spending every quarter (we make the same assumption as before about the effect on consumption spending of changing disposable income through taxation). The series runs:

$$0 + \tfrac{1}{2} \times 6 + (\tfrac{1}{2})^2 \times 6 + (\tfrac{1}{2})^3 \times 6 + \ldots$$

This series eventually approaches a total value of 6 billion dollars a quarter, of 24 billions a year.

for which the public would not themselves choose to spend their own money, and that they tend to push into areas best handled by private businesses—have cause to reject Route I and (still more) Route II. On the other hand, those who are afraid of deficits and growing government debt have reason to prefer Route II, since it alone provides for a balanced budget.

Route III is to be shunned by those who fear increasing government debt, but, on the other hand, should be chosen by those who are concerned to prevent an increase in government expenditure.

The assumption that private investment is unchanged

Our reasoning so far has been very limited by the assumption made that private investment remains unchanged, no matter which Route is pursued.

An increase in tax rates (Route II) tends to discourage private investment; a decrease (Route III), to encourage it. A rise in consumption expenditure (all Routes) induces more investment expenditure. A rise in the public debt (Routes I and especially III) may, if businessmen retain their present attitudes, tend to discourage private investment. A large rise in government expenditure (Route II) may discourage private investment.

All these Routes, therefore, have opposed effects on investment. Route I combines higher consumption (stimulating) with a deficit (probably somewhat depressing). Route II combines higher consumption (stimulating) with increased taxes and heavy government expenditures (depressing). Route III combines higher consumption and lower taxes (stimulating) with a very large deficit (probably depressing).[9]

---

[9] A report to the United Nations on full employment policies makes an interesting suggestion: that when unemployment becomes greater in a country than the accepted tolerable range (perhaps 3 to 5 per cent) for three successive months, a specific schedule of lowered income and sales tax rates and raised expenditures should automatically go into effect. But the executive branch of the government is to be given power to cancel the application of this compensatory program where there is clear evidence that the rise in unemployment is due to other causes than a fall in effective demand. *National and International Measures for Full Employment.* New York: United Nations, 1949.

Our first reasoning, which took into account only the effect of these three Routes on consumption, must, therefore, be considerably qualified by consideration of the uncertain effects of each of them on private investment. If the net effect on investment of a given Route is stimulating, smaller changes in government tax rates and/or expenditure are needed. If the net effect on investment of a given Route is depressing, larger changes in government tax rates and/or expenditure are needed to achieve full employment.

It is even possible that the depressing effect on private investment might more than offset the direct stimulus of the given Route, so that its over-all influence is depressing! It is certainly possible that a disjointed set of timid measures might have such a result. But our war experience, and certain other reasoning (pp. 326-328), strongly suggests that this is a fringe-end possibility only—that any reasonable set of measures, vigorously undertaken, will not lead to a reduction of private investment. Assurance of sustained markets gives an overriding incentive *not* to reduce private investment.

Evidently, different *kinds* of revenue sources (both taxing and borrowing), and different *kinds* of expenditure will have various effects both on consumption expenditure in the economy and on investment. The kinds of taxes and expenditures and the kinds of other policies carried on by the government may be more important than the balance struck on the books, more important than whether the government is balancing its budget or running a deficit.

B. Qualitative Aspects of the Budget

Different *kinds* of revenue sources (both taxing and borrowing) and different *kinds* of expenditure will have various effects both on consumption expenditure in the economy and on investment. They determine, within limits, not only the total amount of expenditure, but also the relative quantities of private consumption, private investment, and government output in the economy.

1. Government Revenues

The government can obtain funds in two ways; it can tax and it can borrow. Taxation is ordinarily much more depressing on private expenditure than borrowing.

Most depressing: Taxing   (a) Consumption taxes; (b) Income taxes
Least depressing: Borrowing (c) From individuals; (d) From commercial banks

a. Consumption taxes

Taxes levied on consumer goods are depressing because they lead ordinarily to higher costs of commodities and to lower wages. If a portion of the purchasing power directed toward consumption is siphoned off by government, the only possible result is to cut the physical volume of production of consumer goods and to reduce the level of employment. There will be also some lessening of investment in consumer goods production, and so still less employment.

b. Income taxes

These taxes also are depressing to the extent that they cause lower consumption spending and lessened investment. The more progressive they are (that is, the more sharply the percentage rates of taxes rise for larger incomes), the greater the proportion of the total tax that will come from higher-income groups and the smaller the proportion from lower-income groups.

It is usual to argue that the more progressive a tax is, the less it reduces consumption: it is reasoned that a dollar taxed from a poor man will cut his consumption spending by almost a dollar, whereas a dollar taxed from a rich man will cause him mainly to cut his savings while he spends on consumption nearly as much as before. In other words the marginal propensity to consume, $\triangle C/\triangle Y$, of the poor is supposed to differ sharply from that of the rich. But in fact, as we have seen before (p. 149), only very little increase in consumption can be obtained by even drastically progressive taxes. The marginal propensities to consume of rich and poor differ only a little, even though their average propensities to consume differ much. A careful survey made in 1941 by bureaus of the Department of Labor and Department of Agriculture indicates that even if disposable income were made completely equal through taxing the rich and subsidizing the poor, consumer spending would rise by only 3 to 6 per cent.[10]

So far we should conclude that progressive income taxes are only mildly less depressing on consumer spending than consumption taxes. The conclusion becomes still weaker when we remember that a large proportion of consumer expenditure is imitative—keeping up with our neighbors, or at least maintaining a standard of living not too much below them. Greater equality of disposable income would mean less incentive to emulate people who are better off, and to that extent would actually lower consumption.

In addition, the more progressive the income tax schedule, the more it will discourage investment.[11] For the potential investor is faced with the choice of "Heads the government wins, tails you lose." If the investment is profitable, the government taxes away much of the profits; if it is unprofitable, the investor bears the loss.[12]

From all these considerations, it is not certain that a million dollars taken from the public in income taxes cuts private expenditure less, or appreciably less, than a million dollars obtained from consumption taxes.

The corporate income tax and the excess-profits tax are

---

10 Harold Lubell, "Effects of Income Redistribution on Consumer's Expenditures," *American Economic Review*, Vol. XXXVII (March, 1947), pp. 157–170; and Vol. XXXVII (December, 1947), p. 930.

11 But if the individual is already subject to high tax rates because of his large income, the government subsidizes part of any loss incurred on a project through reducing the taxes he must pay.

12 Recent corporate plus personal income taxes have been very high. Tax rates for 1945 on the earnings of stock held in a typical corporation by an investor with one dependent, whose income from other sources was $51,000, reduced his return to 1.3 per cent if the corporation earned before taxes 10 per cent, and to 3 per cent if the corporation earned before taxes an extraordinary 50 per cent. (Data of L. Robert Driver, in *Cleveland Trust Company Bulletin*, October 15, 1945.)

usually judged more depressing to expenditure than the personal income tax. They especially discourage the risky investments of small enterprises in new processes and products—a kind of investment that is very useful toward increased employment and productivity, and toward diminished concentration of production and economic power. The lack of progressiveness of the corporate income tax, and loss carryover provisions (p. 274) diminish but do not eliminate the depressing effect on investment.

c. Borrowing from individuals

This is not very depressing to private expenditure. People lend to the government out of savings they have made. Ordinarily, they do not lend to the government at the low interest rates the government pays,[13] unless they have been unable to make safe investments elsewhere paying higher rates. In other words, much of the funds borrowed by government would otherwise have been idle.

There is only a minor qualification to be made to this reasoning. During wartime the government carried on savings-bond campaigns to induce people to cut their consumption expenditure and to "buy bonds till it hurts." These campaigns probably succeeded in persuading patriotic people to diminish their consumption; but such a depressing effect on consumption expenditure is unlikely during peacetime.

d. Borrowing from commercial banks

Such borrowing is not depressing on private expenditure, assuming that the Federal Reserve, by its open-market operations and other policies, supplies member banks with sufficient reserves so that they can continue to lend to the government. The member banks are then not faced with a choice between lending to private business *or* to the government, but are able to do both. There is, therefore, no reason to expect any decrease in private investment.

---

[13] Series E savings bonds pay 2.9 per cent if held to maturity. This is the highest rate paid on any government security.

We have, in the foregoing paragraphs, been making a survey of the sources of government funds from one point of view only—the extent to which obtaining funds from the given source will contract private consumption and investment expenditure. The merits and demerits of a given taxing or borrowing policy are not exhausted by this kind of analysis (pp. 265-267).

2. Government Expenditures

The main principle we follow is that any government expenditure must be justified on the grounds that the government can use the resources in question more effectively for the general good than could private individuals. If this is not true, stimulus to employment must, instead, be sought through reduced taxation and other measures to stimulate private consumption and investment expenditure.

Government expenditure should be for socially useful goals— the most useful goals attainable—and should be administered with the utmost efficiency to obtain the maximum of output from each dollar. This does not imply that the output made available through government spending must be sold for money: additional schools can contribute more to social income and welfare than additional toll bridges. But it does mean that the government should spend its funds in channels of the highest existing social need, and that the management and production methods utilized should, in general, be the most efficient possible. Men should not dig with hand shovels if steam shovels are obtainable.

Sometimes a compromise is necessary with the aim of efficiency, implied by "immobilities" and by the morale objective of employment. If the skills of the men who are unemployed are not usable toward goals that the community needs most, then it may be best to have these men use their skills in second-best channels. If musicians are unemployed, it may be best to use them to give concerts, even though the community needs new houses more than concerts. How far such compromise should go depends on the individual situation.

A second principle follows from the policy of retaining and encouraging free, private enterprise. It is that government expenditures should not compete with private enterprise, unless for special purposes such as the control of monopoly or the avoidance of private control of critical social activities (uranium processing, military research, and the like). The government should not set up its own retail groceries and clothing stores. Instead, the government expenditure should, so far as possible, be in channels that will induce more private expenditure. Among such complementary expenditures are: river valley development; research on industrial problems, available free or at moderate cost to businesses, especially to small businesses; road-building and airfield construction; and subsidy of construction projects whose risk would not otherwise be undertaken by private contractors.

a. Housing, general construction, and other public works

(1) The construction industry is one that so far has conspicuously failed to use extensively the mass production techniques that have cut costs and expanded output in other industries. It is also conspicuously a prey to various kinds of monopolistic extortions. In no other basic industry is government research likely to be so richly rewarding as in construction, and in no other industry is vigorous antitrust action likely to serve the public interest so effectively. The lumbering auto that Detroit sold for $2000 in 1920 had been developed by 1951 into a far better car that sold for about the same price. But the house that sold for $8000 in 1920 was not much improved by 1951, and sold for roughly double. Any measures that can improve the poor record of the industry and so get a better product to the consumer at a lower price will be aids toward the potential vast expansion of investment in construction.

The 1930's coincided with a low period of the 17-year building cycle, and World War II still further postponed private construction. Between 1945 and 1951 construction was at remarkably high levels, and we gained steadily on our deficit. But the need for adequate housing continues, especially among low income groups. Full employment raised postwar incomes; but even at the booming income level of 1949 one family in seven had an income of less than $1000 a year.[14] Such families can afford only substandard housing, which menaces the health, morals, and morale of themselves and others.

Thus there is a continuing need for direct government construction or government subsidy to private construction. Over a 10-year period, 2 million or more homes must be constructed with government aid if an equal number of families are to have decent housing. A construction program for such housing and for the other public works mentioned below might require 8 to 10 billion dollars a year.

(2) Aside from housing, there are other kinds of public works that would rank high on a priority list of social needs. Among them are hospitals and schools, which might be financed by federal grants to state and local governments, especially to those in poor areas unable to support adequate facilities. Good medical and educational facilities are an investment in the health and ability of a people. The full return does not come immediately, but it is eventually richly rewarding.

(3) Further river and valley development on the Tennessee Valley Authority model may be directed toward cheap power production, flood control and irrigation, waterway improvement, and erosion control. Repeatedly in recent years the Missouri and its sister rivers have jumped their banks; and people, houses, barns, hogs, cattle, and topsoil have tumbled down their muddy torrents. Before, during the 1930's, three-quarters of a million people fled from drought within its drainage basin (the Dust Bowl). Under the Pick-Sloan plan to tame the Missouri system, 107 dams and reservoirs are

---

14 *Economic Report of the President,* January 1951, p. 226.

scheduled to be built by 1966, regulating river flow, irrigating farms in seven states (Montana, Wyoming, Colorado, the Dakotas, Nebraska, and Kansas), providing navigation on new waters, and producing one and a half million kilowatts of hydroelectric power. The program has been sharply criticized as not being integrated, but some control plan has been much needed. Further development is possible in the Colorado and Columbia river systems and elsewhere.

(4) The carrying of electricity to as many as possible of the one million or more farm homes without electric current is an important step toward lightening drudgery and bringing fuller living to the country. Where farm homes are far apart, the returns would not justify private investment, but many new power lines are justified from the public point of view by the nonfinancial return of better rural living.

Both (3) and (4) above have the special merit of stimulating additional private investment in the long run, though within a few years only the net effect would doubtless be discouraging.

(5) Land conservation and forest improvement will find a place in federal expenditure. Erosion control, land reclamation, drainage, and irrigation are matters of the first importance. In addition, our forest resources will demand more and more attention as we come to realize increasingly that their quantity is limited. They require thinning to favor the growth of sound timber, and control of blight, and are available for further development of recreational areas.

b. Education, medicine, social security

It is to the interest of the United States to move toward equal opportunities for education and medical care for all its citizens. But the ability of poor communities to provide the facilities is much less than that of rich communities, even though some of the poorest tax their citizens heavily. Additional argument for equalizing of such opportunities by federal action comes from the fact that some of the residents of rich localities and states draw their incomes from property and businesses in the poor areas. Professor Hansen has suggested a program to pay educational grants-in-aid to all states to cover a minimum outlay per student of $80, at an annual cost of $2.5 billions. Real expenditures per student for school construction were actually less in booming 1951 than they had been in 1939.[15] An effective medical program could cut the cost of serious illness to middle- and low-income groups who now find it a financial catastrophe; and it could provide adequate care to rural areas. We have mentioned before the extension of social security as an essential element in expanding consumption. Such extension is an essential aid toward a new higher minimum standard of living.

c. Subsidy of consumption

We have seen that about two-thirds of United States gross expenditure is ordinarily for consumption. The large volume and wide range of consumer goods suggests the possibility of using consumer subsidies on a large scale—they were running at the rate of about 1.8 billion dollars in a year in 1945—to reduce the cost of consumption items basic to our standard of living.

The War Food Administration estimated, for the winter of 1943–1944, that nearly 60 million people in the United States were spending less on food than would purchase a "good minimum diet." A moderate program developed under the provisions of the Aiken-LaFollette bill of that time would have substantially raised the food consumption of 16 million of the lowest-income groups (who average $275 or less per person per year on food expenditure), at an annual cost to the federal government of 420 million dollars.[16] During World War II

---

15 *Economic Report of the President*, January 1952, p. 7.

16 The bill proposed that food stamps be issued to families in income ranges whose average expenditure for food was below the minimum. Hence, it proposed a revival of the prewar food-stamp plan. A revised version designed to increase food consumption of households that spent more than 40 per cent of income on food was presented June 15, 1945. (Senate Bill 1151, 79th Cong., 1st Session.)

and afterward, the British have emphasized the production of subsidized, and hence very cheap, "utility grades" of food, clothing, and other consumption goods.

The stamp-plan type of proposal—stamps valid for purchasing being issued to low-income groups—makes the price of such goods low only to those particular income groups. The subsidy of "utility grades" of commodities increases the real income of all persons who decide to buy those grades.[17] Any kind of consumer subsidy has the result of helping further to put a floor beneath the standard of living by making less expensive the food, clothing, or shelter entering into the consumer's budget.

Secular and Cyclical Policy

The basic pattern of the government budget—the quantitative and qualitative character of revenue and expenditure—turns on the question of to what extent there is a secular problem of low production and employment.

With respect to cyclical fluctuations, so far as is possible, the fiscal system should have an automatic flexibility, and not require special policy decisions to be made. A principal argument for basing government support primarily on income taxes is, as we have seen, their automatic countercyclical variability: they absorb much less money income out of the economy in time of depression than in time of prosperity. Consumption taxes do not have this merit; their take is more nearly stable. Among government expenditures, social-security benefits also have this desired built-in variability: unemployment compensation and other payments grow much larger in time of depression. Many other government expenditures do not vary appreciably. Expenditure on defense, internal order, veterans, education, public health, interest on the debt, and the like cannot or should not be subordinated to counter-

---

17 But commodities ought not, in general, to be completely free: buyers must have incentive to economize in their use. The lower the price of goods, the more wastefully they will be used.

cyclical policy.[18] But most public works are postponable, and it is possible to vary the amount of support given through loans or subsidies to private housing construction, private consumption, and the like.

Often the timing of policy decisions is most important. It is crucial whether a countercyclical policy is introduced before a cumulative downswing or upswing has gathered momentum. In the former case, if action is delayed and distress deepens, the task is greater: expenditure must go first for relief and for shoring up tottering strategic businesses and banks (that is, for offsetting the effects of contraction) rather than directly for expanded production.

C. The Burden of Public Debt

The government can obtain its funds either from borrowing or from taxing. The former, we know, has a much less depressing effect on private expenditure than the latter. The conclusion easily follows that, when more expenditure for output is wanted in the economy (more production and employment), the emphasis should be shifted toward getting a larger proportion of government revenues from borrowing, rather than from taxing. But perhaps such a plain conclusion is upset by the consideration that borrowing means more public debt, and that public debt can have such real and psychological "burden" that the depressing indirect effects of public borrowing on private expenditure more than offset the stimulating direct effects.

This is a melancholy conviction, if it has to be accepted. For it means that our society has no major weapons against depression except those that encourage private expenditure without involving government borrowing. And these have disadvantages of their own (Route II above) or are so weak that we can be certain of suffering heavy unemployment occasionally

18 The federal government cash budget for calendar year 1950 allocated nearly three-quarters of total expenditures to such channels: military services took 32.7 per cent, veterans 21.2 per cent, interest 9.8 per cent, and "international security and foreign relations" 9.8 per cent.

or even chronically. Our mixed-capitalist economic system will not survive long if it tolerates heavy unemployment.

We now consider the real and psychological burden of public debt. We spend more time on the matter than its logical importance merits. But the emphasis given to the matter in current newspapers and magazines seems to demand considerable attention.

Views on Public Debt

The fear of a large public debt is ancient among scholars and businessmen. Some perspective is given on our present problem by seeing what has been thought in the past.

Opinions on the British debt

Lord Macaulay wrote of the public debt owed by Britain through the Napoleonic wars:

At every stage in the growth of that debt it has been seriously asserted by wise men that bankruptcy and ruin were at hand. Yet still the debt went on growing; and still bankruptcy and ruin were as remote as ever. When the great contest with Louis XIV was finally terminated in the peace of Utrecht, the nation owed about fifty millions [of pounds sterling]; and that debt was considered . . . by acute and profound thinkers as an incumbrance which would permanently cripple the body politic. Nevertheless, trade flourished, wealth increased; the nation became richer and richer. Then came the War of the Austrian Succession; and the debt rose to eighty millions.

Pamphleteers, historians, and orators pronounced that now, at all events, our case was desperate. . . . Soon war broke forth; and under the energetic administration of William Pitt, the debt rapidly swelled to a hundred and forty millions. . . . George Grenville, a minister eminently diligent and practical, [conceived] that the nation must . . . sink under a debt of a hundred and forty millions, unless a portion of the load were borne by the American Colonies. The attempt to lay a portion of the load on the American Colonies produced another war. That war left us with an additional hundred millions of debt, and without the Colonies whose help had been represented as indispensable. Soon, however, the wars which sprang from the French Revolution tasked the powers of public credit to the utmost. When the world was again at rest the funded debt of England amounted to eight hundred millions. . . . It was in truth a gigantic, a fabulous debt; and we can hardly wonder that the cry of despair should have been louder than ever. But again that cry was found to have been as unreasonable as ever. After a few years of exhaustion, England recovered herself. Yet like Addison's valetudinarian, who continued to whimper that he was dying of consumption till he became so fat that he was ashamed into silence, she went on complaining that she was sunk in poverty till her wealth showed itself by tokens which made her complaints ridiculous.

The British national debt at the end of the Napoleonic Wars was about twice the national income of the time. The federal debt of the United States at the end of 1950 would have had to have been almost double to bear that same proportion to the United States national income of 1950. But this simple comparison underemphasizes the magnitude of the British debt: interest rates were much lower in the United States of 1950 than they had been in the England of 1818, and so the sums required to pay interest on a given debt were smaller. Despite this huge debt, the British economy led the world in the nineteenth century. A large debt is plainly compatible with rapid economic progress.

United States views on the public debt

Businessmen are inclined to blame depressions on government activities that they dislike. Among causes cited by businessmen have been: extravagance in government expenditure, enormous taxation, the level of the national debt, depreciation of the currency, uncertainty as to the future monetary standard, the disturbed value of gold and silver, undue influence of agitators, class legislation, unfavorable and reckless legislation in Congress, want of confidence in the government, and possession of power by the Democratic party. Corresponding to this diagnosis, they have recommended: reduce the salaries of officers of the government, abolish all unnecessary offices of the government, introduce rigid economy in government, maintain local self-government with no federal interference, check legislative derangement of the currency, make use of good judgment and hard work, restrict the power of the President, and enact laws against communistic schemes.

The above sounds much like a diagnosis of the depression of the 1930's, but it was, in fact, collected in the 1880's,[19] as explanations of the depression of 1874—1879! This does not disprove the validity of the explanations, but it does suggest that the psychological responses of businessmen have remained the same whether or not the causes of the two depressions were the same.

Senator Sheridan Downey in 1939 (when the federal debt was 40 billion dollars, or under one-sixth of its value at the end of World War II) expressed the average man's alarm at a constantly rising public debt:

Where will this process end? Are we to increase our government deficit several billions each year—indefinitely? We know that is out of the question. Our public debt would mount to astronomical heights, and as it did, confidence in public credit would sink to lowest depths. Before long government finances would collapse, dragging down with them our banks and insurance companies, already loaded with Federal bonds.[20]

At a lower level of analysis, John T. Flynn, at the end of World War II, was apprehensive over the size of the debt: "Now we are at the end of our rope. . . . We must realize that the federal government is soon going to be broke." [21]

On the other hand, the authors of *An Economic Program*

---

19 From the First Annual Report of the Commissioner of Labor, 1886. Quoted from the testimony of Theodore J. Kreps before the Temporary National Economic Committee, April 8, 1940; in the *Verbatim Record of the Proceedings*, Vol. 13, pp. 2–3.

20 *Pensions or Penury*. New York: Harpers, 1939, p. 91; quoted in David McC. Wright, "The Economic Limit and Economic Burden of an Internally Held National Debt," *Quarterly Journal of Economics*, Vol. LIV (November, 1940), p. 117.

21 "The Handwriting on the Cuff," *Reader's Digest*, Vol. XLVIII (January, 1946), pp. 10–14. Henry Hazlitt's *Economics in One Lesson* (New York: Harpers, 1946) furnishes stimulating—and untrustworthy—reasoning on the debt and related economic matters.

for American Democracy argue that there is no burden at all
to a public debt:

> If we look at the whole nation as a going concern, we see that its
> internal debts, business and governmental, are merely another aspect
> of its assets. Debt in the broad sense is the obverse of investment. . . .
> Individual debtors do, of course, get into trouble by improvident
> borrowing. But for the economy as a whole, trouble comes only
> when the nation falters in the course of its economic expansion.
> . . . The expansion of debt at a rate sufficient to absorb the na-
> tion's savings is both sound and necessary. This rate could be exces-
> sive only in the sense that the rate of saving itself was excessive. . . .
> It is ridiculous to maintain that debt in general must be repaid.
> The mere attempt to repay debts all around . . . would result in
> complete economic paralysis.[22]

At the end of the revolutionary period the United States
federal debt was over 79 million dollars, which was high compared to the national income of the time, perhaps relatively
higher than the debt of the middle 1930's. By 1836, this was
all paid off out of large customs and land-sales revenue, and
the federal government, embarrassed by large surpluses, distributed its excess funds to the states on three separate occa-
sions. At the beginning of the Civil War, the federal debt
was under 100 million dollars, but at the end of the War it
had risen to the seemingly large figure of 2.3 billion dollars.
By 1914, the debt had fallen to under 1 billion dollars. It
rose during World War I to 25 billion dollars (a little over
one third of the national income of 1919). Eleven years of
surpluses thereafter reduced the debt to under 16 billion dollars by 1930. After that its rise was rapid: to a net total of
40 billion dollars in 1939, and 253 billion dollars at the end
of 1945 (about 1.6 times the national income). In December
1950 it was 219 billion dollars. War expenditures have been
by far the chief cause of increase of our Federal debt; the
Great Depression of the 1930's is a secondary cause.

The debt of state and local government owes its rise in re-

---

22 Gilbert, *et al.*, *An Economic Program for American Democracy.* New York:
Vanguard Press, 1938, pp. 63–65.

cent years mainly to expenditures undertaken in the 1920's on highways, sewage disposal and water supply, and educational buildings. Its net total was 4.6 billion dollars in 1916, 13.7

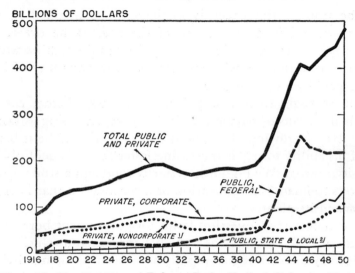

Chart 22. Net Public and Private Debt, End of Calendar Year, 1916-1950

Source: Elwyn T. Bonnel and Allen E. Turner, "Public and Private Debt in 1950," *Survey of Current Business,* Vol. XXXI (September, 1951), p. 20. The dotted line represents individual and noncorporate private debt. The data for public, state, and local debt are for June 30 of each year.

billion dollars by 1929, and 16 billion dollars by 1939. During World War II it fell in consequence of lessened relief needs and higher state and local tax revenues (both results of high federal war expenditures). By 1950, the total was 20 billion dollars.[23]

Until recently the total private debt of the nation was much larger than total government debt. Private debt is classified as corporation debt, and mortgage and nonmortgage debt of individuals. These altogether totaled 75 billion dollars in

[23] *Saving, Investment, and National Income.* TNEC Monograph No. 37 (Washington, 1941), p. 81; *Survey of Current Business,* Vol. XXVII (September 1947), p. 14. The figures for debt are for the end of the year.

1916, 158 billion dollars by 1929, and 245 billion dollars in 1950.[24]

The Nature of the Burden of Public Debt

The man in the street is inclined to be alarmed at the growth of public debt because of the analogy he draws between private and public debt. He thinks of the spot *he* would be in if he were faced with an ever increasing quantity of bills to be paid by a certain date.

But we ought to go a step further and ask whether the individual's means of paying off his debts are increasing as fast as his debts are growing. If so, he is no worse off; and he is better off if his ability to pay is increasing faster than his debt obligation is growing. We do not necessarily condemn a student who borrows to finance his education or a corporation that borrows to expand its plant.

The same sort of question holds for government borrowing. We should ask whether the national income (on which taxes are levied) is increasing as rapidly as interest payments due on the debt are increasing. And, in considering policy for the future, we should remember that well-advised government expenditures can cause an annual rise in the national income much exceeding the annual rise in interest payments due on the debt that is financing those expenditures.

Chart 23 presents this more significant kind of comparison: interest payments are shown as percentages of the national income. By this measurement the weight of the 1950 federal debt is less than that of the Civil War peak. By contrast, the simple and misleading dollar comparison shows an 11,100 per cent rise.

There is another matter that the man in the street is apt to overlook—the major difference that exists between private and public debt. If *A* comes to owe *B* $5, then *A* is to that extent worse off; but if the government debt rises by 5 billion dollars, the whole economy is not worse off by that amount. For

---

24 *Survey of Current Business, ibid.*

though it is true that the government (or the people whom the government represents) owes 5 billion dollars, it is also true that people within the same economy *are owed* 5 billion dollars. The people owe the money to themselves through their agent the government. For every dollar of debt, there is a dollar of credit.

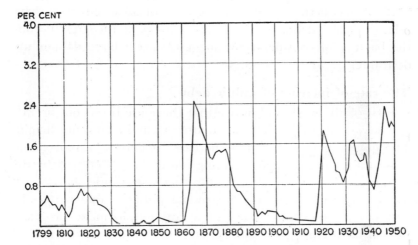

PER CENT

Chart 23. Interest on the Federal Debt Shown as a Per Cent of the National Income.

Source: 1799-1939, Committee on Public Debt Policy, *Our National Debt after Great Wars.* New York: The Committee, 1946, p. 9. 1940-1950, *Survey of Current Business,* July, 1947, p. 23; July, 1950, pp. 9, 12; February, 1951, p. 9.

It is, therefore, true that, from the point of view of the whole society, the U. S. public debt is primarily a *transfer* problem.[25]

It is often argued that borrowing shifts the cost of war or of depression to the shoulders of a future generation. Our reasoning shows this cannot be true. If public debt is accumulated during a war, it is owed by members of the post-war generation to others *of their own* generation. It cannot be owed to those who lived during the war. The transfer of interest

25 Save for an insignificantly small proportion that is held abroad.

or principal is always from present taxpayers to present bondholders.

To say that a public debt is essentially unlike a private debt (in that it is owed by the people of an economy to themselves and so involves only a transfer problem among the members of an economy) is not to say that it is a matter of indifference to a society as to whether or not it has a large public debt. Sometimes it may actually be advantageous for an economy to have a large public debt. In the United States at the present time the balance of considerations suggests that a large debt is undesirable.

The rate of increase of public debt

First of all, we should notice that there are limits on the *rate of increase* of public debt, no matter what its absolute height. The government should not increase its debt so rapidly as to cause inflation (through spending money newly created by the banking system or money that otherwise would have been saved). The government's borrowing policy is one part only, and not an inevitable part, of a full employment program. But so far as this goes, the extreme limitation on the rate of borrowing is that it should be no greater than will secure full employment. It should not overstep this into the range where an excessive price rise results.[26] (Or, if excessive demand exists, funds should be accumulated to pay off the public debt, but not at so fast a rate as will cause unemployment.)

Second, as a possible limit in the rate of increase of debt (and also on the height of the debt), the public might be reluctant to buy more government bonds. Perhaps they have come to distrust the government. This is, however, very unlikely so long as the government continues to pay interest on

---

26 The fear that any increase in national debt threatens inflation is nonsense. A high enough rate of increase of debt will lead to price rises as the government spends the borrowed funds, even if unemployment exists generally. Prices will rise primarily in bottleneck areas where resources are inadequate to meet the increased demand. But a moderate rate of increase of debt, when general unemployment exists, will lead mainly to higher output rather than to higher prices.

its already issued bonds, and this it will certainly do—above all, if it is attempting to sell more bonds to the public. In any case, the banking system could be coerced, whether or not we like the idea, into buying more government bonds; or the Treasury could, under a new law,[27] sell bonds directly to the Federal Reserve banks. This limit, therefore, is not of first importance.

The burden of a large public debt

The disadvantages, or "burden," of a large public debt arise out of the circumstances that, though the debt is owed by, and to, people within the same economy, different people owe (that is, pay taxes) from those who are owed (that is, own government bonds). The burden consists of frictions and institutional changes.

1. The tax system must be expanded in order to provide money for interest payments on the debt, and perhaps also payments on the principal. The Internal Revenue Division of the Treasury must hire tens of thousands of people to mail forms, keep the records, and pursue delinquents. Furthermore, businesses that pay taxes find that the cost of the necessary record keeping can add up to 5 or 10 per cent of the tax paid. If the people occupied by tax administration were not so engaged, they would be available to produce other services or goods for the economy. The larger the debt, the greater is this real cost of tax collection.

2. No tax structure is ideal, but moderate faults do not matter very much so long as the taxes collected are small. As the taxes grow larger, the deficiencies become more burdensome. (a) For administrative reasons, there must inevitably be restrictions on the allowable averaging of income, or carryover of losses, for the purpose of tax calculation. Such restrictions mean that capital goods industries are burdened more by taxes than the more stable consumption goods industries. This effect

---

27 The Second War Powers Act of 1942 authorized the Federal Reserve to purchase bonds directly from the Treasury up to a limit of 5 billion dollars.

can be very undesirable. Similarly, individuals with fluctuating incomes will be taxed more heavily. (b) The larger the absolute volume of taxes, the less the possibility of altering the structure of the taxes. The system becomes more unwieldly and rigid, and is unable to adapt itself to changing objectives of taxation. But from time to time, the society will want to tax private expenditure more, or less, relative to savings, and will want to influence the allocation of resources differently.

3. A large volume of debt tends toward a rigid inequality of distribution of income, because fixed interest payments are due to individual holders of the bonds who are, on the whole, the richer part of the population.

4. At the end of 1950 about 24 per cent of the federal debt was held in commercial banks. The larger the debt, the more our banking system tends to become an agency for the holding of government bonds rather than a system concerned with lending funds to business. It thereby becomes increasingly dependent on Treasury policies with respect to the management of the debt. Some economists believe that this change in the banking system is not healthy.[28]

5. Finally, we come to the political effects of large public debt. The existence of the debt gives incentive to the formation both of *rentier* pressure groups, who will gain from higher interest rates on the bonds, and stable or falling prices in the economy, and inflationary pressure groups who will push for a higher price level and so a lower "real" volume of debt.

The effect of a large public debt on private investment

What we have listed above with respect to the "burden" of a public debt has implied that that burden is moderate. It consists mainly of frictional problems of transfer. These frictions increase as the debt grows, but no definite limit is implied beyond which the debt cannot rise. Rather the increasing frictions will at some point bring sufficient political pressure

---

[28] Cf. John H. Williams, *Postwar Monetary Plans*. New York: Alfred A. Knopf, 1944, pp. 87–111.

on the government to cause it to alter its policy so as to diminish the relative size of the debt (pp. 329-332). It is risky to prophesy where that psychological point would be: at present national income levels one may hesitantly suggest it is probably many times higher than our present debt. Such an altered policy would not necessarily carry any indirect disadvantage to the economy.

But suppose businessmen do not believe the reasoning we have surveyed and on ill-founded grounds are afraid of debt and so afraid to invest. They may prophesy gloomily that a "day of reckoning" is at hand, and succeed, as John Flynn does, in fearing both inflation and deflation at the same time.[29] If so, the stimulating effect of government fiscal policy will be offset and nullified by the contraction of private investment expenditure. It is on this psychological ground that the use of the government budget to increase expenditure, output, and employment in the economy is often opposed.

What can be said about the argument? First, in so far as the fear of large public debt is exaggerated and superstitious, originating in a wrong analogy drawn between private and public debt or in other false reasoning, it would appear that the best prescription is education. When the Millerites predicted that the world would come to an end on October 22, 1843, business was paralyzed in many a county and town of the United States (save for a brisk traffic in white cotton sheets to be used as ascension robes). Likewise, business is injured by any other belief, whether well- or ill-founded, that induces apprehension and alarm.

It is right for the spokesmen of business to present their objections strongly before the forum of public opinion when government loan expenditure is so managed in direction and timing as to introduce obstructions to private business activity. But it is regrettable if objections are advanced out of a mis-

---

29 *Ibid.* Notice that the fear of inflation (continuously rising prices) will lead people to buy more real property, and so will stimulate employment and production. There is also a lesser influence toward lower production, to the extent that some businessmen are dismayed by the prospect of unpredictable rises in costs.

understanding of the simple truth that the whole community benefits when resources going to waste in idleness because of deficient private spending are set to work through government fiscal policy. When objections do arise out of misunderstanding, the remedy is evident: clear information to the end that the whole community—business managers, labor, and consumers—can know what is going on and so can cooperate intelligently in policies directed toward the general good.

Second, if we look to statistics of the 1930's, there is no particular evidence that government deficit spending as such had any depressing effect on business investment. Such an effect would tend to show itself in a uniform decline in business investment. But although by 1937 railroads and public utilities had recovered to a level of only 56 per cent of their 1929 plant and equipment investment, mining and manufacturing had achieved an 81 per cent, and agriculture a 93 per cent, recovery.[30] The data suggest that special industries have special problems,[31] not that business was suffering from any pervading lack of confidence as a result of government action.

If these two lines of argument are correct, we are justified in giving only passing attention to the argument that a large public debt will curtail private investment.

Policy toward a huge and increasing public debt

1. The disadvantages of a large public debt, as we have seen, are indicated not by the size of the debt, but by the proportion of the debt to the national income, or if we want to be more precise, by the proportion of interest payable to the debt to the national income. A timid government policy—fearful of debt, spending mainly for necessary relief, acting late and weakly to offset declines of national income—may well lead to

---

[30] Data of Laughlin Currie, reproduced in H. H. Villard, *Deficit Spending and the National Income*. New York: Farrar & Rinehart, 1941, p. 347. The above follows his analysis of pp. 355–357.

[31] The poor showing of utilities may partly reflect the special depressing effect of the Tennessee Valley Authority, and the Public Utilities Holding Act, and the good showing of agriculture partly reflects the influence of the Agricultural Adjustment Act. But these are specific policies affecting specific industries.

persistently low levels of income and employment. Under such circumstances, the debt will grow but the national income will expand slowly or not at all. Hence, the frictional "burden" of debt will increase.

One of the best methods for encouraging private investment (and so minimizing the task of government) is to give assurance to business of a large national income continuously rising as population and productivity increase. Even if the government must continuously go in debt in order to maintain full employment output, the "burden" of debt may not increase. Under plausible assumptions,[32] the debt will increase only at the same rate that the national income increases. So, paradoxically, the burden of public debt may very likely be smaller with a vigorous government loan expenditure policy directed toward full employment than it would be with a timid policy that tries to balance the budget and tolerates considerable unemployment.

2. Suppose that, through bad luck or bad policies or a mischievous combination of the two, the size of the federal debt should over the next decades grow rapidly *relative* to the national income. This is the specter haunting those who most fear a rising debt. What then would happen?

The frictional burdens of debt would increase steadily, and at some point political pressure would force into action a policy to reduce those burdens.

(*a*) The debt might be reduced by achieving an excess of taxes over government expenditures. But presumably this plain way out is blocked by a continuing deficiency of private consumption and investment expenditure in the economy, despite all the indirect means of encouraging such expenditure that can be mustered. The attempt toward a budget surplus

---

32 Evsey D. Domar, "The Burden of the Debt," *American Economic Review*, Vol. XXXIV (December, 1944), pp. 798–827; and "Rejoinder," Vol. XXXV (June, 1945), pp. 414-418. The critical assumptions are that the average proportion of the national income saved is a constant and that the government borrows on the average a constant percentage, g, of national income. If the national income grows at a constant percentage rate, r, then the debt will approach a proportion of the national income equal to g/r.

would then push the economy into a low level of employment and output, which it is the prime objective to avoid.

(*b*) The debt might be repudiated. The federal government might announce some dismal morning that it will no longer redeem or pay interest on its securities. But such action is so extremely unlikely that we need not give it any serious consideration. The government would not repudiate its debt because of the catastrophic blow it would bring to precisely those people and institutions that had trusted the government most and so bought its securities in quantity. The commercial banking system, which holds about 24 per cent of the debt, would collapse immediately. There would be drastic political repercussions. In addition, the government would ruin its own credit and make difficult or impossible any fresh borrowing. Finally, there are other and better ways to diminish the burden of debt.

(*c*) The debt is expressed in terms of dollars. Hence, monetary and other policies aimed at higher price levels in the economy would diminish its relative size. If average prices rise by 25 per cent, then the holder of a bond (or other obligation expressed in dollars) can buy only four-fifths as much as he could if prices had not risen.[33] The *real* debt, in terms of goods and services, has obviously diminished in size.

There is much to be said in favor of a gradually rising price level, say 1 or 2 per cent a year. It stimulates business investment since the worth in dollars of property is constantly increasing. It facilitates price adjustments within the economy since price rises are psychologically easier to adjust to than price declines. It may have some influence toward a more equal division of wealth: monopolistic sellers have lower returns in so far as they carry on rigid price policies, and the wealthy have lower real assets in so far as they hold their assets in dollar obligations. But on the other hand, persons of mod-

---

[33] If prices rise by 25 per cent, then $80 of goods at the old prices will now cost $100.

erate means are apt to protect themselves less adequately against rising prices than the wealthy: they have much of their funds in the form of bank accounts, insurance, and bonds, rather than in the form of real property. Older persons who are living on annuities and others with fixed salaries will be injured by rising prices. For these and other reasons, if government policy is directed toward rising prices, the rate of price rise should be very moderate. It is, therefore, still possible for a rising burden of debt to exist.

(d) Finally, it is possible for the Treasury to pay off part or all of the debt through funds obtained by sale of its securities to the Reserve Banks. We have mentioned that the Second War Powers Act authorized such direct borrowing from the Reserve Banks up to 5 billion dollars. Our suggestion is that the limit be raised. The interest paid by the Treasury to the Federal Reserve for the purpose could be only a service fee to cover the expense of the banks.

The manufacture of money by banks is a cheap and simple process; it consists essentially of an entry in the books, giving a claim on the bank to the person for whom the entry is made. These entries, or deposits, on which checks are drawn, make up the dominant part of our money supply, and are the medium by which over nine-tenths of payments are effected. There is no adequate justification for paying extravagantly for the service of bank manufacture of money, as we are now certainly doing. It is estimated that in 1948, over half the total income of commercial banks was obtained from government bonds.

The proposal that the government borrow directly from the Federal Reserve (or for that matter issue new currency itself) is not very radical, if by *radical* we mean that reputable specialists in the field are all opposed. Professors Fisher of Yale, Angell of Columbia, and Simons of Chicago have supported a similar proposal for issuing "new money" to buy up the debt, and a bill involving this principle has been before Congress.[34] Simeon Leland [35] concludes that the case against the proposal is weak, and Philip Wernette [36] has made it the mainstay of his full employment proposal.[37] To recommend the proposal implies trust in the federal government to use its fiscal powers wisely. The very great advantage of the proposal is that it frees the government once and for all from the bogy that in peacetime we may not be able to "afford" full employment. It underlines the basic truth that money is the servant and tool of the economy, not its master.

We can conclude that serious worry over the ominous implications of large public debt is unfounded. A more sensible worry is whether the loan-financed money was spent more effectively toward the general good by government than it could have been by private individuals. The objective of a balanced budget is a very secondary matter compared to the objective of full employment and high output. And the latter objective may often suggest that part of the expenditures of government should be loan financed.

But nothing that we have said denies that *management* of the public debt is likely to be a major concern and problem of the Treasury and Federal Reserve during the next several decades. One critical element in the problem is the possibility that the public might unpredictably and in large volume sell bonds to obtain cash, and *vice versa*. Such "flight" between bonds and cash would imply rapid fluctuation in the volume of total demand, and cause disturbances in the banking system.

---

[34] Introduced in the House by Representative Voorhis, July 2, 1945. See pp. 242–245.

[35] Former Chairman of the Board, Federal Reserve Bank of Chicago; since 1948 Dean at Northwestern University.

[36] Sometime President of the University of New Mexico, and Professor at the University of Michigan.

[37] *Financing Full Employment.* Cambridge: Harvard University Press, 1945.

CHAPTER EIGHTEEN

The Mobility of Labor
and the Location of Industry

SUPPOSE THAT A POLICY OF INCREASED EXPENDITURES IN THE economy has been undertaken, with the aim of increased employment and production. To the extent that productive facilities—land, equipment, and especially labor—are not distributed by location and by industry in accord with the direction of demand, there will be pockets of unemployed resources in some places at the same time there are scarcities of resources and rising prices elsewhere. The construction of a dam in the state of Washington will not much relieve the distress of unemployment in New York, and public works construction may not do much to lessen the unemployment of local textile workers, writers, and artists.

In time, equipment and plant can be adapted or built to meet the demand, and—often with still more delay—labor will will move and be trained to the needed skills. But in the meantime the localized scarcities and price inflations persist. Our program is threatened with failure on two counts; unemployment continues, and prices are rising.

What can be done? Where the increased total expenditure is obtained in part through government expenditure, some moderate compromise is desirable with the principle of public spending only in channels where there is the greatest social need for output. Some small proportion of expenditure can be justified because it makes use of resources that would otherwise be idle, even though the product is not of first social importance. We have spoken of this before, and say no more of it here.

If we assume the direction of demand is given, then we are left to see what can be done to improve the location of industry and/or increase the mobility of labor.[1]

The basic economic logic is simple. Local unemployment can be reduced in either of two ways: by moving surplus labor to where the jobs are, and by training and retraining labor for skills in demand; or by moving industry from areas where it is scarce to areas where it is in surplus. The problem is, therefore, how to get the right balance between the movement of labor away from, and the movement of capital and management into, the surplus area or occupation.

If the labor in question can, in the main, move easily to where its services are in demand, while local resources are so scanty that new industry there would operate under a continuing cost disadvantage, then the bulk of the adjustment should take place through an outflow of labor. But if most of the labor is firmly attached to the locality, and if the local area is suitable for further development then the adjustment should take place mainly by an inflow of industry. (This reasoning can be transferred without change to the question of whether labor should be moved *occupationally*—that is, trained in the skills of another occupation, or whether industry using the old skills should be developed.) Whether industry or labor should move depends on whose *social cost of movement* is less. When the best adjustment is reached, the social cost of moving (say) an extra 100 workers and their families away from the surplus area equals the social cost of moving into or originating in the area a business employing 100 workers.

The difficulty in evaluating the importance of each element in social cost [2] is great, and the room for disagreement there-

---

[1] The term *labor mobility* as used here refers not only to movement from one geographical area to another, but also "movement" from one occupation or skill to another.

[2] P. 336.

fore considerable. There is also considerable danger of delaying or blocking necessary structural adjustments in the economy. So far as reliance is placed on government decisions and subsidies we should be wise to fear pressures brought to bear for sectional and private advantage. To the extent that we fear such pressures, we will want to restrict the extent and the detail of the political intervention we judge desirable.

The Mobility of Labor

Unskilled people move much more readily from one occupation to another than from one place to another. The store clerk and the farm hand cheerfully and promptly throw up their jobs when the near-by shipyard expands. Skilled and specialized people are less likely to find other near-by tasks that their skills "fit" and that are attractive enough to induce them to leave their present jobs.[3] They may move across the continent or halfway round the world to take the right job.

Young men and women just beginning their working lives and little attached to particular jobs change their locations fairly readily. But even young people are often reluctant to leave home and friends to look for jobs in distant places. Immobility increases when people marry and acquire families and furniture that must also be moved. Finally, there is a "hard core" among the work force of older people who are nearly totally immobile. They have put their roots down in a given locality, bought property, and have made friends and a place for themselves. No economic change short of complete collapse will divorce them from the community.

In England and other countries of western Europe, immobilities have been sufficient to allow continuing wide divergences of wages between near-by locations, in some cases divergences persisting for centuries. Incomes per person in

---

[3] The census of 1940 classifies less than half of the working force as unspecialized. Of the 49.5 million in the working force, 26.2 million are listed as possessing special skills. A large proportion of the remainder also possess skills that they value.

the United States varied in 1949 from $1591 and up for six widely scattered states in the North and on the West Coast, to $876 and under for eight southern states.[4]

Such variations do not, of course, mean that there is no migration from low-income to high-income areas, but only that such migration as occurs is not sufficient to compensate for the continuing advantages in resources, equipment, and techniques of the latter areas. There has been in recent years a continuing outflow of people from the Southeast to the West and North, but not in sufficient numbers to offset the birth rate; and so population has increased in spite of migration.[5]

The total social cost of the geographical movement of labor includes the cost of building new social facilities in the expanding area: housing, streets, schools, shops, water systems, and so forth. It also includes the cost of movement of household goods and the psychological cost of breaking ties with home, friends, and kindred (sometimes offset, or more than offset, by the education and stimulus of new scenes). The social cost per person of such movement evidently is slight if a few only of the more mobile workers are involved. The cost rises rapidly as increasing numbers of relatively immobile workers are moved.

Similarly, movement from one occupation to another requires one to become accustomed, physically and psychologically, to the new situation; and may involve the time and expense of retraining.

Measures to increase labor mobility

1. So far as is possible, a society ought to encourage the occupational and geographical mobility made necessary by expanding or contracting industry through directing of young

---

[4] *Survey of Current Business*, August 1950, p. 13. To some small extent price differences tend to compensate for these income differences.

[5] During the War, the attractions of jobs in the expanding war industries were sufficient to increase factory wage earners of San Diego and Wichita in late 1942 to 6 times their 1937 numbers. In Norfolk, Seattle, and Portland (Oregon) the increase was 2 to 2½ times.

people into "jobs with a future," rather than into blind-alley work in contracting fields. The labor supply in a declining industry ought to be furnished by older workers, who will gradually retire from work at about the rate the industry shrinks. (That the average age of coal miners—coal mining being a contracting industry—is over fifty is desirable: less displacement of existing workers is in prospect.) No compulsion is implied by this recommendation; it is only that there should be available to young people full information on the prospects of various occupations, good advice on their own abilities, and effective training toward the occupation of their choice. Increasing labor mobility in this way involves no "cost" to the individuals concerned: rather it means opening the door of advancement to them.

2. The labor market ought not to consist of the haphazard hawking of labor services from one shop door or factory door to another. Obviously, this kind of procedure is wasteful of time and morale. The supply of and demand for labor should be matched with each other in one agency, or in cooperating agencies that have widespread coverage by occupations and areas. The present state employment services are evidently less effective than the United States Employment Service of wartime, unless they maintain complete cooperation.

3. The unemployment-insurance program should be formulated and administered with the aim in view of encouraging labor mobility. Our Federal-State unemployment-insurance program now operates under provisions that vary from state to state. Modern systems disqualify from benefits workers who refuse suitable work—that is, *suitable* in view of the skill the job requires, the rate of pay it carries, and, finally, its distance from the worker's home considered together with his ability to commute or move. In some cases, disqualification from benefits should follow refusal to take training for the jobs that are available. The rights of the individual can be safeguarded through his retaining the right of appeal to higher boards.

The longer the period of unemployment, the greater the presumption that the employee's former work no longer needs him, and the more the justification to the administrative agency of cutting off benefits unless the worker accepts a job elsewhere or in a new occupation. The existence of general full employment adds sanction to this policy; encouragement of idleness is no part of the aim of social insurance.

4. Retraining programs should be readily available, with full information about the current and anticipated demands of the labor market available to the worker. It is essential that retraining be undertaken promptly as soon as it is clear that demand for the worker's old skill has permanently declined. Otherwise, the graduates of retraining will be discredited in the minds of employers, since only those will go through it who could not easily be placed.

The British White Paper on Employment favored planned training programs carried on, so far as possible, in the factory or shop, where the trainee can see ahead the job for which he is preparing. There would be clear distinction between the position of a person on unemployment pay and one who had embarked on a training program, so that the latter would feel he was no longer unemployed, but had started on a new job. The allowances paid to trainees is to be larger than the unemployment benefit, but smaller than the wage he is likely to receive during his first subsequent employment.[6]

5. Trade unions may restrict entrance of workers into new trades, and so reduce labor mobility. The restrictions take the form of (a) rules limiting the number of apprentices and helpers permitted, (b) support of license laws that require the possession of a license or certificate of competency as a condition of practicing a given trade, and (c) high admission fees to members of the union or simple refusal to admit new members. This latter restriction is significant only where there is a closed shop, union shop, or preferential-shop agree-

6 Command Paper 6527, "Employment Policy," p. 14.

ment with particular employers; otherwise newcomers can obtain work without joining the union.[7] Licensing rules may have some, or complete, justification. Usually, the public interest is injured by the other restrictive rules, since they hinder the adjustment of labor supply to changes in demand for labor. They ordinarily evidence a psychology arising from continued job scarcity. If the United States succeeds in maintaining full employment over the future years, the incentive for such restrictions will diminish. Pressure for the removal of restrictions, brought by workers who have been discriminated against, will then stand a better chance of success.

6. Some advantage might be gained from a carefully designed program to grant removal and traveling expenses to people for whom jobs are available in distant areas. But there is much doubt whether the results would justify the administrative cost. The Industrial Transference Board, set up in England in 1928 to assist movement to other areas, found that a considerable proportion of those moved through its help returned soon. The attractions of the family unit and of the old location were strong. The bulk of the permanent transferring that took place was voluntary.

If attractive jobs are available elsewhere and people know about them, there will be a substantial volume of *voluntary* migration. The migration will be by those who judge their chances of success in the new job greatest relative to their chances at home, and who are best able to move. These are precisely the people who, from the social point of view, ought to move.

The Location of Industry

Where ought an industry to be located? (1) From an economic point of view industries should be where they can most

---

[7] Sometimes unions require employers to show preference in hiring to local union members before hiring union men from any other area. This rule demands that employers employ the most ineffective local men before they hire any outsiders. On these restrictions see Sumner H. Slichter, *Union Policies and Industrial Management*, pp. 9–97. Washington: Brookings Institution, 1941.

efficiently utilize the resources of the economy. (2) Social considerations suggest that some weight be given to avoidance of concentrating in one area industries subject to wide parallel fluctuations of output. The steel industry and other heavy industries furnish examples. Industries dependent on foreign markets are also vulnerable. To avoid the growth of blighted areas of heavy local unemployment, it is desirable to favor the complementary growth of the more stable consumer-goods industries. Also there is social advantage in decentralizing areas of extreme concentration of population. (3) Finally, in a world that has not yet renounced war as an instrument of national policy, strategic considerations will have some voice —even in such a relatively secure nation as the United States. Industries basic to defense should be dispersed, and distant from likely channels of attack.

The interest of the whole society is best served when all three of these considerations are taken into account and balanced against one another. Our special concern of reducing frictional unemployment suggests, where social and strategic considerations do not oppose and where there is not significant difference of efficiency between possible locations, that industries should be located where there are continuing pools of unemployed people. The argument is stronger in so far as the unemployed are unable to move to other areas and/or have skills that are needed in the industry in question.

The importance of industrial relocation as a means toward diminishing pools of unemployment is lessened by two considerations: (1) A considerable amount of time is often required for establishing new industries. If this is true, *temporarily* unemployed people will not be helped by an industrial-relocation policy. (2) When there is long-continued local unemployment, people have greater mobility—that is, more incentive and more opportunity to search for new situations elsewhere. But there remain many intermediate and special cases where a location policy for industry is worth considering.

Such a policy would need to be carried into effect through use of the powers of government. However, *continued* subsidy for an industry must be justified on noneconomic grounds (social or strategic considerations) if it is to be justified at all. And once again, if we fear that government decision and action on location matters will be biased by the logrolling of local pressure groups, we will conclude that such action should be restricted to a very limited sphere.

During the interwar period, the British Government carried through several policies to attract industry to what were then Depressed Areas. Firms were circularized to ascertain whether they might not be willing to establish plants in the Areas; after 1936 loans up to 10,000 pounds were offered at low interest rates to firms establishing plants in these Areas; payment, in part or whole, of local taxes, income taxes, and rent was offered to such firms for a limited number of years; and finally Trading Estates were established, which built factories for sale or lease to small manufacturers, and managed the industrial community that later grew up.[8]

More recently, the Planning Room of the Board of Trade in London has made available to businessmen who are considering expansion of their plants or the locating of new ones, information on labor supply, transportation, rates, gas, water, electricity, and factory space available. No power of compulsion is held by the Board of Trade, but nearly all the 400 firms who came there in its first half year took the advice offered to them.

The White Paper on Employment contemplated forbidding establishment of new factories in areas where serious disadvantages would result, and of encouraging, by a number of inducements, the establishment of new factories in suitable areas. Priorities are to be given for building and extending factories in those areas; consideration will be given to the

---

8 *Economic Stability in the Postwar World*, pp. 220–221. Geneva: League of Nations, 1945.

needs of special areas in the placing of government contracts; the Trading Estates are to be continued; facilities lor long- and short-term-loan capital, and even share capital are to be provided promising firms which establish themselves in accord with government policy; and finally, munitions factories already in the areas are to be retained in munitions production, or promptly leased or sold for civilian production.[9]

We do not suggest that the above policies are necessarily desirable for the United States. Some of those tried in England before World War II were ineffective—namely, the circularizing of firms, and even the offer to pay rents and taxes for a limited time for firms establishing themselves in the Special Areas. They do suggest the possibilities open to us if the need should be considerable, and if we trust that the pressure of local interests will not significantly distort government policy.

In general, businesses are alert to find areas where effective labor is in surplus. Eastman Kodak and Kraft Foods, among others, built plants in Georgia after the War, because they were attracted by a good supply of skilled labor. An Arrow Shirt factory was set up in the Mesabi area of northern Minnesota during 1947 because mechanization of iron mines had left a labor surplus there.

But the Federal government could be useful through maintaining a bureau of information on matters relevant to industrial location, whose advice would take into account the three relevant considerations—not only the economic, but also the social and strategic. This function appears to be a logical extension of the present business-information service of the Bureau of Foreign and Domestic Commerce of the Department of Commerce. No local agency—no state or city bureau—can present information and advice free from suspicion of bias.

---

[9] Command Paper 6527, pp. 11-12.

CHAPTER NINETEEN

Price Level Policy

General price rises as full employment is approached

WE HAVE SEEN THAT THE CLOSER THE ECONOMY MOVES TO A full employment level of output, the more the tendency for average prices to rise. As total money expenditure grows and demand swells for various kinds of goods and services, sellers are in an increasingly favorable position. Businessmen become conscious that they can raise prices and still sell their production. Labor unions and individual laborers find their bargaining power to extract higher wages increased: employees have less fear of the unemployment that might follow a strike or unsuccessful collective bargaining, and they know that the withdrawal of their labor will cause more loss to the employer than if demand were slack.

Price rises occur first in "bottleneck" lines of goods, where demand is especially heavy relative to supplies, owing to some combination of large increase in money demand and small increase or none in supplies. If demand continues to grow, the bottlenecks multiply, and price rises become general through the economy. (But prices may rise sharply when unemployment is still heavy. This will be true if labor unions are strongly entrenched in strategic industries and press urgently for higher rates even when many are unemployed in their industries, and if monopolistic businesses are inclined to advance prices on slight encouragement.)

The more readily labor moves into bottleneck occupations

and the more readily businesses can be set up and expanded to produce goods in special demand, the more price rises will be smothered by a flow of increased production. A higher level of production and employment can then be attained without price rises.

The Aim of Short-Run Stability of Average Prices

The decline of average prices in time of depression is the consequence of a drop in demand. Faced with shrinking demand, businessmen in search of markets and laborers in search of jobs compete prices down to a lower level. The price decline is greatest in those areas where prices are directly set by competitive pricing rather than by administrative decision.

A government anti-depression policy that aims at pushing the price level lower is, therefore, a policy that mistakes one disease for another. The basic trouble is a collapse of demand, not the failure of prices to fall rapidly enough.

But no sooner have we made this statement than we ought to qualify it: (1) There may be in certain areas and at certain times strategic prices, in which a moderate decline would encourage increased investment. It is sometimes argued that housing is such a field. (2) A dictatorship or a democracy possessing strongly supported price and wage boards could lower internal prices by *fiat*,[1] and so, by giving foreigners a better bargain, increase foreign buying. This is mainly a policy for a small country, whose foreign trade is large compared to its internal trade (so that the internal stimulating effect is significant), but whose foreign trade is small compared to international trade generally (so that there are no important repercussions from other countries who now face stiffer competition). For any country a simpler way of giving the foreigner a better bargain would be through judicious currency depreciation.

---

[1] An ordinary deflationary policy would achieve lower prices (*via* open market operations, higher interest rates, fiscal policy measures, and so forth) *through forcing unemployment* on the economy. Hence it is not a cure for unemployment.

Apart from these moderate qualifications, the reasoning holds: anti-depression policy will find small advantage from aiming at a lower price level. Much of what we have said (pp. 235-236) against thinking that lowered average wage rates would alleviate depression is directly applicable here.

Is the converse policy desirable? Should an anti-depression policy *aim* at higher prices?[2] The ending of price declines will, of course, have its favorable effect on business expectations; and price rises (as under the NRA codes of the 1930's) may have a still further favorable effect through encouraging anticipatory buying. Professor Schumpeter felt that the NRA appreciably favored recovery: ". . . it pegged weak spots within industries, stopped spirals in many places, mended disorganized markets . . . even Blue Eagles do count for something when, objective conditions for revival being given, it is broken morale that is the matter."[3] But price rises also have their negative aspect because, as we have seen, any given money demand will now purchase a smaller quantity of output, and so lead to a lower level of employment than if prices had not risen.

In all cases, rapid price movements will have sharp disadvantages of the sort we list below (pp. 351-355).

We conclude that central policy directed toward averting or alleviating depression should not rely on major price changes as a means.[4]

Interrelationships of Prices

This conclusion does not mean that an economy should aim at stability of individual prices. From the point of view of the whole economy, the function of individual prices is to attract

---

[2] Of course, increased expenditure on output will, to some extent, lead toward higher prices as an indirect result.

[3] Joseph A. Schumpeter, *Business Cycles*. New York: McGraw-Hill, 1939, pp. 992, 993.

[4] If in depression, price *discrepancies* are objected to (some prices having fallen much more than others), an increase of general demand will usually tend to correct them through raising most those prices that had fallen most.

resources (through higher pay) into those uses where they contribute most to the social output, and to apportion the output of the economy among its members. If the pay of welders in Detroit rises, more welders tend to move to Detroit, and more people train themselves to the trade; or if the price of tobbaco rises, farm land and labor shift over from growing other crops to growing tobacco. If shirts are scarce, their prices rise and consumers buy fewer. Since there are continual changes in consumer demand, frequent changes in techniques of production, and some underlying changes in the resources available in the economy, we should expect repeated changes likewise in the prices of finished products and in the prices paid for resources. (The alternative mechanism to shift resources is more drastic: localized unemployment or excess demand.)

But since, at the best, we can hope for only a rough approximation to an ideal balance in our use of resources, daily or even monthly changes in the prices of commodities are not necessary. For some rather perishable commodities, which suffer a considerable annual variation in supply or demand, it is reasonable to expect a dozen or more significant price changes in the course of a year. Many food products fall under this heading—fluctuations in the price of eggs, for example, are plotted in Chart 24. For other commodities on which the dominant influence is decrease in cost of production (rayon in Chart 24), and/or decline in demand (coal) it is desirable and to be expected that there should be a considerable fall in price over the course of the years. Such a fall in price is consistent with a rather high degree of short-run monopolistic power.

On the other hand, we should not leave the impression, with respect to individual prices, that "whatever is, is right." There is a striking movement in the price of shoes in Chart 24: price changes have been rather few; price declined hardly at all in depression and rose rapidly during recovery. The evi-

dence is strong that monopolistic pricing is a major explana-
tory element. The rigidity of prices through the recession

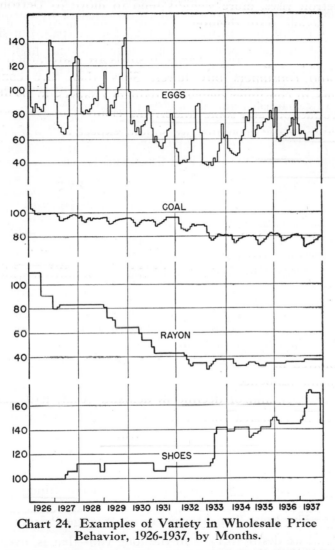

**Chart 24. Examples of Variety in Wholesale Price
Behavior, 1926-1937, by Months.**

Source: Department of Labor, Bureau of Labor Statistics, in National Resources
Committee, *Structure of the American Economy.* Washington: Government
Printing Office, 1939, Part I, p. 127.

might be defended from the point of view of its influence on the general economy (p. 257), but the drastic rise in recovery is plainly undesirable. It appears not to reflect basic supply and demand conditions, nor to be justified by encouragement of technical improvement over a longer span, but simply to evince the power of monopolistic sellers to exact high prices.

Another kind of undesirable price movement is the wide "destabilizing" kind of fluctuation that exists in the prices of basic raw materials and agricultural products.[5]

TABLE 16

PRICE CHANGES IN BASIC COMMODITIES 1936–1938

	Percentage 1936 Low to 1937 High	Changes 1937 High to 1938 Low
Wheat (Liverpool)	+75	—60
Corn (Chicago)	+133	—77
Sugar (London)	+48	—24
Coffee (New York)	+49	—49
Cocoa (New York)	+129	—62
Wool, Merino (London)	+45	—42
Cotton (New York)	+27	—45*
Rubber (London)	+91	—60
Copper (London)	+100	—48
Lead (London)	+99	—53

* Low in November, 1937.

These drastic price changes seem to be, in large part, a result of speculative buying when prices are rising in the upswing of the business cycle, and of speculative selling when prices are falling in the downswing of the business cycle. Such changes are disruptive of production and consumption relationships, rather than a guide to their efficient functioning.

The Long-Run Movement of Average Prices

Should we desire to have in the long run—that is, over peri-

[5] Data from *Economic Stability in the Postwar World*. Geneva: League of Nations, 1945, p. 83.

ods of a decade or more— (1) constancy of average prices, (2) a movement upward, or (3) a movement downward?

Some economists argue for a secular gently falling level of prices, on the ground that this is the most effective way of sharing the gains of technical progress throughout the economy. Wages are supposed to remain fairly stable. There will be a short-run rise in profits in the progressive industries, but in the longer run, management and capital will be attracted into those areas, and with rising output prices will decline. The effect is to make the more abundant products increasingly available among all members of the population, including those with fixed incomes.

• Other economists reason that a gently rising price level is desirable. There will be some injury to people whose incomes remain fixed or nearly fixed. But this is seen to be offset by the encouragement to investment and business enterprise generally that rising prices will give (it is assumed that this encouragement is needed) and by the greater ease of making economic adjustment thought to result from an environment of rising prices.

Employment and the Control of the Price Level

It is unlikely that any *plan* for a stable, gently rising or gently falling price level will actually be realized over the course of the years. The price level is likely to be a by-product of the level of employment and output achieved and of the reactions of firms and individuals of the economy to that level. The significant questions to ask are these: As the level of effective demand rises, sales expand, and unemployment shrinks, to what extent will business entrepreneurs strive for higher prices, either through administrative price decisions (for monopolistically competitive concerns) or through bringing pressure on Washington? And to what extent will labor unions strike for high wages? These are questions of human psychology, on which we may be optimistic or pessimistic, but to which we are not able to give precise answer.

We want an economy in which prices are kept down by the competition of producers for markets and of workers for jobs, rather than by significant use of price controls, rationing, and priorities (pp. 132-133). When we defined "full employment" as employment of all but a margin of 5 per cent of the frictionally unemployed,[6] we were making a guess about the amount of surplus capacity and labor that must necessarily exist in order for their competition to keep prices approximately stable.

Within a range, therefore, unemployment can be looked on as a cost that the economy pays for the self-seeking of groups within it. The greater the sense of social responsibility on the part of management and labor, the smaller, within limits, the quantity of unemployment needs to be.

---

[6] This, of course, did not mean that 5 per cent of the individuals in the working force would be permanently out of work, but only that at any one time 5 per cent would be changing jobs or for other reasons be temporarily unemployed.

CHAPTER TWENTY

Inflation

DURING WORLD WAR II, AND ESPECIALLY IN THE YEARS FOL-
lowing, the fires of inflation were circling the world. They
showed no conclusive signs of burning themselves out after several years of peace, and gained renewed vigor with the arma-
ment expenditures induced in the West after the invasion of
South Korea in mid-1950. The problem in these postwar years
was a universal one, in controlled as well as free economies—in
Soviet Russia and England, in Poland and Greece, in Brazil,
China, and even the United States—although the American
dollar still seemed literally as good as gold to the people of
most other countries.

The Harmfulness of Inflation

Why should prices not be allowed to rise rather freely, as
they did, for example, during and after World War I? In
other words, why is inflation [1] an evil?

One might be inclined to talk in terms of the money saved
by government and private buyers if prices are kept low. The
OPA estimated that, if prices had risen in World War II as
they did in World War I, by the end of 1943 the government
and civilians would have spent 101 billion dollars more than
they did for supplies. The government had actually saved half
its expenditures.[2] But such an answer is superficial. The loss

---

[1] *Inflation* is a continued, considerable rise in prices, resulting from an excess
of money demand for goods and services over supply, the supply being valued
at the prices of a base period.
[2] OPA, Price Control Report 12.

to government and civilians cannot be measured in this way, because if prices had risen freely in World War II, incomes to civilians would have risen and tax receipts of the government would also have risen.

I. A fundamental objection emerges from unevenness of the effects on real incomes. During inflation some people and firms are able to obtain high prices for their products or services. Prices of raw materials, of farm products, and of certain kinds of labor usually rise most. Other people find their money incomes unchanged or even reduced. Firms selling goods in backwater districts do badly. People on annuities or pensions, and those working in many kinds of white collar jobs find their money incomes at the same level as in peacetime or, at best, only a little higher. But people dependent on these sources of money income face higher prices, like everyone else, when they come to buy. Their real incomes are, therefore, cut. In addition, any savings held in the form of cash or of claims on cash shrink in real value as the inflation progresses.

The net result is that some people do very well indeed as the inflation continues, but others are forced into poverty. A deep sense of unfairness pervades the economy; bitterness grows. Such a society is divided and weakened on the rack of internal dissension and hostility.

2. The falling purchasing power of labor incomes that have not risen appreciably, coupled with a growing sense of unfairness, is likely to lead to work stoppages and strikes. These will be unequally successful, depending on the situation of particular employers and the bargaining power of particular unions; and so the sense of unfairness continues. If strikes are numerous in strategic industries, industrial production as a whole is held back, with a consequent tendency toward still higher prices.

3. Continued price rises in any area stimulate the hoarding of inventories by manufacturers, wholesalers, retailers, and consumers: some of these people decide it is better to buy now

rather than later, regardless of whether the commodities are to be consumed or processed or resold. To the extent that the output of the economy is lying idle in excessive inventories, it is being used ineffectively. As supplies dwindle because of hoarding, more of the time of businessmen and consumers must be taken up by the search for assured supplies. This is an inefficient use of their time.

4. Uncertainty about cost-price relationships to be expected in the future discourages some lines of production, and so reduces production there.

5. In wartime, a fifth undesirable result is especially important. Some of the goods and services that rise most in price are luxury items, those not essential either to war purposes or civilian welfare. High prices attract into the production of such goods labor and resources that ought to go toward necessary purposes, and so lower output of the necessary goods. This effect suggests that if the controls are to be loose anywhere, it should be in the area of essential goods.

6. If the price rise is considerable, it tends to lead toward a subsequent depression. The incomes and savings of people whose incomes have risen little or not at all are dissipated in the buying of food, housing, and other necessities, and so there is an influence toward the eventual drying up of the market for other goods. The market for these latter may also shrink because the prices seem "unreasonable." In addition, the speculative buying and producing arrangements set under way by the price rise are unstable: they are apt to change suddenly into selling and bankruptcy when the speculators become fearful of the future and the producers find prices no longer rising and windfall gains no longer obtainable.

7. Finally, if higher output and employment is an objective of the economy, then rising prices are undesirable because they mean that policy directed toward that end is being hindered or frustrated. The added money outlay by private buyers or by the government is partly "going to waste" in higher prices rather than having its full effect in increased output and employment.

Catastrophic Inflation

If the rate of rise of prices in an economy is moderate, people do not change their buying habits much. Although some people, as we have seen above, anticipate a continued price rise and decide to hold their assets in the form of goods rather than money, most people continue to use their incomes to purchase goods or to hold in the form of cash in the same patterns they had followed before. The expectation of continued price rises does not dominate their thinking.

But once the rate of price increase per year exceeds a certain figure the expectation of continued price rises becomes a dominant influence. Everyone is convinced that prices will be higher next year, next month, even next week, than they are today. Therefore everyone has incentive to spend on goods any money he receives, and to spend at the earliest possible moment. The person who keeps cash on hand or claims on cash is considered idiotic: he should spend his money now, before prices have risen further.

The choice open to an economy under inflationary pressure is, therefore, not between, say, a 5, 30, or 50 per cent yearly increase in prices, but between a manageable and an unmanageable degree of inflation. The point at which the inflationary psychology takes hold is not precisely predictable. Perhaps it will be at 20 or 30 per cent, perhaps at a still higher figure. Nor is the degree to which it takes hold predictable. Beyond some moderate rate of price rises, more and more people decide to get rid of their cash and obtain goods instead (that is, the velocity of money increases), and there is growing danger of an overwhelming mass movement to do so. If and when people come to make bargains not on the basis of present prices, but on the basis of what they expect prices to be a week or a month hence, the rate of rise of prices can be astronomically great.

Once this inflationary psychology is firmly established in the population, all attempt to control the rate of price rises collapses. No laws can thwart the overwhelming impulse present in every individual to save himself by spending *now*.

The inflations in Germany and France following 1914 severely damaged the middle classes who held savings in the form of cash, bank deposits, or securities payable in marks or francs. The internal political divisions of France in 1940 and the growth of totalitarianism in Germany in the 1930's were significantly associated with the previous inflations of war and postwar years. During and after World War II internal weakness and political conflict in many nations followed the social upheaval of major inflations.

The Roots of the Postwar Inflations

Inflation is the result of a continuing and decided excess of demand over the value of production at current prices. It comes from too much spending just as plainly as depression comes from too little spending.

The causes of the inflations after World War II are—just as in other postwar inflations—to be found in the production and financial phenomena of the war. It is easy, and common enough, to point to scapegoats—profiteers, unions, hoarders, drones—but the explanation is not there.

Suppose that an economy, like that of the United States in 1941, is at much less than full employment, and then a major war breaks out. A considerable increase in output is possible and desirable. The government can increase its spending—for war supplies and for the armed forces generally—and find the main effect in higher production, with only a moderate rise in prices. Logically, the government *should* spend in excess of tax receipts, financing the difference from public loans and from bank borrowing or printing new money. These last expand the money supply and so encourage a net increase in spending for output. The economy moves toward full employment.

Later, when the economy attains approximately full employment, as did the United States by 1942, the problem becomes different. Inflation is now a threat. But the government will not order fewer uniforms, ships, planes, and tanks, because it fears inflation. The overriding purpose is to win the war. The government *wants* to avoid inflation, but it *must*—if the war is of any size—cut the flow of production into non-war civilian uses to a minimum, and raise the share going to war purposes to a maximum.

The principal tool of government for doing this is its taxing and borrowing policy. (1) As much money as possible is taken away from the civilian economy in order to diminish spending there. Consumers are taxed as heavily as their morale will stand, and businesses are taxed as heavily as is possible without reducing returns to the point where production shrinks. In addition, the public will be urged to buy bonds "till it hurts"—not to get money into the Treasury, but to get it away from civilian spenders. (2) In a major war government spending considerably exceeds receipts from taxes and borrowing from the public. The difference is newly created money. In the United States the new money (deposits) comes mainly from the banking system, as the government borrows there. In less developed countries, like that of China, the new money (paper currency) is simply printed. The new money is paid out into the hands of government contractors, soldiers, and government employees—and as the government and these recipients spend, prices move upward until civilians generally are no longer able to afford the goods and services wanted by government for its war purposes.

The poorer the taxing system of the government and hence the less its success in getting the public to buy bonds, and the greater its expenditures, the more rapid the rise in prices.

The pace of inflation

Suppose that in a year of approximately full employment gross output is worth at current prices 210 billion dollars, made up of 180 billions of expenditure by consumers and businesses, and 30 billion dollars of expenditure by government. Then suppose the rate of government spending rises to 60 billion dollars. Output cannot change appreciably, assuming continued full employment and negligible gains in productivity.

If consumers and businesses should happen to cut their spending by 30 billion dollars, all is well. No price rises result. But if they spend as before, prices must rise by 14 per cent. For the volume of output that was previously valued at 210 billion dollars can be sold for 240 billions only if prices rise by 30/210, or 14 per cent.

Nor is this the end of developments. (*a*) Traders, manufacturers, and farmers have received windfall gains of 30 billion dollars. A considerable part of this will be taxed away, since it is subject to high income tax rates, and some part of the remainder will be saved. Say that roughly 10 billion dollars of these windfall gains flow into additional spending in the next round. (*b*) Employees will be stimulated to present higher wage demands, since the prices of things they buy have risen. Where labor is specially short and unions are powerful, these demands will be at least partly successful. The resistance of employers to wage boosts is less because of high personal and corporate income tax rates to which they are subject at full employment levels of production, and because they can readily pass on their increased costs in higher prices. Suppose that 5 billion dollars of increased wages are paid out, and all goes into consumer spending. (*c*) In the first round, the government was buying 60/240, or 1/4 of the national output. If it wants to continue to use this proportion of the national output, it must now raise its spending to 65 billion dollars. (Private spending is now at the rate of 195 billion dollars, which, when government spending of 65 billions is added, makes up a total product of 260 billion dollars. 65 billions is 1/4 of 260 billions.)

In this second round prices have again risen, but by less than in the first round. Assuming as before that there are negligible changes in the physical volume of output, then since its value has risen from 240 billion dollars to 260 billions, prices have risen by 20/240, or about 8 per cent.

And so the inflationary process continues. We can generalize that if, when full employment already exists, a substantially larger share of output is consumed by any one segment of the economy, prices will rise at first abruptly, then more slowly, as the months go by.[3]

Any increase in production or decrease in demand will dampen the price increases. Any fall in production or increase in demand will increase the rate of price increases. An increase in the excess of exports over imports will tend toward more rapid inflation, and *vice versa*.

Open and repressed inflation

Rapid price rises bring strong public sentiment for price control. The injustices of the price rises are plain: traders, producers, speculators, and those in debt are getting better off; creditors, fixed income receivers, and those whose incomes rise only slowly are hard pressed. In extreme inflations rapid enrichment goes on side by side with impoverishment and starvation.

But price controls are not necessarily of much use. The likely first step is to impose them on goods and services basically important in the standard of living. But higher prices had checked demand and stimulated supply to the point where the quantity demanded was no greater than quantity supplied. At the legal prices, lower than would exist on a free market, more goods are demanded by consumers and their production may be discouraged. Hence demand is now greater than supply. Sellers find their shelves emptied soon after they are stocked; warehouses are empty. The available supply goes to those who get to the store first or who are favored by sellers.

Consequently public sentiment soon builds up for a system of rationing the scarce goods in the interest of fair distribution. If the rationing system is fairly well enforced, then in-

---

[3] Cf. J. M. Keynes, *How to Pay for the War*. New York: Harcourt, Brace, 1940, pp. 61 ff.

centives suffer. (*a*) The real money is ration tickets, and these are shared equally. Hence the factory worker and coal miner have no motive to try to earn more money than they are legally allowed to spend. Effort languishes; absenteeism grows (in part perhaps because people are scrounging around the countryside for food they can't get through the ration system); production falls; and inflationary pressure is stronger than ever. (*b*) With the prices of basic goods controlled and their quantities rationed, people now have money in pocket that they would otherwise have spent on the controlled goods. They are likely to spend most of this money on other, luxury goods. As prices rise in the uncontrolled areas, labor and other resources are attracted into production there, and output of the basic necessities sags further.

Both of these problems—decreased incentives and distorted allocation of resources—were critical in the Europe of 1946–1948.

The logical next step is to extend price and rationing controls over the whole of the economy. As the complexity of the system grows, enforcement becomes increasingly difficult. Violations are hard to check because both buyer and seller want to violate the law: the buyer is willing to offer more than the legal price, the seller is glad to receive more. In 1946 the price of common nails in New York, under OPA controls, was $6.11 a keg. An ordinary small house required four kegs, or about $24 worth at the legal price. But it was difficult or impossible to find nails at the legal price, and so no builder hesitated to buy his nails from black-market sellers at $15 a keg. The $36 more per house that the nails cost was nothing compared with the loss of construction time from waiting around in hope of finding nails at the legal price. Illegal buying and selling—the so-called "black market"—can spread from special areas until it becomes the main channel of trade. The laws grow increasingly unpopular and disregarded; enforcement grows spasmodic and ineffective.

The postwar inflations

These hard lessons of experience have been spelled out in many countries of the world. (*a*) Warring nations uniformly expanded their currencies, and emerged from the war with the quantity of money expanded many times over the prewar level. Neutral nations felt repercussions also. Germany's money supply was in 1947 some 10 to 12 times larger than the 6 billion reichsmarks in circulation before the War. By January, 1948 Japan's money supply of 220 billion yen was nearly 60 times larger than the 3.7 billions of 1939. The United States money supply rose from 33 billions in June, 1939, to 109 billions in June, 1947, or 3.3 times.[4]

(*b*) At the same time there was the pent-up demand of consumers for goods not obtainable during war, and the need of businesses to replace and modernize equipment. Some countries needed to repair war damage to factories, ships, houses.

(*c*) Inflationary pressure has been aggravated in the United States and some other countries by the wage demands of powerful trade unions and by the prevalence of a depression bias in thinking carried over from the 1930's. Predictions were common at the end of the war that there would be over 6 million unemployed within 9 months after V-J day. The United States government did not even try to prepare for monetary and fiscal policies to check inflation.

(*d*) Though the United States escaped war destruction, it did face after the War inflationary stimulus from a large rise in foreign buying, financed by imports of gold, sale of foreign assets in this country, and by our foreign aid program. The excess of exports over imports was nearly 8 billion dollars in 1946, over 11 billions in 1947, and over 6 billions in 1948.

Countries with weak governments, which were not able to tax and borrow from the public any large proportion of their total expenditures, have suffered most from inflation. Newly created money was the source of much of their expenditure,

4 Demand deposits adjusted plus currency outside banks.

and the money supply rapidly expanded. Inflation was especially intense in Greece and China, where civil wars demanded
heavy government spending. In China the budget deficit in
early 1948 was running at about 300 million dollars a year
(in terms of United States money). During 1947 the largest
denomination of paper money currency was the 10,000 dollar
bill CNC (Chinese National Currency). It fell in value during
the year from 88 cents in American money to around 7 cents.
$3020 in stamps carried a postcard to the United States. In
January, 1948, a new 100,000 dollar note was issued; it dropped
three-fifths in value by late February. As the government's
fortunes in the civil war declined the fall in the value of the
money accelerated. For a time after World War II, until it was
made illegal, businessmen in China reckoned their debts and
credits in American dollars. Sometimes checks drawn on
United States banks would circulate as money in China for
seven or eight months before turning up in the United States
dirty and dog-eared.[5]

The inflation in Hungary exceeded all known records of the
past. In August, 1946, 828 octillion (1 followed by 27 zeros)
depreciated pengös equalled the value of 1 prewar pengö. The
price of the American dollar reached a value of 3×10^{22} (3
followed by 22 zeros) pengös. This triumphs considerably over
the German record of 1923, when the American dollar cost
10^{12} (1 followed by 12 zeros) reichsmarks.

When the value of domestic currency has fallen drastically
and keeps on falling, a baby carriage or a box may be necessary to carry enough money to buy anything substantial. In
Germany of 1923 a larger box was needed to carry money to
the grocery store than to bring back the groceries bought.
Fishermen and farmers in 1947 Japan used scales to weigh
currency and change, rather than bothering to count it. Prices
rose some 116 times in Japan, 1939 to 1948.

---

[5] "The Fire that Rings the World," *Fortune*, Vol. XXXVII (April, 1948),
pp. 201-202.

People flee from a weak currency to money substitutes. This in itself cheapens the currency further: people pass on any currency they receive as soon as they can; the velocity of money rises. During the period of the French Revolution, 1790–1796, the government increased the supply of money (by issues of paper *assignats*) 20 times, but prices rose 200 times. This means that, if output was unchanged, the velocity of money increased 10 times. (For a time the government tried to keep down the price rise by threat of the guillotine for violations of price and rationing controls.) In Germany by the end of 1923, living costs had risen about 1200 times above their 1913 level. In the last two years of the inflation, the quantity of money increased 10 times; prices rose 90 times. The velocity of circulation of Chinese National Currency in 1947 was reported four or more times faster than that of a sound currency. When the Hungarian pengö was weakening most rapidly in late 1945, prices rose perceptibly from day to day, even from hour to hour. Employees ran outdoors as soon as they received their pay, to buy whatever they could.

Where there are reasonably effective price controls and rationing, any money in excess of what is needed to get the allowed ration is nearly worthless. Barter, with all its inefficiency, becomes the normal method of exchange; and goods are diverted increasingly from legal channels into the illegal markets. As people learn to avoid the police in black market activities, they are schooling themselves in crime. Theft and violence increase. It is easy to rationalize crime when the uneven hand of inflation is scattering riches and starvation haphazardly.

When in 1947 the military government and unions in the Ruhr wanted to persuade miners to produce more coal by mining on Sundays, they had no success. The 10 extra marks of Sunday pay earned nothing that could be bought on the legal market, since in six days a miner earned enough to buy all the goods to which his ration tickets entitled him; and on the black market 10 marks bought less than an ounce of butter, or 1/20 of a pound of sugar.[6]

The farmer in western Europe was often completely on a barter standard in the early postwar years. He had only disdain for currency, which brought him nothing he wanted. Kitchenware, thread, clothing, jewelry (for investment), tools, the offer of a day's labor—these were what would lure forth the hidden pig or sack of potatoes.

United States Price Control in Wartime

Chart 25 portrays the course of wholesale prices in the United States since 1749. In the Revolutionary War they rose 202 per cent; in the War of 1812, 47 per cent; in the Civil War, 117 per cent; and in World War I, 127 per cent.[7]

A striking contrast is evident in Chart 26 between the price movements of World War I and those of World War II. During World War I retail prices rose 50 per cent and wholesale prices, 93 per cent. In World War II retail prices rose 36 per cent, and wholesale prices, 35 per cent. *During* World War II prices hardly rose at all after 1943.

The much smaller price rise in World War II existed despite the fact that this was a relatively "bigger" war for the United States. A larger proportion of our total production went to war, leaving a smaller increase in goods available to consumers; and purchasing power in the hands of consumers increased by a much greater proportion.[8] In other words, supply to civilians increased less than in World War I, and potential civilian demand increased more.

Evidently, during World War II our price control measures were more effective than during World War I. Three kinds

6 *Ibid.*, pp. 80-81.

7 The percentages are calculated from the average of the new year of low prices just preceding the war, to the year of highest prices during or just after the war.

8 The proportion of total output going to war purposes was, in World War I, 25 per cent; in World War II, 44 per cent. Checking accounts rose 43 per cent in World War I, 105 per cent in World War II. From *Senate Hearings on Extension of the Emergency Price Control Act*, pp. 1558-1567; revised in S. E. Harris, *Price and Related Controls.* New York: McGraw-Hill, 1945, p. 13.

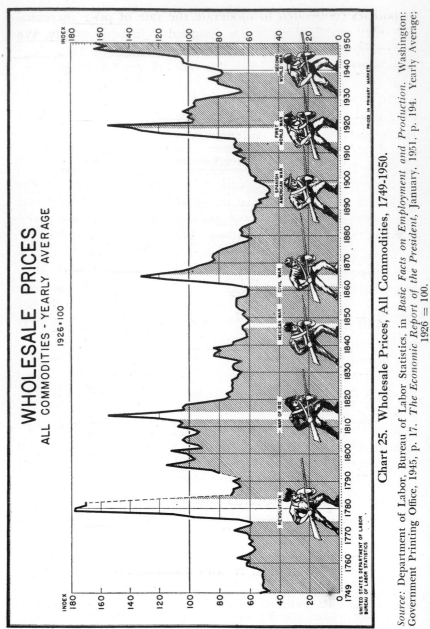

Chart 25. Wholesale Prices, All Commodities, 1749-1950.

Source: Department of Labor, Bureau of Labor Statistics, in *Basic Facts on Employment and Production.* Washington: Government Printing Office, 1945, p. 17. *The Economic Report of the President,* January, 1951, p. 194. Yearly Average; 1926 = 100.

of policies cooperated to moderate the rate of price increases.

1. One set of measures was designed to increase supply. We increased the number of workers and the length of the average work week; we sought to simplify and standardize products, to

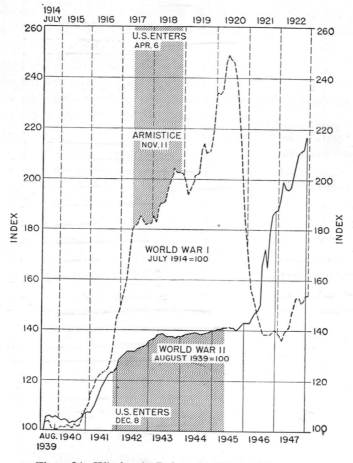

Chart 26. Wholesale Prices in World War I and World War II, All Commodities.

Source: Data through June, 1945, from Department of Labor, Bureau of Labor Statistics, *Basic Facts on Employment and Production.* Washington: Government Printing Office, 1945, p. 19. Data after that time are adjusted from the *Survey of Current Business,* Vol. XXVI (April, 1946), p. S-4; Vol. XXVII (January, 1947), p. S-4; and *The Economic Report of the President* (January, 1948), p. 120.

concentrate production in a few efficient plants; we tried to reduce exports not for war purposes and to increase imports. These measures and others had a considerable measure of success: civilian supplies had increased by about 26 per cent during the last half of 1944 as compared with the average for 1939.

2. We tried also to limit demand. We rationed goods to consumers, and we controlled the flow of materials and labor to businessmen through priorities, allocations, and manpower controls. All these tended to check demand through making the attempt to buy more than specified quantities illegal. If our ration stamp called for only 5 pounds of sugar, we could not (legally) buy the 10 pounds we should have liked. We further checked demand by taking money away from the public through drastic increases in taxes and through bond buying campaigns. Controls on wage and salary increases checked the rise of incomes, much of which flowed promptly into spending on the market.

Such efforts to increase supply and to check the increase of demand were helpful, in fact essential; but they would not in themselves have been sufficient to prevent a drastic price rise.

3. As a direct measure to control price rises, the OPA (Office of Price Administration) established legal price ceilings. Price ceilings were established under one of two principles: either (a) they were set in accord with some formula that related them to *costs* in a particular business, or (b) they were set on the historical principle. This meant that prices were frozen at some previous level or at some maximum percentage above that level. Such ceilings were adjusted (usually upward) from time to time as changing costs and political pressures made advisable.[9]

The Postwar United States Inflation

Between V-J day and the spring of 1951 there were four major upward surges in the price level. The first came in the

---

9 Over 60,000 regulations, rules, price lists, and directives were issued by the OPA during the war, nearly half the 134,248 directives, orders, and proclamations issued by all divisions of the government.

winter of 1945–1946 and spring of 1946. Price controls were still in effect, but the regulations were eased, and manufacturers, unions, and the public were in no mind to cooperate with the controls as they had during wartime. The second was in the summer and fall of 1946 when price controls were first suspended and then abolished. The third took place in the summer and fall of 1947. The fourth, after some decline in 1949, was rapid and sustained after the outbreak of the Korean War in June, 1950.

But price rises over this whole period were, compared to dramatic experience abroad, very mild. Occasionally prices would level off for a time. The American public generally, like its economists at the end of the War, was morbidly afraid of deflation and unemployment. A break in the stock market in the fall of 1946 and a collapse of farm prices in the spring of 1948 were taken as signs that the inflation might be ending of itself. In 1949 there were more emphatic signs of the inflation ending: considerable price decline in certain lines, and an appreciable rise in unemployment during the middle of the year.

Except for a short period in mid-1949 employment was steadily at higher than "full employment" levels, and production, after immediate postwar dislocation in late 1945 and in 1946, was also at unprecedented levels. Despite the plague of rising prices, the United States had never been so prosperous.

Fallacies about the United States inflation

During these postwar years we heard strange arguments about how to cure inflation. Errors of policy have been made, both by the Administration because it had been misled by economists to feel that deflation and unemployment was *the* postwar danger, and by Congress which enacted into law a policy alleged to check inflation that instead clearly fed its fires.

1. A whole set of fallacious arguments are associated with the doctrine that increased production is an important road

out of inflation. If an economy is already at full employment, can production be substantially increased? Of course the answer is that it cannot.

Any rise in productivity (more production from the same input of resources) would help, but in the past this has averaged only about 1.7 per cent a year. It is not likely that over-all productivity could rise at a rate exceeding 2 or 3 per cent a year. This rate would not help much within several years, but the advocates of the doctrine seemed to have convinced themselves that rising production could stop further price rises within a few months.[10] The argument was at least 97 per cent wrong.

A special case of this general argument was pressed during the year following V-J day. If only the wartime price ceilings were taken off, it was said, production would bound upward so vigorously that prices must soon fall to ceiling levels or below. The inflation would be promptly scotched. The emptiness of this doctrine was soon proved by the facts in the months following removal of price ceilings in 1946. The reason why it is fallacious is seen as soon as we remember again that the economy was approximately at full employment. Any possible increase in production in one industry—where, say, ceiling prices had been so low as to discourage production—would be offset by a drop in production elsewhere, as men and materials were bid away from other employments.

But it is easy to understand, too, how manufacturers, farmers, and employees, fretting under ceiling prices on *their* products and services, could manage to persuade themselves that the doctrine was sound.

Not much different was the remarkable theory adopted by Congress in early 1948, that lower taxes and lower government revenues would help to check inflation. The reasoning was that business investment would be encouraged by lower

---

10 Any increase in overtime possible in the economy would mean that increased incomes (and spending) would parallel increased output. Furthermore, the productivity of overtime workers is likely to be low.

taxes, and with more plant and equipment in use, production would soon rise. But heavier expenditure for plant and equipment—if, in fact, it resulted—would add to inflationary pressure *now;* and the hoped-for rise in output could not be significant before some years in the future. This is no road out of inflation.

2. A second fallacy is that prices increased inordinately during the inflation. This was urged by people who explain inflation by the scapegoat method: that speculators and profiteers are to blame. It is an error of the "left," just as the first fallacy is an error of the "right."

There are several ways to measure the pressure on prices. We present below the June, 1939—June, 1947 rise in money supply and disposable income[11] as indications of the increase in demand, and the rise in hourly earnings of manufacturing employees as a clue to increase in costs of production. With these we compare the price rise of the same period.

(Averages for the year)	1939	1950
Money supply (Demand deposits adjusted plus currency outside banks)	100	336
Disposable personal income	100	289
Average hourly earnings of manufacturing employees	100	231
Wholesale prices	100	201
Consumers' price index	100	173

Rises in demand and in costs have considerably exceeded rises in prices.

Those who are inclined to blame profiteers for high prices may point to the swelling figures for corporate profits. Before taxes, corporate profits rose, from 1939 to 1950, to 613 per cent of the 1939 level (6.5 billion dollars to 39.8 billions); and profits after taxes rose to 442 per cent (5.0 billion dollars to 22.1 billions).[12] But a considerable part of this profit rise is an illusion. Profits are figured after *legally allowed* depreciation

---

11 F. Machlup, "Misconceptions about the Current Inflation," *Review of Economics and Statistics*, Vol. XXX (February, 1948), pp. 17-18, corrected for an error in calculation.

12 *Survey of Current Business*, July, 1950, p. 9, and February, 1951, p. 9.

charges are subtracted. These charges are clearly far too low to replace capital: the costs of capital have more than doubled since before the war so that both current reserves and reserves accumulated during wartime are insufficient to replace equipment wearing out and worn out.

We know that some firms were making very large profits in these postwar years if we figure profits as a percentage of capital. But at the huge full employment output of 1950, profits as a percentage of gross output were still small. If we took away all corporate profits after taxes except about 5 billions (a rough estimate of the additional reserves needed to keep up plant and equipment), price could have fallen by a little over 6 per cent.[13] This is something, but not a drastic change. Furthermore, our reasoning assumes that production would continue undiminished as these profits are taken away, that entrepreneurs and investors are willing to take risks and meet losses without any hope of offsetting gain.

But would prices to ultimate buyers have fallen by even this amount? If factories lowered their prices, most dealers would probably have kept final prices at existing levels since they could sell all the output to eager buyers at those prices. And if prices did fall, what would the buyers of these products do with the money thus saved? Probably most of it would be spent for other kinds of goods, perhaps farm products, where prices would promptly rise still higher.[14]

3. There is also the argument that monopolists are to blame for high prices. This has, in part, been answered already. The suggestion is a plausible one, but the facts are directly to the contrary. Competitive prices—those of agricultural products and raw materials—rose most in the United States inflation, just as they normally do in times of expansion. The output of farm products is not greatly expanded during booms; hence rising demand has its chief effect in raising prices.

[13] 22.1 billion dollars of profits after taxes, minus 5 billion dollars of additional reserves, equals 17.1 billions. 282.6 billion dollars is gross national product in 1950. 17.1/282.6 equals 6.1%.

[14] Machlup, *op. cit.*, p. 20.

In the "monopolistically competitive" (or administered price) area output rose greatly during the war, and prices rose slowly then and after the war. Prices were clearly lower during 1950 and 1951 in this area than they would have been if competitively determined. Such prices are fixed by decisions of business managers: prices were often kept so low that firms were forced to ration their product among buyers. Producers could have received much higher prices if they had wanted.

The "gray market" of post-OPA days was not an illegal market, since there were no legal price ceilings. A two-price system prevailed—a low price being paid by factory customers, to whom the scarce production was rationed out; a high price by less favored buyers in the general market. Often buyers obtained a part of their needed supplies direct from the factory at low prices, the rest in the gray market at higher prices.

The main gray market items were, in 1947 and 1948, steel, chemicals, building materials, newsprint, and rayon yarn. Prices were running at two or three times the factory price, but the margins varied sharply with changing conditions. Some 5 per cent of steel supposedly went into gray market channels in 1948—original buyers often promptly resold at the higher free market prices. The volume of sales of all products in the gray market was estimated at over a billion dollars.[15] The used-car gray market was conspicuous. Buyers of new cars from reputable dealers at list prices—or at not far above list prices—often drove them promptly over to used car lots for a gain of $500 to $1000.

The varying gray market premium on products was a sensitive measure of the excess of supply over demand at list prices.

Why did these "monopolistic" producers not charge the highest price they could get? Public relations was a major factor. The heavy demand was thought a temporary matter; in a few months it would be over; but the ill will created by hiking prices could plague the industry long into the future. The $5

---

15 "That Daffy Gray Market," *Fortune*, Vol. XXXVII (May, 1948) , p. 95.

a ton raise in certain steel prices in 1948 caused national discussion and criticism, including appeals for an antitrust investi-
gation. In addition, labor unions would be encouraged to demand higher wages, which could not be reduced when boom
days were over save at the cost of strikes and intense resentment.

But whatever the motives, it is clearly contrary to fact to
blame "monopolistic," or administered-price, industry for the
price rises.

The Way Out of Inflation

What can be done to meet the problems of inflation? (1)
There was in the postwar period always the happy possibility that the inflation would come to a natural end, and
prices level off. Business investment would eventually fall off
as postwar replacement and expansion needs were met. Consumer buying would decline, as wartime scarcities of cars,
washing machines, radios, and the like, were gradually eliminated. As European recovery proceeded and if international
tension lessened—which it did not—the need for government
expenditures would shrink.

(2) We have already seen one thing that should *not* be
done: taxes should not be reduced while inflationary pressure
continues. Instead higher taxes are desirable, to the extent that
equity permits, in areas where production will not be checked.
Funds can be accumulated to pay off the public debt; or, if an
investment boom continues a threat, the funds can be allowed
to accumulate as an idle Treasury deposit in the Federal Reserve. Refinancing of the old debt, to the extent that is necessary, should be by borrowing from the public rather than
from commercial banks.

(3) No less important is the reduction of public expenditures by deferring or dropping all projects not urgently needed
for defense or other purposes. A surplus of taxes over expenditures is a critically useful step toward checking inflation.
In no serious inflation has a budget surplus been maintained.

(4) The encouragement of consumer saving is desirable. If it is politically possible, limited compulsory savings might be introduced. People are required to buy government bonds in amount equal to a proportion of their income tax. The bonds cannot be cashed, save in hardship cases or unless a recession threatens, until three or four years in the future.

Assuming that government and business absorb a constant proportion of output, this policy does not reduce the quantity of goods and services people consume today. They can still buy the full employment output of consumer goods. They could buy no more if they were permitted to spend all their incomes (and force up prices). But they will, under this policy, have savings to spend in the future, at a lower price level than otherwise and in a more stable economy.

(5)More drastic inflations than that of the United States have justified recall of old currency and blocking of bank accounts, with a smaller quantity of new money issued in exchange.

In Belgium where, under German occupation, the money supply had swelled from 65 to 183 billion francs, the postwar government called in all existing currency, issued new currency in fractional amount, blocked all bank accounts in excess of their 1940 levels, imposed a heavy tax on war profits and a 5 per cent tax on all wealth. The Greek government at one time adopted the novel policy of selling imported goods to its people at black market prices, destroying the money so received. In Italy, three separate capital levies were carried out in 1947.

(6) A check on bank lending is crucial, lest other deflationary measures be offset by more bank loans. Central bank policies can be aimed at reducing reserves or requiring higher reserves. Discount policy may be used to raise interest rates. The reversal of the Italian inflation in October, 1947, is associated with sharp restrictions on bank lending. Banks were required by the legislation of Minister Einaudi to invest a specified part of their funds in government securities for de-

posit in the Bank of Italy, or to deposit directly in a blocked account at the Bank of Italy. In the United States, in September 1948, required bank reserves were raised by 2 per cent for all classes of demand deposits, as a move to restrain expansion of bank credit. (But the main effect was to cause the banks to sell government securities they owned to the Federal Reserve. With the proceeds, their reserves were increased to the required level.) Required reserves were lowered after 1948 as an anti-recession measure; and then raised again in 1951.

There is always the danger that one, or a group, of these deflationary policies will be carried too far and transform an inflation into a cumulating recession. The problem sometimes appears, as one economist phrased it, like trying to dim the light by pulling the light switch down toward *Off*.

(7) What about direct controls—price ceilings, priorities or allocations of scarce industrial supplies, consumer rationing? Agreement was limited on this matter among 10 economists who discussed inflation in the *Review of Economics and Statistics* in February, 1948. Most of them seemed willing to accept only a very modest program, no more; or perhaps a stand-by program to be used only if the inflation got much worse. The economists feared that controls would abruptly lead to misuse of resources in uncontrolled luxury channels and that black markets would appear and multiply.

There is no painless road out of inflation. All the policies suggested above hurt someone: they check income or loans to people, or they increase taxes and savings to take funds away from people. The only program that can cure inflation is one of reducing demand; but no one likes to have *his* demand reduced. Politics, "the art of the possible," will conflict with the recommendations that economists are at different times inclined to make. The Congresses of 1946–1951 were of various minds about the emphasis to be placed on these various policies, and the extent to which they should be laid aside as no longer needed, or re-imposed when inflation seemed more threatening.

Index